W9-AUE-337

SUPER *foods*
FOR CHILDREN

SUPER *foods*
FOR CHILDREN

michael van straten
& barbara griggs

contents

LONDON, NEW YORK, SYDNEY, DELHI, PARIS, MUNICH and JOHANNESBURG

This book is dedicated to the memory of Jason and Ninka

Senior Managing Art Editor Lynne Brown

Project Editor Janice Anderson

Art Editor Glenda Fisher

Designer Bernhard Koppmeyer

Food Photography Simon Smith, Trish Gant

Model Photography Vanessa Davies

DTP Designer Karen Constanti

Production Controller Melissa Allsopp

First published in Great Britain in 2001
by Dorling Kindersley Limited,
80 Strand, London WC2R 0RL

Copyright © 2001 Dorling Kindersley Limited
Text copyright © 2001 Michael van Straten
and Barbara Griggs

All rights reserved. No part of this publication
may be reproduced, stored in a retrieval system,
or transmitted in any form or by any means,
electronic, mechanical, photocopying, recording,
or otherwise, without the prior written permission
of the copyright owner.

A CIP catalogue record for this book is available from
the British Library.

ISBN 0 7513 1264 9

Reproduced by Colourscan, Singapore
Printed and bound by Mondadori Printing S.p.A.
Verona Italy

see our complete catalogue at
www.dk.com

nutrition without numbers

'What's for supper, Mum?'

'A rich source of protein and energy, children, with useful amounts of vitamin C, calcium, essential fatty acids, a little iodine, and some valuable B-complex vitamins.'

In the real world, this answer does not add up to a delicious fish pie. But more and more, it is the way that nutritionists, dietitians and self-appointed experts would have us think about our food.

Children do not eat fats, carbohydrates, vitamins and minerals, they eat food. But the numbers approach is highly profitable for many food-manufacturing giants. It allows them to add a few cheap nutrients to poor-quality food, and to persuade you that it is healthy for your children.

Jelly confectionery, which is over 80 per cent sugar, is described as containing 'real fruit juice and vitamin C'. A fromage frais is said to be 'made with all the valuable constituents of fresh milk and enriched with calcium, riboflavin and vitamin B_{12}'. You have to work out for yourself that it is 12½ per cent pure sugar. A popular chocolate-flavoured rice and corn breakfast cereal comes with '8 vitamins + iron' and is described as good 'for maintaining healthy bones'. Not so good for children's teeth, though: it is 38 per cent sugar.

Claims to be 'low-fat' or 'fat-free' are another instance of food manufacturers' sleight-of-hand. They have encouraged the public to believe that the greatest threat to health comes from over-consumption of fats, and equally, that it is fats that are chiefly responsible for today's hugely increased incidence of obesity. It's a belief that does not square with the facts. Between 1980 and 1991, consumption of fat in the USA declined by nearly five per cent, while the number of seriously overweight adults rose by nearly eight per cent. It is sugar consumption that has rocketed: average daily intake in the USA is a staggering 35 teaspoons.

The same patterns of junk-food eating and little or no exercise are producing an epidemic of obesity in the UK and Australia, too. A horrifying study published in the Lancet in 1999 showed that at age six, 10 per cent of British children were already obese, while by 15 the figure had risen to 17 per cent. A study in Queensland, Australia, found that nearly 10 per cent of schoolchildren were obese, and noted that a third of the family food budgets went on fast food.

what food slogans really mean

The term 'low-fat' can be misleading. 'Low-fat' crisps are still 21 per cent fat. Yogurt is a low-fat food, anyway. All too often, the 'low-fat' claims are designed to distract you from all the other unhealthy things going into those crisps,or that fruit-flavoured yogurt devoid of fruit and crammed with sugar as well as strings of E-numbers. 'Sugar-free' or 'light' is another useful term for food manufacturers. It means that sugar has been replaced by artificial sweeteners, the safety of which is open to question (see Danger Foods, pages 66-9).

The magic nutrition-by-numbers game is just as popular with the fast-food chains. It allows them to emphasize the one or two good nutrients in their products in order to distract attention from the horrendous amounts of fat, salt and sugar with which they come packaged. It allows them virtually to suggest that a burger, chips and coke is a thoroughly healthy meal for a growing child.

It is often claimed that children ate a healthier diet in the 1950s, despite rationing and shortages, than today's youngsters. This was not because mothers were especially knowledgeable on nutrition. Most may not have known that a grilled lamb chop supplies 28g of protein, 12mg of fat, 2mg of iron and 0.22mg of pyridoxine (vitamin B_6). What they did know was that a grilled lamb chop, a baked potato and a helping of fresh green vegetables added up to nourishing food for their families.

problems in feeding today's children

It is not that we have lost the instinctive knowledge our grandparents possessed for knowing what is best for us and our children. Rather, we are living in a more complex and more stressful world.

Today's children, more often than not, have two working parents. Food shopping becomes a once-a-week trip to the local supermarket, often involving the whole family, when seven days' eating is purchased in one go, and shelf-life becomes a major criterion of excellence.

One of the fastest-growing sections of the modern supermarket is the range of ready-made meals from the cook-chill cabinet. These instant meals, which can wait days in the fridge or be frozen for future use, can be a boon to the frantic home cook, and a wonderful stand-by in emergencies. But they can never be a substitute, gastronomically or nutritionally, for food freshly prepared in your own home.

Outside the home, children have almost unfettered access to a huge range of unsuitable foods that parents can do little about. A recent research project found that UK children spend £365 million a year on snacks – crisps and savoury snacks, sweets, fizzy drinks – on their way to and from school. And there are all those fast-food chains and burger bars where teenagers with plenty of pocket money like to gather with friends.

making home-cooking easy

While today's parents have to make extra efforts at home to ensure that their children are regularly fed healthy and nutritious food, they are helped by today's greatly improved food-buying network and convenience shopping. Local greengrocers and supermarkets open early in the morning, and many stay open round the clock; there are farmers' markets, farm shops, and organic home-delivery services. And of course there is the ever-expanding shopping mall of the Internet.

Even for busy working parents, it doesn't require all that much effort to stop off on the way home and pick up chicken breasts and fresh vegetables for a stir-fry, or half-a-dozen eggs, fresh herbs, new potatoes and salad stuff for a summer evening omelette supper; or a chunk of Cheddar and a good wholemeal loaf for Welsh rarebit. All these foods are superfoods. You will find them described in detail in this book, and there are recipes using them in many delicious, easy-to-make dishes.

The popular perception is that cooking is fun to watch on TV but a chore to do in your own kitchen. It is certainly true that most of the recipes in this book will take longer to prepare than the time it takes to unwrap a packet and put a meal in the microwave.

However, most of the recipes here are for simple dishes that require little culinary skill to cook, and a fairly short time to prepare. Your decision has to be whether these short moments of your leisure time are worth sacrificing – or, indeed, enjoying – in order to give your children the best chance of a long and healthy life.

Superfoods for Children takes you back to the old-fashioned principles of real home-cooking that looks good, tastes good and will definitely do you and your children good.

healthy eating need not cost the earth

Serving up healthy, nutritious meals for your family need not work out any more expensively than feeding them a diet of chips, burgers, crisps, biscuits, frozen pizzas, tinned spaghetti hoops, fish fingers, chicken nuggets and cheap ice cream.

Even the seriously healthy stuff – the organic meat and poultry, eggs, fruit and vegetables, bread and rice which once cost a lot more than ordinary fare – is now generally less expensive than in the early days of its production.

Even if some manufactured food is cheaper, that doesn't make it great value. And if you look at the enormous profits the food manufacturing giants make, and the astronomical sums they can afford to spend on advertising their junk foods, you might begin to wonder: are you really prepared to sacrifice your child's health to their profits?

Because these profits are based on using the very cheapest ingredients – refined white flour, white sugar, the cheapest margarines or vegetable oils,

poor-quality meat; on boosting their flavour or colour with a few chemicals; and on giving them child-appeal with plenty of sugar and fat.

Buy one of those six-packs of crisps, for instance, and you'll be getting half-a-dozen 24g (less than 1oz) packets. They'll cost you four to five times the price of 500g/1lb potatoes at your greengrocer; and more than a third of their weight will be fat. They'll be very salty, too. And they certainly will not have been made from the best potatoes available on the market. For half the money you could give your family wonderful new potatoes, or crispy baked potatoes with delicious real butter.

You can take it for granted that the chicken in those chicken nuggets and the beef in frozen burgers will be from cut-price factory-farmed sources; that the flour in biscuits, cakes and pies will be the cheapest white; that the fish in those fingers may be little better than sludge, and that the 'fruit' drink may contain little more than 10 per cent actual fruit. You can be sure, however, that at least two ingredients will be lavishly supplied in many of these foods. Sugar and salt. And every shopper and cook knows how cheap those are.

cut down the costs

Most of the so-called 'junk foods' do not actually form part of a proper meal anyway. They are the extras: the packets of crisps and other savouries children buy on the way home from school, the ice creams and cokes taken on any family outing, and the soft fizzy drinks which have replaced plain water in so many families: millions of children growing up today assume that a 'drink' is something out of a bottle or carton, rather than a glassful of water from the tap.

Cut down on these extras and you'll have a lot more money to spend on real food at mealtimes: your children won't have had their appetites ruined in advance, either.

Eating food when it's in season and locally grown is another way to slash the food bills. Out-of-season grapes and strawberries, green beans and new potatoes imported from countries where it is summer sooner than where you live, or hot all the year round, will always be more expensive than when they're in season. And jetlag won't enhance their nutritional value by any means.

Unless yours is a vegetarian family, meat and fish will always be the biggest items in the weekly food bill. But it is only quite recently, and only in wealthy Western countries, that meat has come to form the centrepiece of the meal, with vegetables no more than accessories to the feast. Millions of people throughout the world live long, healthy and active lives on diets based mainly on grains and pulses, with just a little meat or fish for extra flavour. In China and in India, around the Mediterranean and in much of Latin America, this is the normal way to eat, and wonderful food it is too. Even when you're planning dishes which are based on meat, such as stews, casseroles, shepherd's pie or lasagne, you can always replace some of the meat with vegetables, and sometimes they can be substituted for it altogether.

Organic food *is* notably more expensive than conventionally-farmed produce. But the prices are beginning to come down as more and more farmers opt for organic. And as well as supermarkets, there are fast-growing numbers of farmers' markets where prices are much more competitive, there are local box schemes which are often excellent value, and there are organic retailers advertising on the Internet. Shop around for the best bargains (see Resources, pages 214-15).

grow food at home

If you have a garden, however small, you can grow at least some of your own food organically. Grow rocket for salads, sorrel for soups, and plenty of spinach: all three grow fast and easily without too much looking after.

Give the children a corner to grow their own food: they'll be much more likely to eat radishes, sweetcorn or spring onions that they've proudly produced themselves. Even if you only have a backyard, balcony or window sill, use it to grow many of the herbs which contribute health as well as wonderful flavours to everyday eating: thyme, mint, chives, parsley, basil, oregano and rosemary.

nutrition on a plate

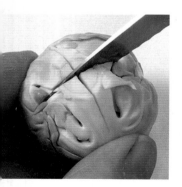

Small bodies need good nourishment to get them through their active days. The brains of children are even hungrier than their bodies, voracious in their need for oxygen, energy and key nutrients. The foods that best supply these essential nutritional requirements are described here.

eating healthily

Follow the simple, practical guidelines illustrated by our plate for life and your family will get all the superfoods needed for health. The plate is divided into five sections and, if you visualize it when you are shopping, planning the day's eating or thinking about the next meal, you'll never be far from eating healthily all the time.

A baby's first foods are necessarily few in number and must be carefully chosen. Once past babyhood, children benefit greatly from eating a wide range of foods, typified by the contents of our plate for life.

A third of the plate is filled with the vitality foods: all kinds of fruits, vegetables or salads. Another third is filled with energy-giving foods: starchy carbohydrates including potatoes, pasta, wholemeal bread, brown rice, oats and sweetcorn. The final third is divided into two larger segments and a much smaller segment.

One of the two larger segments is filled with the body-building foods, with lots of protein: lean meat, fish, poultry, eggs, beans, lentils, nuts and seeds. The other is made up of body- and bone-building dairy products: milk, yogurt and cheeses.

The tiny segment is the place for fats, olive and other vegetable oils and treats such as butter, cream, sugar, chocolate, ice cream and the white flour in croissants, french bread, pasta and pizzas.

getting the balance right

The proportions of different types of food on this plate represent the ideal balance for healthy eating. Use these proportions as a guide, and you will always give your children enough starchy food for energy, enough protein for growth, enough fruit, vegetables and salad for vitality, and enough calcium for strong bones, while keeping the

amount of fats, oils and dairy products within heart-healthy bounds. And there's still room for treats.

You'll only have to look at the meal you're putting in front of your children to know if you've got it right or wrong. A bowl of tomato soup with a crusty roll and a glass of milk; a home-made burger with oven-baked chips, peas and carrots; and fresh fruit salad with cream scores A+, because there are plenty of the vitality foods, plenty of the energy foods, enough protein and body-building foods, and a little cream as a treat.

A cheeseburger and fries, with a milkshake, apple pie and a large cola drink, in contrast, rates only a C-. The meal provides adequate protein, but it also supplies masses of fat and salt, a huge amount of sugar, and just a scrap of tired lettuce and a little apple to represent the vitality foods.

You do not have to follow the proportions on the plate rigidly, or worry too much if the treats get out of hand from time to time: just try to stick to the general proportions. If your children are eating plenty of fruit and vegetables and the good energy foods, enough protein and enough body-building foods, and small amounts of healthy oils you can forget about adding up the numbers and percentages. Your children will be getting all the vitamins and minerals, trace elements and essential fatty acids, protein, carbohydrates and fats they need, and all the fibre as well.

A plate for life

Plan children's meals in the proportions of foods on this plate, and you will ensure they eat a healthy diet.

• Vitality foods – fruits, vegetables and salads – fill a third of the plate.

• Energy foods – starchy foods such as potatoes, pasta, wholemeal bread, brown rice and oats – also fill a third of the plate.

• Body-building protein foods – lean meat, fish, eggs, pulses and nuts – fill 15 per cent of the plate.

• Dairy foods, mainly milk products, also take up 15 per cent of the plate.

• Fats, including butter, cream, oils and sugars; foods based on white flour; and 'treats' should cover no more than 3 per cent of the space on the plate.

33% starchy foods

33% fruits and vegetables

15% protein

3% fats

15% dairy food

carbohydrates

Carbohydrates are found in fruits; in grains such as wheat or rice; in pulses such as peas, beans and lentils; in starchy vegetables like potatoes and carrots; in milk; and in sugar and honey. Carbohydrate foods are energy foods, and children need plenty of them, not only because they are naturally active and use up a lot of energy, but because they need energy for growth, too.

The best carbohydrate foods – wholemeal bread, brown rice, whole oats, beans, lentils, and fruits – supply more than just energy. They also contain important nutrients, and are rich in fibre to keep the digestive system functioning efficiently.

When these foods are refined or heavily processed, as are white bread and white rice, for instance, they lose not only large amounts of vital nutrients, but most of their fibre too.

To take just the white flour that goes into our bread as an example: compared with wholemeal flour, white flour contains much less zinc, which children need to build resistance and to help with brain work; a great deal less magnesium, which is vital for the nervous system, and also for the absorption of calcium for the development of strong bones and teeth; and significantly less of the protein that is essential for body-building. Token amounts of major nutrients are added back when flour is baked into bread, but not for other uses. Much the same losses occur when rice and maize are refined. And the white sugar produced when sugar beet and sugar cane are processed has absolutely no nutritional value at all, except for a lot of energy-giving calories which have been styled 'empty' for this reason. Brown sugar and honey at least contain traces of some key nutrients.

carbohydrates and glucose

There is another downside to highly refined carbohydrate foods. When they are eaten, the sugars they contain are broken down into glucose during the process of digestion. Glucose, or blood sugar as it is also called, is the fuel our bodies run on. The glucose circulating in our bloodstream after a carbohydrate meal is transferred to cells for instant use, and any surplus is converted into glycogen and stored as fuel in the liver, ready to be 'switched on' for use whenever it is needed. The hormone insulin, which is secreted by the pancreas, is responsible for this storage job.

Eat a slice of wholemeal bread, a dish of lentils, or a few ripe apricots, and the sugars in them are broken down into glucose quite slowly. But tuck into a couple of biscuits, a bowl of cornflakes, or a chocolate bar, all of which are known as 'high-glycaemic' foods because they are rapidly absorbed, and the sugars they contain will be broken down very quickly into glucose, sending the level in the bloodstream soaring.

The pancreas responds to this abnormal situation by pumping out extra insulin, and blood-sugar levels drop sharply. You are now suffering – if only in passing – from hypoglycaemia or low blood sugar, sometimes called the 'Sugar Blues'. Children who eat a plateful of sugary cereals for breakfast may experience this dive in blood sugar a couple of hours later, making them jittery, unable to concentrate and wanting a little sugary fix.

These fluctuations in blood-sugar levels have been linked to a wide range of health problems. Long-term, they can be responsible for high blood pressure, obesity, diabetes and heart disease in adults. In children, they may be responsible for disruptive behaviour, hyperactivity and an inability to concentrate. One of the commonest symptoms of low blood sugar is fatigue – which may account for the state of permanent exhaustion in which so many of today's teenagers appear to live.

Researchers have recently discovered another consequence of the constant insulin 'highs' produced by yoyo-ing blood sugar levels. Insulin stimulates an enzyme called lipoprotein-lipase, which directs circulating fatty acids into fat-cell storage, thus upping body weight, instead of into ordinary cells to be burnt up by their power-plants, the mitochondria. Children who are constantly snacking on biscuits, crisps, cakes, ice cream and chocolate bars will tend to put on weight – and obesity among children is a growing problem.

vary the carbohydrates

Give children wholemeal bread, brown rice and nourishing porridge oats most of the time, and save the buns, biscuits, pizzas and white rice for treats. The more nourishing foods are more filling and satisfying, too, so children will not keep asking for odd snacks. There's no need to ban sugar, but choose unrefined cane sugar instead of white, and be very mean with it. Honey can often replace sugar, though it should not be given to babies under one year as, in rare cases, bacteria found in honey can cause botulism.

It is a good idea to vary the carbohydrates in your children's meals. Most modern Western diets over-emphasize a few basic foodstuffs – wheat-based ones in particular. Toast for breakfast, bread in some form in the middle of the day, cakes and biscuits after school and pasta or pizza for supper add up to an awful lot of just one food. Growing numbers of children are sensitive to certain foods, which can give them severe digestive and other problems. Top of the list of these problem foods is wheat, closely followed by dairy foods and the orange juice which is most babies' first drink after milk. (See Special Problems, pages 200-213, for advice on recognizing the potential problem foods and how to deal with them.)

protein

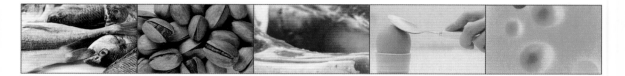

Protein is found in a wide variety of foods including anything made from cereals such as wheat and oats; in rice, eggs, cheese, fish, poultry, meat, nuts and seeds; and in all varieties of beans, peas and lentils. Generally speaking, protein derived from animal sources is a complete protein on its own, whereas, with the exception of soya beans, you need to combine cereals with pulses and legumes to obtain complete protein from vegetable sources. This is commonly seen in ethnic food like rice and peas (black-eye beans) in the West Indies, or chapattis with dal in India.

Protein is essential for the building of every single one of the body's cells and it is constantly being used and replaced. Because babies, children and teenagers are growing rapidly they tend to need more protein in relation to their weight than adults. Pregnant women also need extra protein for the creation of new cells in their growing baby.

In the West, adult protein deficiency is extremely unusual, except in those suffering from eating disorders. It is less rare to find children whose protein intake is marginal or low, as children are more inclined to eat a limited range of foods and to develop passing obsessions with particular foods eaten to the exclusion of others. But don't be too alarmed if your child will only eat baked beans, crisps or chips. 100 grams of each provides 5.1, 6.3 and 15 grams of protein respectively.

Children's need for protein varies with age, and boys and girls have the same daily requirements up to the age of 10. After that age their requirements differ, as the chart, right, indicates. However, this does not denote the amount of protein-containing foods that children need to eat, as no food is made up of just protein. Vegetables contain 5 per cent or less protein, and fruits contain very little. Eggs, cheese, fish, meat and poultry, peanuts, beans, lentils, cereals and bread contain between 10 and 30 per cent protein and usually provide over 80 per cent of a child's daily protein consumption.

The following list of foods, showing the amount of protein in an average portion, will give you an idea of how much protein your children are obtaining from the food they eat:
- 100g/3½oz white fish have 18 grams of protein
- 300ml/½pint whole milk have 10 grams
- two boiled eggs have 14 grams
- 200g/7oz baked beans have 8 grams
- one slice of wholemeal bread has 3 grams
- 60g/2oz of peanuts have 14 grams
- a matchbox-size piece of Cheddar has 12 grams
- an average burger has 10 grams
- one fish finger has 4 grams.

Freezing and cooking do not much alter the amount of protein present in foods, although cooking can make some difference. Slightly cooked proteins are thought to be more easily digested than raw; if you overcook red meat until it is tough, the protein will be less available because the digestive juices will have trouble breaking it down.

Daily protein requirements of children

Age group	Boys	Girls
0-3 months	12.5g	12.5g
7-9 months	13.7g	13.7g
10-12 months	14.9g	14.9g
4-6 years	19.7g	19.7g
7-10 years	28.3g	28.3g
11-14 years	42.0g	41.2g
15-18 years	55.2g	45.0g

The body is not able to store protein, and if excessive amounts are eaten they will be converted into sugars and fats. The idea that feeding your child lots of protein instead of starchy foods because it is less fattening is quite wrong and may well be more harmful to health. It is particularly important not to feed too much protein food to small babies (up to the age of 9-12 months). Their immature kidneys cannot deal with the breakdown products that build up in the bloodstream, and this can lead to serious problems.

It is perfectly possible to raise your child as a vegetarian and still ensure he receives adequate amounts of protein. You will need to take more care to maintain iron and vitamin B_{12} intake, but there is no problem with providing sufficient amounts of vegetable-based protein to ensure normal growth (see Vegetarian Child, pages 104–7).

fats

Science has now established an irrefutable link between heart disease and breast cancer and a high intake of animal fat in the diet. Many Western governments have responded by aiming to reduce the total percentage of calories their populations obtain from fat in their diet. In Britain, the figure recommended is 35 per cent (down from 40 per cent, or 100 grams of fat a day, the current average consumption). In the USA the figure is 30 per cent, the equivalent of 70 or 75 grams of fat in the daily diet, which seems to be the level above which heart disease and breast cancer become more prevalent.

As there is growing evidence that the seeds of heart disease are sown in childhood, possibly even in the womb, it is clearly never too early to teach your children eating habits that control their intake of total fats and particularly of saturated fats.

Saturated, polyunsaturated, monounsaturated, trans-fats, cholesterol, omega-3, omega-6 – all fats, all confusing, but are they good or bad? Do children need any of them in their daily diet? The answer to the last question is that they most certainly do: growing children need to derive quite a high percentage of their energy intake from fat – 50 per cent up to the age of one year, and 35 per

cent thereafter. Some fats are essential to enable the body to absorb the fat-soluble vitamins A, D, E and K. The essential point is to understand what kinds of fat there are and how much children need.

Saturated fats are nearly all animal fats: butter, lard, the fat in meat and the fat in cheese, cream and milk. Some vegetables also produce saturated fat, especially coconut and palm. The body is able to manufacture its own saturated fatty acids so you do not need to eat them.

Polyunsaturated fats are found mainly in vegetable oils like soya bean, corn, sunflower and safflower. They also occur in oily fish. They are extremely important and should form a regular part of every child's diet.

Monounsaturated fats occur mostly in olive oil, nuts and seeds and rapeseed oil, and are important as heart protectors.

Essential fatty acids include the omega-6 and omega-3 fatty acids that are vital building blocks of body cells, especially brain and central-nervous-system tissue. Without them, normal

development of the baby's brain during pregnancy and in early childhood can be adversely affected. Recent studies have indicated a lack of some of these essential fatty acids in the diets of pregnant vegetarian women. The omega-6 fats are found in safflower, soya and sunflower oil, and the omega-3s are abundant in oily fish and in soya bean, rapeseed and walnut oils.

Cholesterol

It is generally accepted that levels of cholesterol in the blood are a key marker for an individual's risk of heart disease. But cholesterol is an essential constituent of every cell in the body. Happily, the liver makes all you need so there is no requirement to get it from food.

Trans-fats,

found mostly in margarines, are the real villains. Good natural foods are always preferable to anything manufactured in a factory and margarine is the prime example. Trans-fats are even more dangerous for your child's heart than saturated fats, so sparing amounts of unsalted butter are undeniably better than any margarine.

keeping a watch on calories

Calorie content is a main reason for being very careful with a child's fat intake. Of all the components of our food, fat contains the highest number of calories by weight and, with the exception of fat-reduced spreads, all fats – whether saturated, unsaturated or essential fatty acids – will give very nearly the same number of calories in every 100g/3½oz (more than twice as many as starchy foods). One hundred grams of boiled new potatoes contain only 76 calories. But turn the potatoes into chips with added fat and the potatoes will give 253 calories.

We get 50 per cent of our daily fat intake from meat, milk, cream, cheese, eggs and oily fish; 30 per cent from butter, margarine and other fats and oils; and 8 per cent from food items such as biscuits, cakes and pastries.

The first step towards ensuring children do not get more fat than they need is to cut down on all the visible fats (i.e., the ones you can see): butter, cheese, cream, the fat around steak or chops, or on the outside of a slice of ham or bacon. Much more difficult is to avoid the hidden fats in meat products like sausages, salamis, pies and pastries, and in biscuits, cakes, Danish pastries and chocolates. These are insidious and the only way to control them in your child's diet is to read all labels very carefully before you buy – and only buy fat-high foods in small quantities occasionally.

The chart below shows just how little of some of these high-fat foods your child needs to eat to provide 10 grams of fat – almost a third of his total recommended consumption for a day.

Fat in foods

The fat content of some foods, eaten in quantity by children, is alarmingly high. The table below lists popular foods and their fat content. A 35g piece of quiche, for example, contains 10g of fat.

Food amount containing **10g (⅓oz)** of fat

Chocolate biscuits	35g	Lamb chop with fat	30g	Cream cheese	20g
Chocolate digestives	40g	Average meat pastie	50g	Stilton cheese	25g
Traditional shortbread	40g	Fried scampi	55g	Cheddar cheese	30g
Sponge cake	40g	Taramasalata	20g	Scotch egg	50g
Cheesecake	30g	Butter, Margarine	12g	Quiche	35g
Fried bacon (streaky)	20g	Lard, Vegetable oil	10g	Potato crisps	30g
Roast duck with skin	25g	Double cream	20g	Chips (frozen)	50g
Pork pie	35g	Single cream	50g	Milk chocolate	35g
Pork sausage	30g	Mayonnaise	12g		

minerals

Because of modern intensive-farming methods, soil that has been artificially fertilized and had the same crop grown on it for years may have had its natural stores of minerals depleted. The crops and the animals fed on them may then contain less than we need, and that can be a health hazard for children.

Minerals and trace elements are of special interest to us, as deficiencies are often overlooked as the cause of illness. From birth onwards they are essential for growth, development, natural resistance and all-round health. Make sure your family gets plenty of minerals by eating all the foods listed here – ideally, organically grown.

Zinc is vital for growth, healthy sex organs, insulin production and natural resistance. Lack of zinc can lead to weight loss, skin diseases, ulcers and acne, loss of taste and smell and brittle nails.

People with anorexia nervosa have very low levels of zinc, so a supplement can really help.

A lack of zinc may be linked to ADHD (see page 206), and could even start before birth if the mother is low on her own intake. Zinc, in food or as a supplement, helps with teenage acne.

Best zinc sources are shellfish (especially oysters), lamb, liver, steak, garlic, Brazil nuts, pumpkin seeds, eggs, sardines, oats, crab, almonds and chicken.

Selenium is a key factor in the immune system. It is also important for giving protection against heart disease, skin problems and increased risk of cancer.

In some Western countries, selenium intake has dropped markedly in recent years. This is all the more alarming in view of the fact that current research shows that normally harmless viruses can become dangerously virulent when living in a body that is deficient in selenium.

This may all seem far removed from your baby or child, but making sure their diet is full of selenium-rich foods is not only protection now but will help protect their health throughout their lives.

Best sources are wholemeal bread made from Canadian and North American flour, Brazil nuts, butter, oily fish, liver and kidney.

Magnesium is essential in many of the body's enzyme functions, and helps maintain a balanced distribution of calcium, potassium and sodium in individual cells. It is vital for growth and also as part of the cell-repair mechanism. It is, in addition, one of the minerals that enables nerve pulses to be transmitted from cell to cell.

Magnesium deficiency can be the result of bad eating habits, malnutrition, anorexia nervosa, inability to eat because of mouth or tooth problems, or poor absorption due to digestive disease. Eating too much uncooked bran increases magnesium loss from the body, as can excessive consumption of fats, vitamin D and calcium. Some prescribed drugs, including some antibiotics and diuretics, can increase magnesium loss, too.

A deficiency of magnesium in the diet can cause hyperactivity in children, apathy, exhaustion, fatigue, cramp, tremors, insomnia, palpitations and low blood-sugar levels. This vital mineral is also required by the body to aid good calcium absorption (see opposite).

The best food sources are soya beans, nuts, wholemeal flour, brown rice, dried fruit and bananas. All green vegetables are also very good sources of magnesium.

Iron combines with oxygen in order to make haemoglobin, the red colouring of the blood. This haemoglobin transports the oxygen from the air we breathe to every cell of the body. Iron helps keep children cheerful and active. Without enough, your child is vulnerable to anaemia, fatigue, depression and palpitations, and will look pale.

Kelp (seaweed), molasses, pig's liver, beef, black pudding, oily fish like pilchards, herring and sardines, shellfish, kidney beans, Brazil nuts, dates, raisins, lentils, chickpeas, peanuts, chicken, egg yolk, soya beans and peas are good sources of iron. A reasonable-sized portion of liver, chilli con carne, or a home-cooked burger or steak, with green vegetables, peas or beans, provides the daily need. Contrary to popular belief, spinach is not the best source of iron, as it contains oxalic acid which makes it more difficult for the body to absorb.

Copper works with iron to make red blood corpuscles, important for bone formation, breakdown of cholesterol and the skin pigment melanin. Deficiency can lead to anaemia, hair problems, raised cholesterol and dry skin.

Children who eat nuts, beef, liver, lamb, butter, barley and olive oil get all the copper they need.

Calcium is a vital mineral for the formation and continuing strength of bones and teeth, and is particularly important during pregnancy, breast-feeding, childhood and in the teenage years. In later life, both women and men are at risk of osteoporosis (brittle-bone disease), which is caused partly by a combination of too little calcium in the diet and poor absorption, and partly by the fact that bones naturally lose density as we get older.

The time to do something positive about protecting bones is in childhood. A diet which contains lots of calcium-rich foods is the first step. And children should be encouraged to be active, play sport and get plenty of fresh air and sunshine, which makes vitamin D (another substance, like magnesium, that is needed for calcium absorption.

Milk, yogurt and cheese are great sources of calcium, so encourage a taste for them in your children and make them part of their regular daily food. Canned sardines with the bones, lots of greens and dried fruit, nuts, beans and good bread are other good food sources of calcium. Eating plenty of them will guarantee your children grow up with strong bones and teeth.

Iodine is essential for the proper working of the thyroid gland, which produces hormones that control many of the body's functions. It also gives some degree of protection against radiation damage to the thyroid. Lack of iodine will cause lethargy, skin thickening, hair loss, growth problems and goitre (thyroid enlargement). Too much, on the other hand, may cause overactivity of the thyroid.

Seaweed and sea fish are the only dependable sources of iodine. But beware of taking too much of the kelp (seaweed) supplements, which can be high in iodine – few of them are standardized – and may cause thyroid problems.

Manganese is needed for the formation of a number of enzymes, bone formation, muscle action and fertility. A lack of it may cause bone and disc problems and high blood-sugar levels. It is found in all wholegrain cereals, nuts and tea – one cup of tea provides nearly half the daily requirement.

Potassium is essential for the proper functioning of all cells and nervous tissue. It is present in all foods except oils, fats and sugars: bananas are a great source. It can be lost into the cooking water of vegetables, so use vegetable water for soups, gravy and stews.

vitamins & antioxidants

Antioxidants have been the great nutritional revelation of the past decade or so. They are powerfully protective plant chemicals found in the bright pigments of fruits and vegetables, and form the body's best defence against attack by unfriendly molecules called free radicals, which are generated both in our bodies and environmentally by pollutants such as pesticides, tobacco smoke and stress. Free-radical damage has been linked with cancer, heart disease, wrinkles, cataracts, and more.

The earliest known antioxidants were vitamins C and E, and beta-carotene, which is turned in the body into vitamin A. It is now known that the pigments which give fruits and vegetables their glowing colours are rich in these wonderful protective factors – so children should feast on brilliantly coloured seasonal fruits and vegetables.

Although health departments the world over are concerned to keep everyone informed about how many vitamins and minerals we should all be taking every day – given as RDA ('recommended daily allowance') figures on many food labels – they make no allowance for the huge variations in the actual nutrient content of today's foods. Intensive growing methods, transporting, storage, freshness and handling can all reduce the level of vitamins and antioxidants in foods. And that's before you buy them, take them home and cook them. The theoretical vitamin content of what ends up on your child's plate is often a great deal more than the reality of what is eaten.

There is also an enormous difference between what children need to avoid deficiency diseases, and the amounts needed to keep them in good health and to protect them against serious illness.

The following list describes in detail what the vitamins do and how much you theoretically have to eat to achieve the RDAs. Obviously, children's requirements vary with age, but from about 11 years old their needs are much the same as the adult quantities that are specified here.

Vitamin A is essential for growth, skin, night and colour vision. Get all you need for a day from: *60g/2oz liver; 45g/1½oz old carrots; 75g/2½ oz spinach, butter or margarine; or 125g/4oz broccoli with 60g/2oz Cheddar cheese in a sauce.*

Vitamin C prevents scurvy, aids wound-healing and iron absorption, and is a vital and protective antioxidant. The daily dose is in: *2 teaspoons blackcurrants, a lemon, half a green pepper, an orange, half a large grapefruit, a kiwifruit, or 90g/3oz raw red cabbage.*

Vitamin D is essential for bone formation as it is part of the calcium-absorption system. Lack of this vitamin causes rickets in children and bone disorders in adults. The action of sunlight on the skin produces vitamin D, so encourage lots of outdoor activities. The Asian community, especially women and girls, is often at risk of vitamin-D deficiency due to traditional clothing that bears very little skin to the sun, diet and lifestyle.

The 10µg that is essential will be obtained from: *1 teaspoon cod-liver oil, 45g/1½oz herring or kipper; 60g/2oz mackerel, 75g/2½oz canned salmon or tuna, or 140g/4½oz canned sardines. Eggs contain the vitamin, too.*

Vitamin B$_1$, Thiamin's main function

is during the conversion of carbohydrates into energy. If you live on a high-starch diet, as some vegetarians do, the need for vitamin B$_1$ increases. Your daily dose can be had from: *60g/2oz cod roe, 75g/2½oz wheatgerm, 100g/3½oz Brazil nuts or peanuts. Oatmeal, bacon, pork, offal and bread are all good sources, too.*

Vitamin B$_2$, Riboflavin, is vital for

growth and for the skin and mucous membranes. *6 eggs, 900ml/1½ pints milk, 60g/2oz liver or kidney, or 250g/8oz Cheddar cheese will each supply the 1.3g you need. Beef, mackerel, almonds, cereals and poultry are also good sources.*

Vitamin B$_6$, Pyridoxine, helps to

release energy from protein. It is essential for growth and the functioning of the immune and nervous systems. It may also overcome some of the side-effects of the contraceptive pill. *Fish, meat, liver and cheese are good sources. A large banana and half an avocado will provide the daily dose. A portion of cod, salmon or a grilled herring will give you nearly all you need.*

Folic acid is vital during a child's growth and

development as well as during pregnancy, and deficiency is linked to birth defects such as spina bifida. Also vital throughout life for protection against heart disease. *The best sources are dark green vegetables, liver, kidney, nuts, wholemeal bread and wholegrain cereals. An average portion of lamb's liver supplies 250µg, spinach 140µg and kidney beans, frozen peas, chickpeas and raw red cabbage all around 75µg of the essential 200µg.*

children and vitamin supplements

The burning question most people ask about vitamins and their children is, 'Do my children need to take extra vitamins?' The theoretical answer is 'No, not if you are all eating a well-balanced diet, and using a wide variety of foods.'

In fact, few people manage to do this, and even fewer persuade their partners or children to do it. Pressures of time, working couples, no school meals, and the relentless march of the fast-food industry all make it more difficult.

Buying vitamin supplements can be very confusing. Do you choose a multivitamin; six individual vitamins (and if so, which ones?); mega-dose, slow-release or vegetarian capsules; tablets made without gluten, yeast, colourings or sugars; a brand with 70 different ingredients, or one with five?

You may also waste money on supplements your children don't need, and which may do more harm than good. Single vitamins and minerals certainly have a place but, as a general rule, they – and certainly, the high-dose ones – are best taken on the advice of a doctor or nutritionist.

If you are giving vitamin supplements to children, make sure that you only buy those specifically formulated for the age of your child and that you do not exceed the stated dose. While current government guidelines recommend that all children under the age of 5 should take a supplement of vitamins A, C and D, as a general rule of thumb, most children should not need anything more than a simple multivitamin and mineral, unless they have some underlying health problem or are on a very bizarre diet. In these circumstances, get professional advice before you start dosing your youngsters.

Note:
'µg' in some of the quantities mentioned here indicates micrograms; one microgram is equivalent to one millionth of a gram.

organic foods

Organic produce is taking an increasingly prominent place in our thinking about food standards. It is grown without the many chemicals of conventional foods, generally tastes better and contains more nutrients, too. It is certainly the kind of food we want our children to eat.

Remember that a baby's central nervous system is developing but immature and that it's immune system is still, like the baby, in its infancy. There has been little research into the effects on very small children of the multiple chemical cocktail that does into much food production. Some leading allergy experts maintain that it is not atmospheric pollution that produces problems such as the ever-increasing incidence of asthma among our children so much as the damage to their immune systems from chemicals and additives in food. It seems only sensible to use as much organic produce in babies' diets as possible to remove one major factor that could potentially be damaging. The same remains true as your baby grows into a toddler, school child, teenager and adolescent.

There are many reasons for trying to bring children up as organically as possible – which is much easier to do than once it was, with an increasing range of organic food outlets, from farm shops to mail order home delivery schemes, and with many supermarkets greatly extending their range of organic foods, both fresh and processed.

avoiding additives

One important reason for going organic is to avoid the huge list of artificial additives that find their way into commercially produced and processed foods, from artificial sweeteners to colouring agents.

Many of the orange drinks that four- and five-year-olds drink so avidly contain very little of the citrus fruit and a great many additives. Avoid all the chemicals and added sugar by giving children pure organic fruit juices diluted 50/50 with water – if they like them fizzy, use mineral water. Look out, too, for the organic juices without added sugar, sweeteners or agrochemical residues that major manufacturers are now producing.

An even more important reason for going organic centres on the question of nutritional value. Without a doubt, organicially produced crops are higher in nutrients than their conventionally-grown counterparts. Studies consistently show higher contents of vitamins A and C in organically-grown fruits and vegetables, for instance. The organic farmer uses traditional methods of crop rotation, green manure planting, composting and organic fertilising to keep the soil in good heart and to replace nutrients taken up by previous crops.

Intensive commerical cultivation relies on artifical fertilisers which replace only the nutrients essential to grow the crops, with scant regard for their nutritional quality. Intensive livestock producers have to use feed supplemented with minerals and vitamins to replace those missing from their own feed crops, and non-organic produce has a much higher water content and contains less of these essential vitamins and minerals.

Other things besides nutrients may be missing, or have a reduced presence, in intensively-reared livestock. Professor Mike Parizza, studying cattle meat at the University of Wisconsin, isolated a special fat called conjugated linoleic acid (CLA), a powerful anti-carcinogen. This essential fatty acid proved to be a key factor in weight control: the more CLA in the diet the more the body stores surplus calories as muscle rather than fat. Professor Parizza's research also showed that the highest levels of CLA were found in beef reared naturally on grass.

It's extraordinary that in all the food legislation there are laws that cover everything from seeds to packaging, from storage to handling, from dairy hygiene to clean food shops, even down to the size and shape of bananas, and from sell-by dates to labelling. But there is no law that makes testing for nutritional quality obligatory.

organic foods taste great

And a final reason for going organic: most organically-grown foods have full, rich flavours and superb textures – particularly important where children are concerned.

Take a bite out of an organic then a commercially grown apple; dip your organically grown stoneground flour wholemeal bread soldier into the yolk of an organic free-range egg and compare it with a finger of white sliced commercial bread in the pale anaemic yolk of a battery egg; savour an organic freshly harvested new potato with any non-organic variety you care to name; you won't need a degree in food technology to tell the difference – nor will your children.

Organic food is best for all these reasons and it does not really matter whether you choose it for taste, safety, or to protect the environment, and it does not matter whether or not you can switch to a totally organic diet, as every organic product you consume is better for your health and better for the planet, too.

Try beginning with organically-grown versions of those foods where the risk of chemical residues are high – root vegetables such as carrots, or lettuces and other salad greens, for instance – or where farm production has been called seriously into question, such as with beef, or, if you have a young baby, with organic formula milk. Such foods can do nothing but good for growing children.

If you're pregnant or thinking of it, feeding young children, suffering or recovering from serious illness, it is really important that you make organic food as big a part of your regular consumption as you can possibly afford to do.

superfoods

Here are over 130 foods – vegetables, fruits, dairy products, grains, nuts and seeds, meats, fish, herbs and oils – that provide the building blocks for *Superfoods for*  *Children's* irresistible collection of recipes and menu plans. Use the foods to build the kind of diet your children need for healthy growth – and which they'll enjoy eating, too.

super vegetables

Green is nature's favourite colour, and green leafy vegetables are the cornerstone of healthy eating, reducing cancer rates and heart disease and increasing longevity. Feast your family on these vital greens, on earthy roots and the many other rainbow-hued members of the vegetable kingdom.

cabbage

Cabbage has for centuries been valued for its healing properties and as a stress-buster. Today, researchers are finding that cabbage also has enormous cancer-prevention value. Studies have shown that where people eat large quantities of cabbage and its close relatives, including the superfoods cauliflower and broccoli, some cancers, such as cancer of the lung, colon, breast and uterus, are far less common.

This anti-cancer effect is attributed to phyto-chemicals (protective plant chemicals), especially glucosinolates, found in all the brassicas. As soon as the leaves are chopped, crushed, juiced or cooked, enzymes are released which convert the glucosinolates into indoles, a group of chemicals that is anti-carcinogenic. Studies with animals have shown that cabbage can have a mild protective effect against radiation, and this may work with people, too, especially if the cabbage is eaten raw.

Cabbage contains healing mucilaginous substances similar to those produced by the mucous membrane of the gut and stomach for their own protection. It is also rich in sulphur, a mineral often in short supply in our diets but vital to healthy skin and joints. It is valuable for chest infections and is a powerful anti-bacterial.

QUICK FOOD IDEA

Use cabbage water and leftover shreds of cooked cabbage to give a quickly prepared vegetable soup a satisfyingly meaty flavour.

Cabbage, like the other brassicas, becomes indigestible if overcooked and loses much of its healing power. Cook it well-washed and shredded in a tightly sealed pan, over a low heat, in a tablespoon or so of water for 2–3 minutes only. When cooked, add a knob of butter and a dusting of nutmeg, or a trickle of oil and lemon juice. Or stir-fry it, or eat it raw in Coleslaw, a salad that many children love (see page 198).

A **rich source** of folic acid, sulphur, vitamin C, beta-carotene and fibre.

broccoli

Another brassica, with the same cancer-fighting properties as cabbage. Eat broccoli raw in florets with a dip (see page 149) or steamed for 2–3 minutes until just tender. Stir-frying is another excellent way to cook broccoli and the other brassicas to enjoy them at their health-giving best.

A **rich source** of potassium and beta-carotene, and a **good source** of iron; the latter is well-absorbed by the body, because broccoli contains vitamin C, which is essential for this process.

cauliflower

Although cauliflower contains the same cancer-fighting compounds as other brassicas, it is less rich in beta-carotene, riboflavin and folic acid, all of which are easily destroyed by over-cooking. Cauliflower is a great crunchy dipping vegetable.

If you do cook it, be sure to add some of its tender young inner leaves for extra vitamin C and beta-carotene.

Interestingly, there is more available beta-carotene in cooked brassica vegetables than in raw.

asparagus

Children love finger-food, and dipping asparagus spears in a little melted butter or mayonnaise is a messy treat. Asparagus is a good resistance-booster because it has huge amounts of beta-carotene, which is also essential for the development of healthy skin and lungs. There is an added bonus of significant amounts of antioxidant and protective vitamin E. Eat asparagus fresh, as it spoils when stored too long.

QUICK FOOD IDEA

Use stalk trimmings and cooking water, plus herbs and seasoning, for a speedily made soup.

A **rich source** of beta-carotene, vitamin E and folic acid, asparagus is also a **good source** of minerals and of fibre.

turnips

Not every child's favourite vegetable, but well worth including in winter soups, casseroles or roasted vegetables, because of their high sulphur content which will help protect young lungs from infection. An old country cure for coughs was made by hollowing out a raw turnip, filling it with brown sugar and giving children teaspoon-size doses of the runny liquid which formed.

A **useful source** of fibre, calcium, phosphorus, potassium and some B vitamins.

carrots

Baby new carrots taste delicious but contain far fewer vital carotenoids than the much darker-coloured old carrots, which contain so much beta-carotene that just one average-size carrot provides enough beta-carotene for a whole day's dose.

Beta-carotene is converted in the body to vitamin A, vital for healthy skin and mucous membranes and, therefore, for the lungs and the entire respiratory system. Vitamin A is also essential for good night vision.

It is now well-established that eating generous quantities of carrots provides increased protection against the risks of some cancers, especially those of the lungs and breast.

Carrots have also long been used in the treatment of diarrhoea, particularly among small children and infants, for whom carrot purée is both healthy food and good medicine. Scrape 500g/1lb dark red carrots, boil in water to cover until very soft, press through a food mill and add boiled water to bring the amount up to 1 litre/1¾ pints. Refrigerate and give over the next 24 hours, the runny liquid through a bottle, the solids by the spoonful.

If possible, buy organic. Carrots readily accumulate alarming levels of pesticide residues – so much so that in Britain official advice is to top, tail and peel them before eating.

A **good source** of beta-carotene, and **contain** reasonable amounts of vitamins C and E.

QUICK FOOD IDEA

Put carrot sticks on the table for children to nibble at while they wait for you to dish up. Serve them with dips (see page 149) or grated in a creamy dressing as part of a crudités starter.

potatoes

Don't deprive your children of potatoes. They are not fattening, but filling, full of energy and rich in a number of good nutrients, including enough vitamin C to keep scurvy at bay even in winter. Obviously, chips every day are not a good idea, but boiled or baked potatoes contain only 100 calories per 100 gramsg/3½oz – and you can dish them up with baked beans, salad, a poached egg, cottage cheese, cold chicken, garlic mayonnaise or spicy chilli to make a cheap and ribsticking meal.

It's worth noting that thin, burger-bar fries are much more unhealthy than old-fashioned fat chips. They absorb far more fat and are covered in salt, both of which are best avoided in any quantity.

Potatoes are a **good source** of vitamin C, fibre, some potassium, folic acid, iron and protein.

QUICK FOOD IDEAS

Potatoes Juventus: peel potatoes and cut into 1cm/½ in cubes. Put in a baking dish with 2 tbsp olive oil, tossing to coat them. Add a couple of sprigs of rosemary and bake till golden and tender.

For healthy mashed potato use olive oil, not butter.

Teaming potatoes with cabbage is a good way to persuade children to eat greens: try Bubble and Squeak (page 174) and Colcannon (page 141).

Sweet potatoes are a tuber, not related to potatoes, but they are so rich in beta-carotene they belong in any healthy diet. Cut them in fat chips and oven roast; cook them with ordinary potatoes and mash together; add them to soups, casseroles or stews.

spinach

Its iron content is not the best reason for eating spinach – sorry Popeye. It is, however, a very rich source of the dark green plant 'blood', chlorophyll, so is valuable both in preventing and treating anaemia. Children may not relish platefuls of spinach, but baby leaves in a salad with crispy bacon and slices of avocado may tempt them.

Spinach contains high levels of two carotenoids, lutein and xeaxanthin, which protect not only against cancer, but more particularly against a major cause of poor sight in later years called age-related macular degeneration. People who eat spinach and other dark green vegetables on a regular basis are less than half as likely as those who do not to develop this disease. It's never too soon to start protecting eyesight.

A **rich source** of the carotenoids, and a **good source** of potassium, vitamin E and folic acid.

onions, leeks, garlic

Onions, garlic, leeks, spring onions, chives and shallots all belong to the same family, the alliums. You might think that these strongly-flavoured vegetables lack child-appeal, but in fact most youngsters love them, as onion rings with their burgers, garlic bread in the pizzeria, or a hearty onion soup on a cold winter's day.

As well as that great taste, onions and garlic are a family medicine chest in themselves. As intensive modern research has shown, they protect the lungs, the heart and the digestive system, as well as being strongly anti-bacterial, anti-viral and anti-fungal. They are also potent cancer-fighters.

As atherosclerosis – the formation of fatty deposits in the arteries – is occurring earlier and earlier in the junk food generations, it is never too soon to start protecting children. Researchers have found that raw and also fried onions can pull down cholesterol levels in the blood.

QUICK FOOD IDEAS

If you've got the oven on, slice off the pointed tips across a whole bulb of garlic and put in the oven in a small ovenproof dish with a drizzle of oil for at least an hour. Then squeeze out wonderful garlic purée on to vegetables.

In winter, roast a whole unpeeled onion along with the baked potatoes and enjoy it with butter.

Wash and trim leeks, lay them in an ovenproof dish with a drizzle of olive oil and lots of black pepper, and bake in a moderate oven until tender.

The onion family is more valued for it's protective phytochemicals than for high levels of nutrients. But spring onions supply some vitamin C, and leeks **contain** vitamin C, folic acid and potassium.

sweet peppers

Sweet peppers come in rainbow colours, but children usually prefer the red, yellow and orange ripe ones to the harder, less ripe green ones – and they are richer in antioxidants, too. Serve sticks of peppers with a dip (see page 149 for some ideas), in salads or in vegetable stir-fries.

A **rich source** of vitamin C and also of the protective antioxidant beta-carotene.

beetroot

Not, please, the horrible pickled things you buy shrink-wrapped in the supermarket. Much better to choose the firm, raw, straight-from-the-ground variety, which, as its dramatic colour suggests, is loaded with anthocyanins which are antioxidants and cancer-fighters.

In Romany medicine, beetroot juice was used as a blood-builder, for patients who were pale and run-down. And in Russia and Eastern Europe, it is used both to build up resistance, and to treat convalescents after a serious illness. Fresh raw beetroot juice is a powerful blood-cleanser and

tonic. It has also been valued for centuries for its usefulness to the digestive system generally, and to the liver in particular – except when, as so often, it is drenched in hyperacid vinegars.

The popular French starter, crudités – a delicious combination of grated raw beetroot, raw carrot and perhaps paper-thin slices of cucumber, dressed with olive oil and lemon juice and garnished with chopped parsley – is a more powerful tonic for general health than a whole bottle of vitamin pills.

A **good source** of potassium and folic acid as well as of calcium.

green beans

When they are young and fresh in summer, green beans make a delicious vegetable contribution to a meal, whether you pick the big flat runner beans or the flat broad beans with the slippery skins. Green beans add colour and interesting texture to meals, and they supply the beta-carotene and

vitamin C lacking in dried beans. Green beans should never be eaten raw; an exception is broad beans which are best eaten when they are young and tender, when they make a delicious salad.

A **good source** of vitamin C, beta-carotene, potassium and folic acid.

pumpkin

Squashes come in a huge variety of shapes and sizes, many of them, such as butternut squashes and those fetching turban-shaped ones, being more widely available than was once the case. But it is pumpkins, those giant orange squashes that come out at Hallowe'en, that are most familiar to us – and they deserve to be eaten and enjoyed as food as well as being hollowed out as decorations for a party.

As their wonderful orange or yellow colours tell us, pumpkins are spectacularly rich in beta-carotene. It is not surprising, then, that in numbers of studies, the trio of pumpkin, carrots and sweet potatoes gave the highest protection against lung

cancer: regular consumption halved the risk of contracting the disease, even for heavy smokers. If you smoke yourself, or cannot persuade teenagers not to, make sure there is plenty of this great trio of vegetables on the menu as often as possible in your home.

In European folk medicine pumpkin is considered to be an especially good food for chest complaints, as well as a soothing, protective food for the entire digestive tract. Add chunks of pumpkin to stews or make it into a cheerful winter soup (see Pumpkin Soup, page 133).

A **rich source** of beta-carotene.

super salads

Salads, with their fresh raw ingredients, put vitality into the daily menu. The tender young leaves, bright red tomatoes, cool cucumbers and fresh herbs of summer bring sunshine straight to our tables, while crisp raw salads of celery and chicory, shredded cabbage and grated carrot make wonderfully light salads for winter.

lettuces

Lettuces are more than just water. They contain good amounts of several nutrients, a little iodine and even a modest amount of iron. As a rule, the darker the lettuce leaf, the higher its beta-carotene content. Because it is grown indoors, iceberg lettuce is the least valuable nutritionally, but it does keep well and kids know it from burger bars, so don't ignore it. Even if you've only got a window box, growing lettuce is a good way to introduce children to growing and eating greens – try cut-and-come-again varieties like mustard and cress or saladisi.

A woman considering pregnancy should bear in mind that 100g/3½ oz of lettuce provides more than a quarter of her daily folic acid requirement. And a lettuce sandwich at bedtime is a far healthier aid for insomnia than sleeping pills. The combined sedative effects of the lettuce and the tryptophan released by the digestion of carbohydrates ensures a good night's sleep.

Sadly, all these nutritional values may be more than counter-balanced by chemical contamination: commercial lettuce crops may be sprayed dozens of times before they reach you. So, always be sure to wash lettuces well before eating them, or buy organic, if possible.

A **good source** of folic acid, potassium and beta-carotene, and **contains** some vitamin C.

chicory

Wild chicory, the ancestor of both our fuzzy endive and fat pale celery, was highly regarded as a food medicine in ancient Egypt, Greece and Rome. Like most bitter foods, it is a liver stimulant and good digestive aid. Tear a few leaves into a green salad to give it crunch.

Chicory is more valuable for its phytochemicals than for its nutrients.

watercress

Hippocrates, who described watercress and its medicinal values in 460BC, built the world's first hospital next to a stream flowing with pure spring water so that he could grow fresh watercress for the benefit of his patients.

Watercress, like its relative the brightly coloured nasturtium, contains a benzyl mustard oil – similar compounds give 'bite' to the related horseradish and radish – which research has shown to be powerfully antibiotic. But, unlike conventional antibiotics, those in watercress are not only harmless to our intestinal flora, they are positively beneficial to the health of our gut. So eat plenty of watercress and you will greatly enhance your natural resistance.

Dr Stephen Hecht, Professor of Cancer Prevention at the University of Minnesota, USA, has recently published a dramatic report on the importance of watercress in the prevention of lung cancer in smokers. Of course, he says, the best way to avoid lung cancer is to stop smoking but, for those who can't, chemoprevention in the form

QUICK FOOD IDEA

Combine chopped spring onions, watercress, olive oil and lemon juice for a salad with 'bite'.

of 60g/2oz of watercress at three meals each day for three days will produce enough of the chemical phenethyl isothiocyanate, also known as gluconasturtin, to neutralize the important tobacco-specific lung carcinogen NNK. Phenethyl isothiocyanate is only released from watercress when it is chewed or chopped.

Because watercress is grown in water, it is specially important to wash it carefully before eating it to remove any waterborne parasites that may be present.

A **good source** of vitamins A, C and E, the powerful antioxidants that protect against cardiovascular disease as well as cancers, and of iodine, essential for the proper functioning of the thyroid gland.

celery & celeriac

Both wild and cultivated varieties of celery have long been popular with herbalists, who use the leaves, stalks and seeds. Most children love the crunchy texture and mild flavour of celery and will happily nibble sticks of it, with or without a dip.

Celeriac is a turnip-rooted variety of celery but it is the bulbous round root which is eaten rather than the stalks. The two smell similar, but celeriac has a less pronounced flavour. Children enjoy eating celeriac grated into fine matchsticks, par-boiled and served as salad with the addition of a creamy dressing.

Nutritionally and chemically, celery and celeriac are similar, but the white bulb of celeriac and

blanched white celery stems do not contain beta-carotene, whereas dark green celery stalks do. Celeriac is a rich source of folate which makes it an excellent addition to salads for women planning pregnancy, and both vegetables supply vitamin C, potassium and fibre.

Celery helps calm the nerves, wrote Hippocrates, and how right he was. Research in both China and Germany has demonstrated that essential oils extracted from celery seed have a powerful calming effect on the central nervous system.

Good sources of potassium; also **contain** reasonable levels of fibre and vitamin C, and some beta-carotene, if green in colour.

tomatoes

Tomatoes are a fruit rather than a vegetable, and most children will enjoy their sweet freshness in the summer – as long as you buy only the brightest, ripest red tomatoes and forget about the insipid watery pale things on sale for the rest of the year. Put a dish of tiny scarlet plum and cherry tomatoes on the table at the start of a meal: children will eat them happily. Tomatoes are extremely rich in antioxidants, especially carotenoids like beta-carotene and lycopene, as well as vitamins C and E, making them good protectors of the cardiovascular system and effective against some forms of cancer.

Tomato ketchup is super-rich in lycopene because the whole tomato, including its skin, goes into the ketchup. Organic tomato ketchup is now available – great for children's burgers.

QUICK FOOD IDEA

For a quick summer pasta, quarter ripe cherry tomatoes and stir them into cooked pasta with plenty of olive oil, some seasoning and a handful of torn basil leaves.

Canned tomatoes lose very little of their nutrients but do gain some extra salt. If buying tomato juice or the traditional Italian passata, choose low-salt varieties.

Sun-dried tomatoes are full of stored sunshine energy: add snippets to enrich a tomato sauce for pasta, tomato soup or stews.

A **good source** of carotenoids, potassium and vitamins C and E.

avocados

Avocados, like tomatoes, originated in South America. They are rich in healthy monounsaturated fats, which makes them especially valuable for children. Since avocados also contain compounds which stimulate the production of collagen, teenagers agonizing over pimples should eat them.

Weight-watching mums who think avocados are fattening are misguided: half an avocado has the same number of calories as two apples and far more nutrients, so don't deprive your children or yourself on that basis.

Because the fats in avocados are very digestible and because they also contain anti-fungal and anti-bacterial chemicals, puréed avocado is an excellent food for invalids, people convalescing from illness, and sick children.

If you need to ripen avocados quickly, store them in a brown paper bag.

Chunks of avocado add a rich, creamy note to salads, or serve them as Guacamole, which most children enjoy, or in the popular Italian Tricolore Salad – slices of bright red tomatoes, cool green avocados and creamy white mozzarella cheese, garnished with fresh basil leaves. There is also a tasty avocado dip on page 149.

A **good source** of essential fatty acids, potassium, vitamins A, C and E, and iron.

super fruits

Fruits, like vegetables, are the most important health-giving and protective foods. To obtain a maximum of the good things in fruit, all children should eat at least two or three helpings every single day. Encouraging your children to eat fruit is a health investment that will last for the rest of their lives.

apples

'An apple a day keeps the doctor away.' Indeed it does. Phenolic acids and flavonoids in the skins of apples have richly antioxidant qualities, inhibiting the growth of bowel- and liver-cancer cells, while apple juice has significant anti-viral properties. Eating five or more apples a week is thought to improve lung function, so ensuring that children eat apples could help keep them free of coughs, bronchitis and even pneumonia and asthma.

And that's not all. Apples are rich in a soluble fibre, pectin, which helps the body to eliminate cholesterol and toxic heavy metals like lead and mercury. The soluble fibre also makes apples a good weapon against constipation. Then, there's the malic and tartaric acids they contain: these help with the digestion of rich fatty foods. Apples are also good for treating diarrhoea. Naturopaths recommend grated apple, left to turn brown and mixed with a little honey, as an effective remedy for diarrhoea. The American BRAT diet (bananas, rice, apples and dry toast) is popular with doctors for the relief of diarrhoea.

The sugar in apples is mostly fructose, a simple sugar that is broken down slowly and thus helps to keep blood sugar levels on an even keel. Modern apples contain very little vitamin C, but some of the old English varieties like Sturmers or Worcester Pearmains are not only delicious but good sources of the vitamin.

A **good source** of fibre, malic and tartaric acids.

melon

This is a fruit with a great taste and real benefits for health. Melon does not a lot to offer in the way of classic nutrients like vitamins or minerals, though the deep orange varieties, such as the charentais, are antioxidant-rich. Melons are a cooling delicious treat in hot weather. A large slice of crunchy watermelon beats any can of fizzy drink for cool refreshment. All forms of melon are mildly laxative without being irritant, making this a good food to give children who are constipated.

Contains some potassium, a small amount of iron, vitamin C and folic acid.

citrus fruits

Oranges – at least when recently picked or juiced – have a high vitamin C content, which accounts for much of their beneficial influence on our health. Vitamin C is enormously important in combating infection and preserving general health, and plays a major part in helping the body absorb iron from other foods.

Oranges also contain beta-carotene, bioflavonoids (contained in pith and segment walls) which strengthen the walls of the tiny blood capillaries, and many other nutrients. Blood oranges, as you might expect, are particularly rich in protective antioxidants.

Oranges are in season and at their juicy best during the winter months, just when the protective nutrients they contain are most valuable, and when their vibrantly fresh taste is most welcome. Too many children only see oranges in juice form: the whole orange, peeled and divided into its neat little segments, is much more fun, as well as richer in fibre. And many children enjoy eating the flesh from crescents of oranges with the skin still on.

As well as vitamin C, oranges also supply a whole spectrum of nutrition, including even protein, calcium and iron. Their high potassium content makes them particularly useful to counter-balance the excess sodium in the crisps and other salty snacks popular with children.

The fruits, flowers and peel of both bitter and sweet oranges have long been used in herbal medicine. The peel contains hesperidine and limonene which are used in the treatment of chronic bronchitis. Tea made from the dried flowers is a mild sedative.

To ensure the best value from orange juice, be choosy about what you buy. Making your own from organic oranges just before you want to drink it is your best guarantee of maximum vitamin C content. The next best thing is freshly squeezed orange juice from your supermarket chill cabinet. But watch out: many of the products in the same-shaped bottles as fresh juice are 'drinks' or 'crushes' which may be full of sugar and may also have been pasteurized, which destroys much of the vitamin C content.

A **good source** of vitamin C, potassium, bioflavonoids, calcium and folic acid.

Lemons are a whole medicine chest in themselves. Lemon juice with hot water and honey is the first thing you give to a child with a cold, a temperature or 'flu. Used in food preparation, lemons not only supply vitamin C but are also a wonderful anti-bacterial. They are friends to the digestive system: a thick slice of lemon in a glass of hot water is an instant remedy for a tummy upset. Used as a gargle or mouthwash, lemons are perfect for sore throats or mouth ulcers.

A **rich source** of vitamin C: add the juice of a lemon to salad dressings.

Grapefruit are also high in vitamin C – the deeper the colour, the more vitamin C the fruit contains. One whole ruby grapefruit can contain a whole day's supply. The pith and skin between segments contain bioflavonoids, so don't scrape them all away. The pink ones are sweeter, too, so are more palatable for children.

A **rich source** of bioflavonoids and vitamin C.

Clementines, mandarins, satsumas and other small citrus fruits are all much less acidic than the bigger ones, are easier to peel and have few or no pips, so children can manage them easily.

Rich sources of vitamin C and **good sources** of folate.

berries

Most children love berries, both for their dramatic colours and for their marvellous flavours. Modern research has revealed that colours and flavours are each produced by a host of nature's most powerful healing compounds. They protect against heart disease, cancer, urinary infections, painful joints and skin disorders, and they are generally anti-viral, anti-bacterial and anti-inflammatory.

Strawberries are rich in the soluble fibre
pectin which helps in the body's elimination of cholesterol and toxic metals, such as lead, mercury and cadmium. This, combined with their powerful antioxidant properties, makes them highly effective against heart and circulatory disease. There is also a growing body of evidence that these delicious fruits have anti-viral properties too.

Strawberries contain modest amounts of iron which their extremely high vitamin C content ensures is well-absorbed, making them useful in both the prevention and treatment of anaemia and fatigue: 100g/3½oz of strawberries provides almost twice the body's vitamin C needs for a day.

This is one medicine which doesn't need a spoonful of sugar to help it down. These wonderful berries should be eaten on their own or at the start of a meal in order to achieve their therapeutic best. A few each day during the season is the cheapest, and most delicious, health insurance you'll ever buy.

A **good source** of vitamin C; **contain** some iron.

Blackberries are extremely rich in vitamin E
(wild berries have a higher concentration than the cultivated varieties), which is vital for the protection of heart and arteries.

Their dramatic black colour indicates the presence of valuable plant pigments called anthocyanins, which will help keep your children healthy as the weather gets colder. Add them – at the last minute to preserve their nutrients – to stewed apples, make them into delicious tarts or

pies, or combine them with slices of crisp apple in an autumn salad. Too many children grow up without the faintest idea of where food comes from. Make sure yours enjoy the traditional fun of blackberrying on an autumn afternoon.

A **good source** of antioxidants, vitamins C and E, fibre and potassium.

Raspberries, like grapes, should be on every
hospital menu. This delicious fruit is a rich source of vitamin C: 100g/3½oz provides 75 per cent of the UK RDA. They are also a useful source of the soluble fibre, pectin, and contain small amounts of calcium, potassium, iron and magnesium, all vital to the convalescent, as well as to those suffering from heart problems, fatigue or depression – and all well-absorbed, thanks to their vitamin C content. This makes them the perfect food for a poorly child – or for kids suffering from low spirits or tiredness.

Herbalists value raspberries for their cooling effect – useful in feverish conditions. Naturally astringent, raspberries can do good the length of the digestive tract, helping counter spongy, diseased gums, upset stomachs and diarrhoea along the way.

A **good source** of vitamin C, and useful source of iron, calcium, potassium and magnesium.

Blueberries contain the anti-bacterial
compounds anthocyanins, which have a tonic effect on blood vessels, and are protective of the eyes, making them a true superfood for youngsters who spend a lot of time in front of computer screens. Blueberries are also prized in traditional medicine as a treatment for cystitis and for diarrhoea. In Scandinavian countries dried blueberry soup is a favourite treatment for diarrhoea, as is chewing the dried berries.

Contain small amounts of vitamin C, vitamin B_1 and potassium: it is the natural chemicals they supply that make them medically valuable.

Cranberries are one of the very few fruits native to North America. For centuries Native Americans used these extraordinary berries as both food and medicine. Thanks to the vitamin C in cranberries, early settlers from Europe avoided the terrors of scurvy, as did American whalers in later centuries. Today, no Thanksgiving meal in America is complete without cranberry sauce for the turkey.

Science has recently validated the folk-remedy use of cranberry juice for both the prevention and treatment of cystitis, discovering a substance in cranberries that prevents infectious bacteria clinging to cells in the urinary tract and bladder. Cystitis can affect children as well as adults, and is not uncommon in young girls, so it is worth including cranberries and juice regularly in your menus for preventative reasons.

Cranberries **contain** vitamin C, B vitamins, iron and other minerals.

Blackcurrants are an exceptionally rich
source of vitamin C, containing four times as much as an equivalent weight of oranges. Just 60g/2oz of blackcurrants will give you 60mg of this vital vitamin. And it is particularly stable in blackcurrants – a syrup of blackcurrants loses only 15 per cent of its vitamin C content in a year.

Blackcurrants are also rich in anthocyanins, which are powerful antioxidants as well as being anti-bacterial. Both these qualities are put to good use in the country remedy for sore throats: hot blackcurrant juice sipped slowly. To make this, simmer half a cup of blackcurrants in 2 cups of hot water for 10 minutes, then strain and add some honey. Alternatively, add boiling water to a teaspoon of blackcurrant jelly.

A **rich source** of vitamin C and a **good source** of potassium and antioxidants.

Red currants, although they contain only a
quarter of the vitamin C of blackcurrants, still have plenty: 100g (3½oz) will supply the UK RDA. This makes them valuable for improving the natural function of the immune system. Although they lose some vitamin C when cooked, used as jellies, juices or stewed with other fruits red currants can make an important contribution to the diet of a recovering invalid. The iron, fibre and potassium in them are not lost during cooking.

Herbalists have traditionally recommended red currant juice as a refreshing and temperature-lowering drink for anyone with a fever.

A **good source** of vitamin C, potassium and antioxidants; **contain** iron and fibre.

cherries

Cherries are one of the few fruits not available for twelve months of the year so make the most of them while they are cheap and in season.

Because cherries have a reasonable potassium content and virtually no sodium, the fruit and the dried fruit stalks are an extremely effective diuretic. They are excellent for children with a tendency to constipation, too. For these reasons, cherries are often regarded as a specially cleansing food. Their bright flushed yellow or deep red colours signal their protective anioxidant content.

Cherries are great for the lunchboxes of children old enough to manage the stones: put them in a lidded pot so they don't squash over everything else in the box and there is somewhere convenient to put the stones.

A **good source** of bioflavonoids with some vitamin C and potassium.

apricots

Wonderful ripe apricots, the true colour of sunshine, should be enjoyed as often as possible, while they are cheap and in season. Whereas with most fruits fresh is best, apricots can be eaten fresh, cooked or dried and their nutritional value remains enormous. Their massive content of carotenoids makes them highly protective of skin and eyesight and invaluable for general resistance. They are also one of nature's great anti-cancer foods. Dried apricots are an excellent source of

QUICK FOOD IDEA

Whizz soaked dried apricots in a blender with live natural yogurt and honey.

fibre, iron and healthy energy, so they deserve a place in every child's lunchbox.

A **good source** of beta-carotene and potassium; also **contain** iron and a little vitamin C.

bananas

Bananas are the perfect fast food, even coming in their own packaging. The starch in bananas is not easily digested, which is why children should only eat them ripe, when most of the starch has turned to sugar. This happens when the skin turns a speckled brown. Because ripe bananas are so easily digestible and the fibre in them is mainly of the soluble type, they are good for the treatment of both constipation and diarrhoea, as well as helping to eliminate cholesterol from the body.

The high potassium content of bananas helps prevent cramp and, combined with the easily available energy from the ripe fruit, makes them the ideal snack for active youngsters. One banana contains a substantial amount of vitamin B_6, something that is often missing from children's diets and known to help in the prevention of depression, skin problems and asthma.

A **good source** of potassium, as well as of vitamin B_6 and folic acid.

peaches & nectarines

Velvet-skinned peaches and smooth-skinned nectarines are sisters under their skins, and in fact they are both especially good for your skin – it is no coincidence that an admired English complexion is described as 'peaches-and-cream'.

Nutritionally, there is little difference between the two fruits. They both contain good amounts of vitamin C (nectarines slightly more, so that one will give you a day's requirements) small amounts of fibre, modest numbers of calories, some beta-carotene and minerals. Dried peaches contain far more calories than fresh, but 100g/3½ oz will

provide almost a day's requirement of iron and a third of your daily need for potassium. Forget canned peaches, especially those in high-calorie, high-sugar syrup, because nearly all the vitamin C is lost in the canning process.

Peaches and nectarines should be thoroughly washed before they are eaten, skin and all: don't encourage children to peel them since, as with many fruits, much of their nutritional value is concentrated in the skin.

A **good source** of vitamins A and C, and also **contain** iron.

pineapples

In Hawaii, chunks of juicy pineapple are eaten by old and young as a delicious cure for digestive problems. Scientists explain that this is because the fresh fruit is rich in an enzyme, bromelain, which can digest many times its own weight of protein in a few minutes and only breaks down food and dead tissue, leaving our intestines undamaged. The juice of fresh pineapples, used as an instant gargle, is also an effective folk medicine for sore throats and was once a favourite herbal remedy for diphtheria. This is because pineapples contain compounds with marked antibiotic and anti-inflammatory effects.

Some of these compounds, though not the enzyme bromelain, probably survive the processing that produces commercial juice or canned fruit. But for maximum healing potential, fresh ripe pineapple or freshly extracted juice must be your first choice. Eating fresh pineapple or drinking pineapple juice is a good remedy for bruising sports injuries, such as falls, kicks or knocks. This is because the enzyme bromelain breaks down the accumulating blood in the injured area that causes the bruising to appear.

When choosing a pineapple, go for one that feels heavy for its size as this is a good guide to quality. Forget the old superstition that a pineapple is only ripe if you can tug a leaf out easily – it's nonsense.

A **good source** of fibre, and **contain** vitamin C.

QUICK FOOD IDEAS

Pineapple Iced Lollies: whizz fresh pineapple in a blender or food processor and freeze in iced-lolly moulds. Better than ice cream for a sore throat.

Pineapple Sorbet: combine puréed pineapple with sugar syrup. Freeze, stir, and freeze again.

kiwifruit

Kiwifruit contain almost twice as much vitamin C as oranges and more fibre than an apple. One kiwifruit will give you twice as much vitamin C as the recommended minimum daily intake. This vitamin C content remains very stable; although there are some losses soon after harvesting, 90 per cent of it is still present after six months in store.

Kiwifruit are particularly rich in potassium, a mineral of which Western diets, with their junk food high in sodium, can be dangerously short. The average kiwifruit supplies about 250mg of potassium, but only about 4mg of sodium.

When buying kiwifruit, avoid the rock-hard ones and choose those that are soft enough to yield to gentle pressure. They can be stored for several days in the refrigerator, and should be peeled just before eating.

QUICK FOOD IDEA

Once they've tried them, most kids will adore kiwis. Encourage them by putting one in an eggcup, slicing off the top, and letting children eat it with a spoon just like a boiled egg.

The fibre content of kiwifruit and their particular type of mucilage make them an excellent, but extremely gentle, laxative, ideal for youngsters who are often short of vitamin C and also, especially if they have been eating too much junk food, often constipated.

A **good source** of vitamin C and potassium; also **contain** vitamin E.

exotic fruits

As you would expect, fruits from sun-drenched tropical climes are high in protective antioxidants. As well as insisting on sunscreens and floppy hats, it makes sense to give children extra protection by giving them an abundance of these succulent fruits – where better to eat a mango than on the beach?

Mangoes

are a delicious and health-giving treat, brimful of nutrients. One average-size fruit gives the minimum daily need of vitamin C, two-thirds of vitamin A, nearly half vitamin E and almost a quarter of fibre, as well as useful contributions of potassium, iron and nicotinic acid. It's this great combination of antioxidants in a very easily digested form that should put the mango on everybody's weekly shopping list.

In their native India, mangoes are part of the way of life and are eaten all year round. In the hot season drinks are made from pulped mangoes to replace body fluids. Panna is made from pulped mangoes strained with salt, molasses and cumin, and mango chutney is served with spiced dishes.

Good source of vitamins A, C and E; also **contain** potassium, iron and some B vitamins.

QUICK FOOD IDEA

When mangoes are cheap and plentiful, use them for juice, milkshakes, sauces and iced lollies.

HEALTH WARNING

Mango peel can be highly irritant. Anyone who has previously been sensitized by mangoes can suffer a severe reaction. Even cutting the flesh with the knife you used to peel the mango can cause sufficient contamination to represent a hazard. If dealing with large numbers of mangoes, be sure to wear kitchen gloves.

Papayas

are nutritionally very important. They are a rich source of beta-carotene, which makes them excellent for treating skin problems. An average-size papaya supplies twice the minimum daily need of vitamin C, so the fruit helps boost the body's immune defence mechanisms; and well over a quarter of vitamin A. Because a fully ripe papaya needs no cooking, it can be quickly puréed or mashed to make an excellent and convenient first food for babies.

The most important constituent of the papaya is the enzyme papain, which is a great aid to digestion. In South American cooking, meat is often wrapped in papaya leaves to tenderize it.

A **good source** of vitamins C and A, beta-carotene and fibre.

Guavas

are an extremely rich source of vitamin C: one average-size fruit supplies five days' worth of the minimum UK requirement. There are many varieties, in a great range of sizes and flesh colours. The pink-fleshed varieties are richer in vitamin C than those with white flesh and the content is at its peak in green mature fruits.

Canned guavas can lose up to a third of their vitamin C content during processing, but are still an excellent source of the vitamin and retain the fibre content.

Guava has become popular as a drink but it is sold heavily sweetened as guava nectar.

A **rich source** of vitamin C; a **good source** of beta-carotene, phosphorus, calcium and the B vitamin nicotinic acid.

QUICK FOOD IDEA

Fresh guava purée added to a carton of natural yogurt makes an exceptionally health-giving and delicious 'shake'. Rich in calcium, gut-friendly bacteria, vitamins and fibre, it is a really nutritious addition to breakfast.

grapes

Every child's favourite fruit – especially the seedless varieties – but make sure they are well washed. Grapes are uniquely nourishing, strengthening, cleansing and regenerative. They are useful for anaemia and for fatigue.

Grapes contain enormous numbers of protective compounds called polyphenols; most of these are concentrated in the skin, and there are more of them in black than in white grapes, which is why red wine has earned its reputation as protection for the heart when drunk in moderation. The same compounds help prevent cancer, too.

A **good source** of potassium; also **contain** vitamin C.

dried fruits

Dates are mostly sold semi-dried, although fresh dates are also now quite widely available. Avoid the ones in gift boxes, which are heavily coated with sugar.

Fresh dates provide 96 calories per 100g/3½ oz, but 100g/3½ oz dried dates will give you around 250 calories. Fresh dates contain modest amounts of vitamin C, but there is virtually none in the dried variety.

It is the minerals in dates which are most interesting, especially their iron content. The amount of iron is totally dependent on the variety of date. One or two date varieties are very poor sources of iron, but the vast majority make highly significant contributions.

Their high iron content together with their easily available energy make dates an excellent nutrient for those suffering from anaemia and illnesses which produce chronic fatigue. They are a healthier sweet snack than chocolates or biscuits.

A **rich source** of iron and potassium; **contain** fibre and some B vitamins, including folic acid.

Prunes, which are dried plums, have an unfortunate reputation among children: perhaps if kids weren't told so often that prunes are good for them, they might like them better. As part of a mixed compote of fruit they are good to eat and a great source of instant energy, iron, fibre and a range of vitamins including A and B_6.

Prunes' well-known laxative action is due to a natural chemical that gently stimulates the bowel muscle. Since constipation is common in children, and irritant purgatives should be avoided, a few prunes occasionally will help avoid problems.

A **good source** of fibre, potassium, iron, and vitamins A, niacin and B_6.

Sultanas, raisins and currants have all the nutritional benefits of grapes concentrated in them, making them a wonderful store of instant energy for children and adults alike.

These dried fruits are spectacularly rich in potassium, a mineral useful for counteracting the high salt content of many fast foods and commercial breakfast cereals.

The perfect snack is a packet of raisins or sultanas, particularly when mixed with fresh unsalted nuts (over five-year-olds only) to provide protein as well as energy.

A **rich source** of potassium; a **good source** of iron, fibre and some B vitamins.

HEALTH WARNING

Non-organic dried fruits are treated with the preservative sulphur dioxide. Some are coated in mineral oil, too. Wash them carefully in warm water to remove both ingredients.

---

super pulses

One of the **first food crops** ever cultivated, beans originated in the Middle East thousands of years ago. **Dried beans** and other **pulses** are basic foods and essential in the diets of people all over the world today, being rich in **body-building** protein as well as in sustaining complex carbohydrates.

dried beans

A huge variety of dried beans is available today. There are the white beans of Western traditional cookery; the dark red kidney beans that are essential to Chilli con carne; the small black beans of Tex-Mex cookery; and the tiny green mung beans – most digestible of all the beans – of Indian cooking. Black-eyed beans, aduki, pinto and navy beans, and those speckled Italian borlotti beans are other members of this huge food family.

Weight for weight, beans contain almost as much protein as a good steak, with much less fat – beans are very low-fat – and lots of the soluble fibre that takes care of the heart and circulation. And they're high in complex carbohydrates which supply the best kind of energy for active children.

So, if you're in such a rush that all you have time to do for the kids' supper is heat up a can of baked beans in tomato sauce (sugar-free are best) and toast some bread to put them on, don't feel guilty: you're giving them a really nourishing meal.

Canning has turned beans into wonderful fast food. But canned beans can never have quite the authentic flavour and fresh taste of beans you have soaked and cooked yourself, and, although you need to plan bean-feasts well ahead, you'll only need to spend minutes on actual preparation.

You can also speed up the process. Instead of soaking the beans overnight, put them in a pan with enough water to cover them by 13cm/5in. Bring to the boil and boil rapidly for 2 minutes, then cover the pan, remove from the heat, and leave to soak for least an hour – more if you have the time. Drain the beans and start cooking them.

Soaking beans overnight is useful because the process helps break down the compounds that give beans their notorious reputation for windiness. Many herbs and spices, including winter savory and parsley, also counter the flatulence beans can produce.

Rich sources of B-complex vitamins; the minerals calcium, iron, magnesium and zinc; and protein and soluble fibre.

QUICK FOOD IDEAS

Baked beans on toast

Tuna and beans: flake canned tuna into well-rinsed canned white beans, dress with plenty of olive oil, lemon juice, pepper and a little salt, and garnish with onion rings and chopped parsley.

chickpeas

Like beans, chickpeas need long soaking before being cooked in plenty of water – 1.5 litres/2½ pints for 250g (8oz) dried chickpeas. Chickpeas add a special nutty flavour to spicy stews; they make delicious salads and chickpea flour is used in India to make savoury pancakes or to wrap around meat or vegetables like tortillas. Chickpeas are also a key ingredient of hummus.

A **rich source** of iron, calcium, magnesium, fibre and protein.

lentils

Lentils may have been the first-ever cultivated crop and there are many varieties of them, usually named after their colour, which can be green, red-orange, yellow, brown or black. To get the best value from their iron content, lentils need to be eaten with salads or vegetables rich in vitamin C so that the iron can be absorbed. They need no presoaking and only about 35–40 minutes cooking. They can give body to warming soups and stews, accompany roasts, and make an excellent salad.

A **good source** of B vitamins, fibre and protein; high in iron, calcium, zinc and other minerals.

split peas

Dried peas have been used for thousands of years, made into the solid sustaining soups of medieval peasants, the pease pudding of English cookery, the aromatic yellow purées of Greece, or dressed with oil and lemon and served as a meze with pitta bread. They are sold skinned and split, so need no soaking: cook them for 45–50 minutes.

A **good source** of protein and fibre.

soya beans

Soya beans are the source of such familiar foods as soya drink (also called soya milk), tofu, tempeh, soy sauce, miso, soya oil and TVP (textured vegetable protein). Like all beans, they are great sources of fibre, protein and some minerals. Soya beans also contain plant chemicals called isoflavones which mimic the action of natural oestrogens: studies have shown that the Japanese, who eat soya regularly, have far lower incidences of hormone-related cancers (breast and prostate particularly), and heart disease, than the West. However, isoflavones are found in all legumes, and too much soya can cause thyroid problems unless, like the Japanese, you eat plenty of seaweed; studies of people who eat diets rich in any of the legumes also show up lower rates of cancer and heart disease. Other studies, too, suggest that it is lifelong regular consumption of these pulses that confers protection.

Tempeh and tofu are good meat-substitutes in stir-fries or soups; organic tamari soy sauces add a great jolt of flavour to soups, rice dishes and stews, and miso may help protect against radiation.

A **good source** of protein and fibre.

super nuts & seeds

Think of nuts and you think of a cheap and handy snack, a little packet of something to nibble. But to our hunter-gatherer ancestors, nuts were far more than just a snack: with their high fat and protein content, they were a diet staple, and particularly useful since they were easy to store and transport – when they weren't being eaten straight from the tree.

Eaten as part of a meal, nuts are an excellent source of protein, which makes them a must for vegetarian children. Many nuts contain more protein than beef, and, whereas beef comes laced with saturated fat, the fats in fresh nuts are mono- or polyunsaturated, which favour healthy hearts. Nuts are good sources of antioxidants and they're high in fibre – essential for general health.

So, it is hardly surprising that a famous Seventh-Day Adventist study, which has been in progress since the mid-twentieth century, shows that those people who eat nuts more than four times a week have only half the number of heart attacks of those who eat them only once a week.

Allergic reactions to peanuts and to other nuts, which can in some cases be fatal, are becoming alarmingly common among children (see pages 202 and 204). The widespread use of peanut oil in processed foods and baked goods, and even in nursing mothers' nipple cream, is believed to be responsible for this.

Make sure that nuts are fresh – straight from the shell, if possible – because their high fat content means they easily turn rancid when shelled. Buy nuts in small quantities in their shells or whole rather than broken, and eat them up quickly. Store them in the freezer: they defrost quickly.

For maximum absorption of their mineral content, eat nuts with vitamin C-rich fruits and salads, or toast them lightly. As for those tempting little packets of nuts, avoid them except as treats: they are usually very high in salt and in fat, too.

Nuts are **rich sources** of protein and fibre and of the minerals calcium, magnesium, potassium, iron and zinc; and they are **good sources** of B-complex vitamins, except vitamin B_{12};

Seeds – future foods – are little powerhouses of nutrition. Tossed in a little hot oil for just seconds, they make delicious crunchy additions to salads; roasting or dry-frying seeds helps to release the aromatic essential oils they contain, thus increasing their flavour. Better still, teach your children to sprout them – and grains and legumes too – as then their nutritional value rises dramatically.

Seeds are **rich sources** of protein, essential fatty acids and several minerals.

HEALTH WARNING

Because of the increasing incidence of allergic reaction to nuts – especially peanuts – among children, allergy specialists suggest that children whose families have a history of allergies should not be given nuts to eat in any form until they are five or six years old. Children under three years old should not be given whole nuts, because they could easily choke on them.

almonds

Almonds are such a richly nutritious, body-building food that five or six are as many as anyone should eat at a meal. Almonds are 20 per cent protein by weight, and weight for weight they have a third more protein than eggs. A great energy food, they also contain an oil that is particularly bland and soothing: almond milk used to be given to babies as one of their first foods. For children who have a problem with dairy foods, almond milk, which can be bought in some health-food stores, is an excellent substitute for cow's milk with breakfast cereal. To skin almonds, dunk them in boiling water for half a minute, then drain and pop the skins off between thumb and finger – a nice little kitchen job for children. Bought ground almonds are sometimes adulterated with other nuts, or have a trace of bitter almond – better to make your own in a food processor.

A **good source** of protein, B vitamins, and zinc, iron, calcium and magnesium.

walnuts

Much the best way to enjoy these is by cracking the fresh nuts to dig out that tasty little kernel, a healthy way to end a meal. They are also great in salads, such as the classic Waldorf Salad.

A **good source** of protein, omega-3 fatty acids, potassium, zinc, some B vitamins and vitamin E.

chestnuts

The least fatty and the starchiest of the nuts – flour can be made from them – but richly nutritious as well. All children love the fuss and messy fingers of that wonderful mid-winter treat, roast chestnuts.

Contain vitamin E, potassium, vitamin B_6 and omega-3 fatty acids.

brazil nuts

Eat just one Brazil nut and you've probably taken in one day's supply of your body's requirement for the mineral selenium, a key player in the immune system, and a vital antioxidant which helps protect our hearts. Soils dedicated to intensive farming are likely to be depleted of their selenium content, but there's plenty of this key mineral in the soils of the Amazon rain forest where these nuts are grown. Brazil nuts are high in fat so they turn rancid very quickly: buy only small amounts at a time.

A **good source** of selenium and protein.

peanuts

The world's most popular snack is not actually a nut, but a legume. Peanuts can be eaten raw straight from those funny shells, or roasted, and most children love peanut butter. They are rich in protein, quite low in fat and filled with other nutrients, so peanut butter is a very healthy food for children, but look for brands without extra salt or added sugar. (For peanuts allergy, see page 204.)

A **good source** of protein, vitamin D, fibre, magnesium, iron and zinc.

pistachio nuts

These should be eaten from the shell when they are fresh – if only for the fun of cracking open their tough little shells to get at the green kernels inside. Pistachios have the lowest fat content of any nut, and much of the fat they do have is healthy monounsaturated fat. Their delicious flavour does not need enhancing by roasting or salting: try to eat the unsalted kind.

A **good source** of healthy fats, plus protein and significant amounts of four vital minerals: magnesium, calcium, iron and potassium.

pine nuts

The softest and most delicate of all the nuts, pine nuts are an essential ingredient in the Italian pasta sauce, pesto. They can also be tossed in a little oil for salads, or added to savoury rice dishes.

A **good source** of protein, magnesium, iron, zinc, potassium and vitamin E.

cashew nuts

This delicious nut is always sold shelled and roasted to destroy the film of caustic oil between the two layers of its shell. Avoid the salted ones and choose plain roasted. Cashews are high in healthy heart-protecting monounsaturated fats.

A **good source** of protein, potassium and B vitamins, including folate.

hazelnuts

Deliciously crunchy hazelnuts are rich in the B vitamin thiamin, deficiency in which can make people of any age feel low and lethargic. And they supply the omega-3 fatty acids needed for balance in our diets.

A **good source** of protein, fibre, thiamin, magnesium and vitamin E.

pumpkin seeds

Buy them ready-shelled and dry-roast them in a non-stick pan to add to salads, or as a crunchy snack: they are an exceptionally good source of zinc, vital for our immune systems, our skin and the efficient functioning of our brains.

A **good source** of zinc, protein, fibre, iron, magnesium and potassium,

sesame seeds

Children love the nutty taste of these tiny, light-brown seeds: add them to muesli, toast them and sprinkle on salads or add to rice dishes, or mix into yogurt with honey for a super-snack. Do not buy sesame seeds that are an even cream colour – they have been chemically hulled. The calcium in sesame seeds is easily assimilated.

A **good source** of protein, calcium, zinc, iron and potassium.

sunflower seeds

These go rancid very quickly, when they turn yellow, brown or black instead of their pearly grey: avoid sunflower seeds so coloured. Once bought, eat them up fast. A high-protein snack, they are a useful source of vitamin E and important B vitamins.

A **good source** of protein, iron, calcium and vitamin E.

QUICK FOOD IDEAS

Toasted or tossed in a speck of olive oil, nuts can give a satisfying crunch to salads.

Make your own mixed-nut butter as a change from just peanuts: combine two or three different nuts – perhaps cashews, pistachios, almonds and/or hazelnuts – and drop them into a blender with a little olive oil.

Ground almonds make a great topping for crumbles, either on their own or added to the usual flour-based crumbles. Buy ground almonds in small amounts and use them up within a few days, or make your own in a food processor from whole almonds.

super grains

Unrefined grains have been the staple diet of some of the hardiest and healthiest races on the planet. Richly nourishing, whole grains are an essential part of any child's diet, supplying protein for body-building, carbohydrate for energy, fibre for a healthy heart and digestive system, and essential fats, vitamins and minerals.

wheat

Today, much of the world's bread is wheaten, including the chapattis of India and the pitta of the Middle East. The husk or bran of wheat is rich in fibre, minerals such as iron and calcium, B vitamins and important trace elements including chromium, which helps stabilize blood sugar levels (see page 14). The germ of the wheat is a nutritional treasury, supplying antioxidant vitamin E, B vitamins, minerals and healthy fats. The white flour widely used for bread, cakes, biscuits and other processed foods loses much of its goodness, including zinc, magnesium, vitamin B_6 and vitamin E, when the germ and fibre-rich outer husk, or bran, are stripped out in milling. Thus, only wholemeal flour, which is milled from the whole grain, can claim to be a true superfood.

Bulgur or cracked wheat, a Middle Eastern favourite, retains much of the goodness of wholewheat. Since the grains are already roasted, bulgur can make a nourishing salad after a simple rinse and 10-minute soaking. Add extra-virgin olive oil, massive amounts of mint and parsley, and chopped tomatoes to make the Lebanese salad Tabbouleh; or serve it with Roasted Vegetables (see page 174) for a satisfying supper.

Sprouted wheat is tremendously rich nutritionally and fresh wheatgerm, the germ of the grain extracted during milling, is a superfood for growing children, packed with B vitamins and essential fatty acids. Store fresh wheatgerm in the refrigerator and use it up fast, sprinkled on cereals or in place of breadcrumbs in cooking.

Semolina, made from the hard outer part of wheat, is used in the making of couscous and pasta, both great superfoods, providing children of all ages with lots of slow-release energy.

Note: see Allergies (page 204) for the problems some children have with eating wheat-based foods.

QUICK FOOD IDEAS

Wholewheat pancakes served with apple purée.

Wholewheat pitta pizzas, brushed with oil, topped with sliced tomatoes, a pinch of dried oregano, seasoning and grated cheese, then grilled.

Sprouted wheat with hummus and tomato slices in sandwiches.

rice

For half of humanity, rice is the foundation of their diet, and for centuries it was eaten with only the inedible outer husk removed. This unrefined rice is a low-fat, very easily digested food supplying plenty of energy and useful amounts of some B vitamins.

Brown rice, the whole natural grain with its bran, is more nutritious than white rice and helps stabilize blood sugar levels. Brown rice takes longer to cook than white, but is much harder to overcook. To prepare, wash it well and put in a saucepan with a teaspoon of vegetable bouillon powder and enough water to cover by about the depth of a thumbnail. Cover the pan tightly and cook for about 40 minutes. It can also be cooked in a casserole in a low oven. Brown basmati rice, with a delicious nutty flavour, takes about 25 minutes to cook.

White rice, universally eaten today, is polished to remove the thin outer skin and the germ as well, thus stripping it not only of all its fibre and 60 per cent of its mineral content, but most of its vitamins too, including almost all the B vitamin thiamin, which we need for the digestion of carbohydrates.

'Par-boiled' or 'converted' rice has some of these nutrients driven back into it by steaming.

Rice water, made by cooking 30g/1oz whole rice in 1.2 litres/2 pints water and then straining it, is a traditional remedy for diarrhoea.

QUICK FOOD IDEAS

Cooked brown rice mixed with apple purée is an old country favourite for a soothing and sustaining supper.

If you have leftover cooked rice, fry mixed vegetables – carrots, onions, leeks, cabbage, courgettes, tomatoes, sliced and diced small – in a wok, then add the cooked rice and a cupful of hot vegetable stock. Cover and simmer for 20 minutes.

Use up cooked rice in croquettes: add grated cheese, chopped parsley and a beaten egg to the rice; form into croquettes, dust with flour and fry.

See also Brown Rice Four Ways (page 173).

millet

The only grain that is a complete protein, millet is a richly nutritious food for growing children, low in starch and very easily digested. It contains more iron than any other cereal, and plenty of magnesium. It is also high in silicon, a mineral needed for strong bones, teeth and nails, and healthy hair. Since it is gluten-free, millet can be eaten by children sensitive to the gluten in grains (see page 204). It should always be washed thoroughly several times under cold water and drained before cooking. Try a millet pilaf as a change from rice as a savoury side dish: put 1.2 litres/2 pints water in a pan with a big lump

of butter and a little salt, and bring to the boil. Add 250g/8oz millet (weighed before washing), bring back to the boil, lower the heat, cover tightly and cook for 30–40 minutes, stirring occasionally. The mixture will be thick and porridge-like.

To prepare millet like a breakfast muesli, put a tablespoon of millet in a bowl, add a cupful of milk and a dollop of runny honey. Mix together thoroughly, cover and refrigerate overnight. In the morning, add more milk if necessary, and chopped bananas, berries or grated apple. Millet is an ingredient in the famous health food Five-Grain Kruska (see page 123).

oats

For centuries oats were eaten as a staple food throughout northern and eastern Europe, often in the form of a simple porridge. Until the nineteenth century oats were the mainstay of the Scottish country diet, too, and according to one Scottish physician they produced 'a big-boned, well-developed and mentally energetic race'.

Rolled oats and oatmeal, the milled grain, are both high in protein, rich in minerals including zinc, iron, calcium and magnesium, and they pack in enough B vitamins to rank as a first-class remedy for nerves and exhaustion – just the food for stressed-out teenagers. They're also a rare source of the omega-3 essential fatty acids.

The fibre in oats excites cardiologists, too: in studies at Kentucky University in the USA, high cholesterol levels nose-dived when a diet rich in oats was eaten. And before insulin was discovered, one of the few effective treatments for diabetes

was the 'oat-cure': oats have a remarkably stabilizing effect on blood-sugar levels.

One way and another, in fact, this warming and nourishing food will send children off to school full of energy, and keep them going all morning.

QUICK FOOD IDEAS

Porridge, properly made with fresh oatmeal, eaten with honey and a trickle of cream.

Fresh trout or mackerel rolled in oatmeal or oat flakes, then fried.

When making bread, substitute 30g/1oz oatmeal for 25g/1oz out of every 500g/1lb flour.

2 oatcakes (see recipe page 158) with a hunk of cheese, a glass of milk and an apple adds up to a perfectly balanced quick snack.

corn

Pre-Colombian America feasted on this grain from South America and used every part of it for medicine. But when corn became the staple diet of the very poor in the southern United States and parts of Europe, thousands fell sick with pellagra, the deficiency disease caused by lack of vitamin B_3. For this reason, sweetcorn should be eaten with good sources of vitamin B_3, such as eggs, tuna or milk. This defect apart, sweetcorn is still a delicious user-friendly food that children eat with gusto, especially messy, delicious corn on the cob with plenty of butter. Sweetcorn, fresh or frozen, provides more protein than potatoes, plenty of fibre, useful vitamins and minerals.

The flour from corn is made into polenta, a near-solid deep yellow creamy food that Italians love to combine with roast chicken or dark

aromatic game stews. Popcorn is a healthy snack, easily made at home. Both cornflour and popcorn are made from unmilled corn.

QUICK FOOD IDEAS

Sweetcorn with tuna, sliced tomatoes, parsley and basil, and French dressing for a quick salad.

As a side-dish: melt 1 tablespoon of butter in a saucepan, add a packet of frozen corn, stir, cover and let heat through for 5–6 minutes. Season and add chopped parsley.

To make salt-free popcorn, heat a little oil in a big pan, drop in popping corn, cover tightly and wait for the music!

barley

Probably the oldest of all cultivated grains, barley is rich in useful minerals, with particularly high levels of bone-building calcium, and plenty of B vitamins. In ancient Rome it was valued as a particularly strengthening food, fed to gladiators in training. Tell that to your 10-year-old son! The little beige grains of pot barley are unrefined: eat them in preference to pearl barley, which cooks much faster but has lost a lot of its goodness in refining. Barley is an ingredient in Five-Grain Kruska (see page 123). Herbalists value barley for its uniquely soothing action the length of the digestive tract, and it makes a nourishing and soothing drink for children laid low by mystery bugs or tummy upsets. Most children, well and sick, like Lemon Barley Water.

rye

Rye flour makes coarse and heavy black bread, and the rye bread you buy in shops is usually half rye and half wheat flour for this reason. But rye is a wonderfully warming grain for winter – survival food for millions of Russian peasants through long hard winters – and is rich in fibre. It is also particularly low in gluten. Rye crispbread is a must in the family store-cupboard.

buckwheat

Buckwheat is actually a seed, but it has always been used in grain-like ways – chiefly as kasha, the porridge-like food eaten all over eastern Europe right down to the steppes of Russia. According to the US Department of Agriculture, the protein in buckwheat is complete, and as valuable as that in meat. It is also a rich source of magnesium and zinc, and rich in a flavonoid called rutin, which helps keep the walls of the tiniest blood capillaries strong and elastic. Buckwheat has a fairly strong flavour which some children may not like. To persuade them to try it, make the Buckwheat Crêpes on page 148.

ancient grains

Growing numbers of people are sensitive to certain common foods – over 35 million in the USA, according to the National Institute of Health – and wheat is one of the most frequently cited culprits. Diversifying your diet by eating from a wider range of grains makes obvious sense: the more so since some of the ancient grains are much richer in protein, minerals and fibre than modern wheat. A growing range of these grains, as wholegrain flours, cereals and mixes for baked goods, are becoming available. Look for the following grains in health-food stores.

Kamut

Kamut has been raised in Montana in the USA from a packet of grain shipped from Egypt in the 1970s. Clinical trials conducted in Chicago for the International Food Allergy Association indicated that 70 per cent of those severely allergic to wheat could tolerate kamut. This ancient cousin of durum wheat is lighter and softer in baked goods than wholewheat flour. It is also higher in protein and richer in almost every mineral.

Quinoa

Quinoa, like buckwheat, is a seed rather than a grain. The Incas cultivated it and thought highly of it, perhaps because of its high protein content, as well as its slightly smoky taste. It is available in health-food stores as a wholegrain or flour. To make a creamy porridge, add one part of well-washed grain to two parts water in a pan, bring to the boil, cover, lower the heat and simmer for 12–15 minutes. Fluff with a fork and serve with butter and chopped fresh herbs as a savoury pilaf. Add quinoa to nourishing winter soups.

Spelt

Spelt was the grain of the Roman armies, and highly regarded in the Middle Ages as particularly nourishing, and ideal for building strong bodies and healthy blood. It is actually richer in protein than today's wheat, has more minerals, and special sugars that help boost resistance. Spelt wholegrain flour makes delicious bread, and can be substituted for wheat flour in baking.

Another bonus is that many wheat-sensitive people find they have no problem with spelt.

Amaranth

Amaranth, which has a slightly nutty flavour, was cultivated by the Aztecs and the Incas. It deserves to be on any family shopping list, since this ancient grain is a whopping 16 per cent protein – compared to wheat's 10 per cent or the 7 per cent of rice. It is also a rich source of calcium and has more than three times the iron content of wheat.

super meat

Before grains and legumes were extensively cultivated, meat, fish and fowl were our early ancestors' most reliable source of protein. In today's varied diet, meat still offers valuable protein and other important nutrients for growing children. Of all the areas where 'organic' is really important, meat for children must come first, to avoid the risks of growth hormones, neurotoxic chemicals, antibiotics and, above all, BSE.

beef

Beef has traditionally been one of the most highly sought-after of all meats. There is no denying the nutritional benefit of beef. It supplies most of our dietary needs apart from fibre, though some constituents are present only in small amounts.

The way beef is cooked is nutritionally important. Trimming visible fat before cooking reduces total fat in such dishes as stews and casseroles. Joints should be roasted on a trivet so that the fat drips through into the pan and can be removed before making gravy from the residual juices. Steaks and chops should be cooked in the same way.

Beefburgers made at home from lean minced steak are great for kids, but commercially produced ones are inevitably high in fat. A standard burger isn't bad at only 9g of fat, but a quarterpounder has 20g (about ¾oz), rising to a massive 63g/2oz in a double 125g/4oz burger with cheese and all the trimmings. And that's without the fries!

Beef in small quantities is a good constituent of a normal mixed diet, but advice from the WHO and the Harvard School of Public Health suggests it should only be eaten a few times a month or, if more frequently, in very small amounts.

A **rich source** of protein, and a **good source** of calcium, vitamin C and folate.

Note: not all children will eat offal, but ox and calf liver (and lamb and pig liver, too) are extremely rich sources of nutrients, especially easily absorbed iron and vitamins A and B_{12}, so offering it to children is always worth a try.

HEALTH WARNING

Undercooked beefburgers may contain harmful bacteria. One strain, E.coli 0157:H7 VTEC, gets in at the time of slaughtering and when the beef is minced, is distributed throughout the finished product. This particular strain can cause serious illness and even death. Thorough cooking until there is no trace of pink in the meat or juices is essential to destroy this E.coli bacterium.

lamb

New season spring lamb is always the most tender and has the lowest fat content, though modern breeds are all lower in fat generally. The amount of fat that you get with your lamb depends on the cut, how it is cooked and what you eat: neck fillet and leg are lower-fat cuts. Ideally, most of the fat should be removed before cooking and any that's left on the meat should not be eaten.

A **rich source** of protein, easily absorbed iron, and zinc and B vitamins.

pork (& bacon)

There is a popular misconception that pork is a 'fatty' meat, whereas in fact modern breeds produce pig meat which contains less fat than beef or lamb and very little more than chicken – if you don't eat the skin.

There's no doubt, though, that pork is an extremely good source of several nutrients, while the iron it contains is haeme iron, which is much more easily absorbed and used by the body than that of other meats. Some of the chemicals used in producing ham and bacon are known to be carcinogenic if consumed in excess, particularly the nitrites. Both products are also high in salt and should be eaten sparingly.

A **rich source** of thiamin (vitamin B_1), niacin, riboflavin (vitamin B_2) and zinc; and a **good source** of vitamin B_6, phosphorus and iron.

rabbit

Delicious, delicately flavoured, high in protein and low in fat, joints of rabbit can be grilled or sautéed, but rabbit stew is the traditional and best method of cooking. Children sometimes have problems with the bones so they're best removed.

To compensate for the rabbit's lack of many nutrients, use plenty of root vegetables in the stew and serve it with a large salad.

A **rich source** of protein; very low in fat; also **contains** minerals and B vitamins.

venison

Venison, farmed rather than wild, is making a comeback in supermarkets, so if your children are adventurous with their food, why not give it a try? Flavour and texture are superb and it contains only a third of the calories and half the fat of beef, and even less than chicken.

Prime cuts should be cooked very hot and for just enough time to be medium rare. Otherwise, marinate before cooking. Red wine, oil and herbs are common marinades in Europe and the UK, and buttermilk is a US favourite. English slow-cooked venison hotpot with lots of vegetables, and the American hunter's campfire recipe cooked in coffee and cider vinegar, are both wonderful.

A **rich source** of protein and ultra-low in fat; also **contains** zinc, iron and B vitamins.

super poultry

All poultry is a **terrific source** of **protein, B vitamins** and **minerals**, which makes it an ideal food for growing youngsters, a real boost during periods of **intense activity**, both physical and mental, and an excellent superfood for **convalesence** after illness. Chicken, especially, is a versatile food that any child can enjoy.

chicken

Until the time of factory farming and intensive rearing, chicken and turkey were luxury meats. Both are now so cheap that they are everyday foods, but the price we pay is a lack of flavour and texture, a higher saturated-fat content and the risk of chemical residues like antibiotics and growth-promoting hormones. Far better to spend more on free-range organic poultry and eat a little less of it.

Chicken meat contains much less fat than red meats and, as most of this is contained in the skin, it's easily removed. As well as protein, chicken provides easily absorbed iron and zinc – twice as much in the dark meat as in the breast. This makes it excellent food during pregnancy, and a blood- and resistance-builder for children of all ages.

Roast chicken should have all the fat removed from inside the body cavity. It should then be cooked on a roasting rack so that all the fat drips into the bottom of the pan. Don't cook potatoes in this fat: roast them in a separate dish drizzled with olive oil and sprinkled with rosemary. Enjoy the succulent flavour of chicken, but don't eat the skin.

A **rich source** of protein and most B vitamins, and a **good source** of iron and zinc.

wonderful chicken soup

All poultry can be used to make soup, though it is important to remove as much fat as possible from the stock, either by skimming or blotting it off, or by refrigerating overnight so the hardened fat can be removed in the morning.

The traditional Chicken Soup beloved of European, British and American Jewish mothers has more than folklore to thank for its nickname, 'Jewish penicillin'. Researchers have found a special sulphur compound in chicken soup that really does protect against throat and chest infections. The protein content of soups made from chicken and other poultry is also very easily absorbed, which makes them perfect invalid food. It's possible that a poor immune system, chronic fatigue and glandular fever may all be aggravated by poor protein absorption, particularly in the presence of digestive difficulties. Chicken soup could be the answer.

turkey

The modern farmed turkey is a pale and insipid descendant of its wild ancestor in North America. But if you can find a free-range organic bird, you will be well-rewarded. Unlike other poultry, turkey is extremely low in fat, containing only 2.7g per 100g/3½oz. It's rich in protein and supplies some well-absorbed iron and zinc, more in the dark meat than the white.

The low fat content tends to make it a dry insipid bird when cooked unless great care is taken. Generally speaking, the larger the bird, the less it dries out and the better the flavour. Many children prefer delicious cold leftover turkey, which can also be used in curries and hashes.

A **rich source** of protein and vitamin B$_{12}$; a **good source** of other B vitamins, potassium and zinc.

duck

Duck is rich in protein, minerals and lots of the B vitamins. Delicious though the crispy skin is, you will get 29g of fat if you eat 125g/4oz of meat and skin, but only 9.7g if you just eat the meat. Always cook duck on a rack. Prick the skin all over with a sharp fork or skewer first, so the fat layer under the skin can trickle out and fall under the rack as it melts in the heat of the oven. Served with apple sauce, duck not only tastes wonderful, but benefits from the pectins in the apple which help the body eliminate much of the cholesterol from the duck.

With the huge popularity of Chinese food, many children get their first taste of duck served with plum sauce, spring onions, cucumber and buckwheat pancakes in the local Chinese restaurant. You couldn't have a healthier combination.

A **rich source** of protein, iron, zinc, potassium and nearly all the B vitamins.

COOKING POULTRY SAFELY

The vast majority of our intensively reared chicken meat is infected with salmonella bacteria. While this does not present a health hazard when chicken is thoroughly and properly cooked, undercooked chicken is an extremely common cause of food poisoning.

- When cooking chicken and other poultry at home make sure that frozen birds are thoroughly defrosted – 24 hours in a refrigerator – before cooking.
- If roasting, ensure the oven is fully up to temperature before placing the bird inside.
- To check that poultry is cooked, prick the thickest part of the thigh with a fork or skewer to see that juices run clear.
- If barbecuing chicken, it's best to part-cook it first to ensure that it is cooked right through when finished on the barbecue.
- Any poultry which is still pink when you cut it, or has juices that still appear bloodstained, should never be eaten.
- Observe the rules of kitchen hygiene when preparing, handling and cooking poultry (see pages 114–15).

QUICK FOOD IDEA

A delicious pitta filling from left-over cooked poultry. Dice the cold poultry into small cubes. Heat 1 tablespoon olive oil in a deep frying-pan. Add 1 bruised garlic clove, 3 finely chopped spring onions, with their green tops, and 1 medium potato, peeled and diced into small cubes. Sweat gently for 5–6 minutes until soft. Add the poultry, increase the heat and cook for 5 minutes, stirring frequently. Serve hot in warmed wholemeal pitta breads.

super fish

Fish is an **outstanding superfood**. It is rich in **protein**, low in **fat**, and loaded with B vitamins and **precious minerals** from the seas which were the origin of all **life on earth**. Sea fish are particularly valuable for their **high iodine** content. The oily fish are important sources of vitamins A, D and E and the omega-3 **essential fatty acids**.

at the fish counter

When buying **fresh fish** check that the eyes are bright and shiny, not dull or sunken in to the head, that the skin still has lots of scales on and that gills are still red. Fish should always have the fresh smell of the sea. Look for bright clear spots on plaice and well-defined markings on other fish.

When buying **shellfish** check that they feel heavy for their size. All molluscs should be closed. All shellfish should be eaten on the day you buy it. Above all, buy your shellfish from a regular supplier whose reputation you can rely on.

Watch out for additives in **processed fish**. Colourings, preservatives and flavourings are commonly used in the coating of fish fingers, and brown and yellow dyes on kippers and smoked haddock respectively. Growing public concern about additives in recent years has meant that more manufacturers have given up using them and undyed kippers and haddock are widely available.

at home

All fish are particularly nutritious for children as they are easily digestible and quick to cook. Another bonus is that if you buy seasonally some can be extremely inexpensive. If your youngsters already like fish fingers, it won't be too hard to persuade them to be just a bit more adventurous.

As a rule of thumb, all fish take 5 minutes per 2.5 cm/1 inch of thickness to cook, no matter how large the fish or whether it is baked, steamed, grilled or pan-fried.

• When baking, put the fish into a preheated oven. If cooking whole fish, score the surface with two or three deep cuts, brush with olive oil and sprinkle with herbs and lemon juice.

• Steaming can also be done in the oven by wrapping the fish in a loose but tightly sealed foil parcel. For traditional steaming, an ideal and cheap utensil is the Chinese bamboo steamer, which works brilliantly and is easy to handle.

white fish

These are all very similar from a nutritional standpoint, whether sea fish like cod, haddock, whiting, monkfish, sea bream, catfish, red and grey mullet, snappers, plaice, sole and halibut, or freshwater fish like pike, perch, bream or carp. They contain virtually no fat, few calories and plenty of the protein needed by young children.

They all contain the B vitamins but not much iron and, although halibut (which is slightly oily), may contribute a little vitamin A, the white fish do not generally supply fat-soluble vitamins.

Cod and halibut livers are very rich in vitamins A, D and E, but these aren't eaten, just used for the production of oil.

oily fish

Oily fish like mackerel, salmon, trout, tuna, herring, anchovies, sardines, whitebait, sprats and eels contain high levels of eicosapentanoeic acid, one of a group of fatty acids belonging to the omega-3 family. These are known to be essential to healthy cell function, especially in the brain, and their anti-inflammatory action can be extremely valuable in the relief of psoriasis and eczema.

When buying fish canned in oil take great care to read the labels. Avoid those marked 'vegetable oil'

as this is certain to contain a proportion of palm oil which is high in saturated fat. Choose instead fish canned in olive, sunflower or safflower oil and drain off the surplus before serving it.

Oily fish are often smoked to preserve them and, though little of their nutritional value is lost, a great deal of salt is added before the smoking process. Eating large amounts of smoked food has been linked to a higher incidence of cancer, so smoked oily fish should be regarded as occasional treats.

shellfish

These can be divided conveniently into the crustaceans: crabs, lobsters, prawns, shrimps, crayfish and langoustines; and the molluscs: mussels, oysters, cockles, whelks, winkles, clams and scallops. All shellfish contain the same amount of protein and other nutrients as white fish, though they are much saltier. The vitamin and mineral content of the crustaceans is the same as white fish. Molluscs contain much more iron and vitamin A and they are also good sources of zinc, especially oysters, which, together with cockles and whelks, contain as much iron as a fillet steak.

Winkles are an even richer source of this essential mineral, supplying as much as the equivalent weight of meat or poultry liver.

HEALTH WARNING

Shellfish are a fairly common cause of severe food allergy reactions. If children have had one bad reaction, be extremely careful to ensure they avoid eating shellfish again (see page 204).

super dairy products

Dairy products are widely eaten in the Western world, where they are a key ingredient in many of the foods children most enjoy, such as ice cream, milkshakes, pizza, lasagne and summer salads. They are a major source of bone-building calcium, essential for the healthy growth and development of all children.

milk

Milk is our very first food, and the COW'S milk so widely drunk in the Western world is great stuff for growing children. When in the 1930s undernourished Scottish school-children were given a daily pint of milk, their growth rate accelerated about 20 per cent, and there was an obvious improvement in health and vitality.

Milk provides bone-building calcium, plenty of protein, zinc for the immune system and growth generally, and some vital B vitamins, including folic acid and vitamin B_{12}. When the cows graze out-of-doors, their milk is always a rich source of vitamins A, D and E, and of a special fatty acid (CLA) which may help protect against a number of cancers, including melanoma (skin cancer) and leukemia. The vitamins A, D and E are all found in the cream, for which reason children under five – or over, for that matter – should always be given whole milk, not skimmed or semi-skimmed. Even whole milk is over 96 per cent fat-free.

Wonderful food that it can be, however, the milk news is not all good. Bones need magnesium as well as calcium, and other trace elements, all poorly supplied in milk. In many parts of the world, people lack the enzyme lactase needed for its digestion, and millions of people in the West are allergic or sensitive to it. Eczema, asthma, colic in babies and hyperactive behaviour have all been linked with milk, as have catarrh, sinus trouble and respiratory problems (see Allergies, page 204).

Goat's milk is now on sale in every supermarket, however, and children who cannot tolerate cow's milk may thrive on this substitute. The various substitute 'milks' on the market, particularly those based on soya, supply protein, and some are fortified to provide extra calcium, but these drinks lack most of the B vitamins, and other trace elements found in true milk. Some experts are questioning, too, the wisdom of giving small children big regular doses of the isoflavones found in soya drinks, a practice unknown in Japan.

Organic milk is now widely available. Free of the traces of antibiotics, growth-promoting hormones and pesticides liable to lurk in ordinary milk, it is worth the extra cost hundreds of times over for your children's health.

cheese

Cheese is another great food for growing children – though with the possible problems of milk (see page 204) – and one that adds a huge range of wonderful tastes and textures to their diet. The hard **cow's-milk cheeses**, such as Cheddar, tend to be the highest in fat, but they are also the highest in protein, in calcium – a 60g/2oz chunk of Cheddar will supply your day's calcium needs – and in zinc, which is needed by developing brains, the skin and the immune system and which could also help protect children from anorexia and other eating disorders.

Introduce children to a wide range of cheeses, including soft young **goat's cheeses** (older goat's cheeses become much sharper and develop that distinctive flavour which many people dislike), but save the blue cheeses until they are older. Cheeses made from **sheep's milk** may be easier to digest: they include the wonderful Spanish Manchego – in Spain you can choose the degree of maturity and sweetness you prefer – and Greek feta cheese, which is hard, white and crumbly and very good in salads.

QUICK FOOD IDEAS

The ploughman's lunch – 2 or 3 different cheeses, wholegrain rolls, and coleslaw could be a quick, tasty and nutritious weekend lunch.

Granny Smith's Welsh Rarebit (see page 155).

Pizza-style Bread (see page 198).

Greek salad: diced cucumber, chunks of tomato and green pepper, onion rings and black olives, dressed with plenty of oil, lemon juice, fresh herbs and seasonings, with cubes of feta cheese tossed in.

cottage cheese

Most children love cottage cheese, a mild-tasting curd cheese, which is far easier to digest than ordinary cheese, and is very low in fat but still has lots of protein. The Indian cheese, panir, is made from curd cheese pressed solid and cut into cubes. Cottage cheese is so mild that you can eat it with either savoury or fruity accompaniments, and as such it can turn a snack into a fairly square meal. A must for the family fridge – but eat it up quickly: dried-out cottage cheese is not pleasant.

QUICK FOOD IDEAS

Supper for a hot day: cottage cheese with chunks of peach or nectarine, a few strawberries, or a handful of grapes.

Slices of tomato and cucumber tossed with cottage cheese, served on lettuce leaves with plenty of fresh basil, coriander or parsley and a drizzle of extra-virgin olive oil.

yogurt

One of the fermented foods developed by primitive people the world over, yogurt is definitely in the superfood category, not only because it is rich in calcium, protein and some important B vitamins, but also because it is much more easily digested than milk. Its great claim to fame, however, is the wonders it works in the digestive system.

The human gut is host to several billion bacteria. Most of them are good guests, helping protect us from less friendly bacteria, and new research suggests that they may also play a key role in the healthy functioning of the immune system. When these good guys get wiped out by pathogenic bacteria, or by a course of antibiotics, yogurt helps replace them, as long as it is one of the serious 'bio' or live yogurts.

All fresh yogurts, except those pasteurized for a longer shelf life, contain lactic acid bacteria, and may also contain varying amounts of others, such as bifidus. Yogurt makers are getting very serious about the health-giving properties of their product, and many brands – look for the word 'bio', for instance – may contain extra quantities of these useful bacteria. Remember that the fresher yogurt is, the higher its bacterial content; remember, too, that pasteurized yogurts do not contain these bacteria and are no longer 'live'.

Flavoured fruit yogurts almost always proclaim virtuously that they are low-fat or very-low-fat. No doubt they hope this will distract attention from the sugar or sweeteners, colouring, flavouring, stabilizers, emulsifiers and other chemical nasties such yogurts usually contain. Since 100g/3½oz ordinary yogurt contains only a single gram of fat, don't be fooled. And don't waste your money on the long-life newcomers which don't need to be refrigerated. They aren't 'live' any more. Buy thick natural yogurt – Greek for special occasions – and make your own delicious fruit versions. Introduce children, too, to sheep's milk yogurt – which they may like even more: and when they're tiny, give them goat's milk yogurt, even easier for them to digest.

QUICK FOOD IDEAS

Stir puréed fruit, or crushed strawberries and raspberries, or a spoonful of a no-sugar fruit spread into natural live yogurt. Blend with fresh orange juice and water for a refreshing summer drink.

Stir fresh mint, grated cucumber, a little olive oil, salt and a touch of lemon juice into natural live yogurt for a lovely summer salad.

eggs

One of the most important substances in egg yolk is lecithin, which is vital as part of many of the body's metabolic processes, including the dispersal of dangerous fat deposits and cholesterol. Lecithin helps to prevent the development of heart disease and the formation of gall stones and also encourages speedy conversion of body fats into energy. Because of their high lecithin content eggs are an important brain food, contributing not only to memory and concentration, but also to good mental and emotional status. Eggs are also rich in protein, zinc, vitamins A, D, E and B_{12}.

How sad it is that the obsession with cholesterol, especially in the US, has resulted in the humble egg being branded as a black villain in the heart disease story.

Because of recent scares involving salmonella in eggs, people have been turning against them even more. The risk of infection is far, far less in a well-run organic farm where the chickens are not crowded and have large areas of fresh land to roam and feed. Pregnant women, babies and very young children, the elderly or anyone with an existing severe illness should avoid runny yolks or undercooked scrambled eggs. The best protection for everyone is to buy only free-range organic eggs from a certified supplier. They will provide one of the best nutritional value-for-money bargains.

While British and US experts advise no more than three or four eggs per week, the World Health Organisation advocates a total of 10, including those used in cooking. Eggs are an amazing source of high quality protein. Just two boiled eggs supplies a quarter of a day's need which, with their other nutrients, makes them a true superfood for children of all ages. Eggs in almost any form are the perfect quick food for children from older babies to teenagers. We suggest some ideas below.

HEALTH WARNING

Eggs are quite a common cause of allergy (see page 204) and some authorities believe that introducing eggs too early in a baby's diet can increase the risk of allergy. Between six and nine months is usual, but later rather than sooner is advisable if there is a history of allergy in your family. In some children asthma attacks can be triggered by eggs.

QUICK FOOD IDEAS

Eggy triangles: cut medium-thick bread into triangles. Heat 1 tablespoon vegetable oil in a frying pan. Beat 1 lightly seasoned egg smoothly and dip the bread triangles in it. Fry the triangles in the oil until golden on both sides. Drain on kitchen paper.

Flavoured scrambled eggs: lightly cook chopped tomato in a little melted butter and pour scrambled-egg mixture over it. When the egg is almost cooked, sprinkle over a little grated cheese.

Mix chopped hard-boiled egg with mayonnaise and chopped cucumber for a sandwich filling or open sandwich topping.

super fats

Without some fats meals would lose their savour and interest. And without the right fats, children cannot grow and think. Vegetable oils, for instance, provide the fats we need to hold our cells together, insulate us from the cold, supply energy and deliver the important vitamins A, D, E and K.

The whole question of fats is complicated and confusing, but understanding the different types of fats, what they do, how much we need and how much is healthy, is a vital step on the path to nutritional good health (see page 16). All of the healthy fats and oils make a major contribution to the calorie consumption of small children. These calories come in abundance from small amounts of the fats and oils, so it is much easier for youngsters to get their calorie needs from these than from having to eat huge amounts of the bulky foods that would be needed for the equivalent calories.

It is now certain that the seeds of heart disease are sown in childhood, if not before, so getting your youngsters into good habits regarding eating fats is vital to their long-term good health. Unsaturated fats, found mainly in vegetable oils like soya bean, corn, sunflower and safflower and in oily fish, contain virtually as many calories as saturated fats, but they are extremely important for good health and should form a regular part of every child's daily diet.

HEALTH WARNING

Labels such as 'cholesterol-free' or 'low in cholesterol' on foods can be very misleading. It is the percentage of saturated fats that you have to look out for, avoiding foods high in them.

---

butter

Butter is delicious and used in modest amounts it is certainly better than any margarine, most varieties of which are high in unhealthy trans fats (see page 17). Butter is virtually all fat and 60 per cent of that is saturated. But butter is also a rich source of vitamins A, D and E so, used sparingly, it is useful for children. Unlike most dairy products, butter is a poor source of calcium and contains virtually no B vitamins.

vegetable oils

Oils are enormous providers of calories, 899 per 100g. Most vegetable oils contain little saturated fat and good supplies of vitamin E. Exceptions are palm oil and coconut oil, which both contain large amounts of saturated fat, and coconut oil has virtually no vitamin E. It is likely that either of these oils would be a constituent of anything labelled "vegetable oil" so always buy named varieties of oil, or if you're buying foods canned in oil avoid any just labelled 'vegetable oil'.

The polyunsaturated fats in vegetable oils are extremely important because they contain essential fatty acids that we do not make for ourselves.

When used in baking bread and cakes, oils retain most of their nutritional value, but when used for frying the percentage of polyunsaturated fats is reduced: up to 20 per cent in quite a short cooking period.

Sunflower is the richest of vegetable oils in vitamin E. It and **corn** and **safflower** oils are ideal for light salad dressings and for cooking. Their light flavours may make them more acceptable to children than the richer olive oil.

Walnut oil and **hazelnut oil** both contain important essential fatty acids, and gourmets love their strong and characteristic flavours, walnut especially, on green-leafed salads or added to boost the flavour of a stir-fry. These oils may be too strongly flavoured for young palates, although teenagers may appreciate them.

olive oil

Olive oil, although a monounsaturated fat, is a marvellous food-medicine. In traditional folk medicine, it has always been recommended as an enhancer of overall health and a remedy for digestive problems.

Recipes in this book specify 'extra-virgin olive oil' for salads and dressings, but include 'olive oil' for basic cooking such as stir-frying. Extra-virgin olive oil is expensive, but it is the healthiest because the way in which the oil is extracted from olives does not lose any of its rich mineral, vitamin, essential fatty acid and antioxidant content – or its wonderful flavour. Choosing the best possible olive oil – and cold-pressed varieties of other vegetable and nut oils, too – could help your children avoid a range of illnesses from arthritis and joint problems to heart disease and some forms of cancer.

cream

OK, so it's high-fat, but cream is one of life's treats, so don't banish it from your home on that account: and as long as it is healthy organic cream – the only kind we'd give children – that fat is rich in sunshine vitamins A, D and E. Whipping cream is 35 per cent fat, against the 48 per cent of double cream or the 18 per cent of single. Fromage frais or yogurt can often be substituted for cream – rich Greek yogurt is even nicer with a fruit salad than cream, we think.

herbs & spices

Nearly every herb or spice commonly used in cookery has also been employed as a medicine down the centuries. Almost all of them improve the digestion of foods to which you add them and most herbs and spices also have other healing properties that make them great additions to foods for young and old alike.

herbs

Parsley is rich in iron as well as antioxidants beta-carotene and chlorophyll, which make it great for tired, listless teenagers. It also contains good amounts of vitamin C. Add it to soups, salads, home-made vegetable juices and sandwiches.

Sage is a great aid to the digestion of rich fatty foods: add a leaf to the pan when you fry sausages. It is also very effective against infections of the mouth and throat.

Rosemary is a friend to the memory, because it is a stimulant to the brain, and to the nervous system. It is also a good general tonic. Add sprigs to a roast of spring lamb, or warm it in the olive oil in which cubed potatoes are to be baked.

Thyme is a powerful antiseptic and general tonic and has a good aromatic flavour – so it is a must in robust winter stews and casseroles.

Oregano gives pizzas their distinctive wonderful aroma and is also a powerful antiseptic (though it should not be used medicinally during pregnancy). Use it dried or fresh in tomato-based sauces, soups and casseroles.

Basil is the perfect herb for children of all ages, because it is calming and soothing – so it will be good for parents, too. The aromatic oils in fresh basil that produce these beneficial effects have an unmistakable aroma in any tomato dish and every type of salad. It is an essential herb in pesto. Basil freezes well, but loses much of its aroma when dried.

Garlic offers super protection for the heart, lungs and digestive system and is also powerfully protective against all kinds of infection, so give your children plenty during winter months especially. Add it to soups, salads and savoury dishes – and kids love garlic bread.

Mint, the inseparable companion of new potatoes and roast lamb, has an uniquely soothing effect on the digestive system. Try peppermint tea for stomach upsets, too.

Chives are junior members of the great onion and garlic tribe, and add a fresh distinctive note to summer salads, especially cucumber and tomato.

Bay leaves, added to stocks and soups and to bean casseroles, help counter gas and wind. They are a natural aid to digestion.

Coriander is also very beneficial to the digestive process. The fresh green leaves add a wonderfully aromatic and tangy flavour to curries, rice dishes and salads.

spices

Chilli peppers provide a boost to the circulation and are very helpful for the digestion. When cooking for children, try these fiery flavourings, whether fresh or dried, powdered or flaked, in tiny quantities at first.

Cinnamon warms the whole system, to aid circulation and digestion, and is a powerful antiviral, too. Use it in winter cakes, apple puddings and hot drinks.

Cloves are another great winter warmer and antiseptic: use them in bread sauce, dried fruit compotes and apple puddings.

Nutmeg is a warming aid to digestion. Grate it over winter vegetables like spinach, cabbage and cauliflower just before you serve them up.

Ginger turns up in almost every Chinese Indian meat dish to improve its digestibility, protect against toxins and improve flavour. Hot ginger tea will help ward off colds and chills, and children love crystallized ginger. Ginger is an effective remedy for nausea and travel sickness, so it is a good idea to have some crystallized ginger or a can of ginger ale handy when travelling with children.

Cumin is another digestive aid and nerve tonic, adding that unmistakably aromatic note to the kebabs and stews of Middle Eastern cookery. Don't keep ground cumin too long because it loses flavour quickly.

the danger foods

By the time your children are old enough to have reached the big wide world of the playground and the children's party circuit, you will have come to realize that much of the food their school-mates eat for much of the time is not exactly healthy. Foods once known as occasional treats have become part of our children's everyday eating.

According to recent research, as many as 99 per cent of the food products advertised on UK television during children's viewing times is potentially unhealthy for them. And psychologist Dr Aric Sigman, who contributed to the research, pointed out that the advertisements 'were crafted to exploit children's vulnerability at critical stages of their development'.

There's nothing wrong with crisps, chips, cakes and chocolate when they are occasional treats. But the key word is occasional, and they will stop even being treats when children can have them any time they want. Explain to your children exactly why you're being selective – or, as they will probably see it, mean – with their treats. When they are big enough, show them how to read food labels and identify the cosmetic additives and the artfully disguised sugars. Teach them to be questioning about the endless parade of TV commercials aimed directly at them. Gently, little by little, instil into them a sound knowledge of nutrition. Show them how to make healthy choices.

One day your children will thank you; for the time being, you'd better get used to being unpopular quite often. But you know it is worth it.

On these pages is a run-down of the danger foods and drinks that you need to think twice about before giving them to your children.

caffeine

Tea and coffee are not drinks for small children. The caffeine in them renders them powerful stimulants which can easily make children edgy and hyperactive. The tannins in tea can interfere with the uptake of vital nutrients, including iron and magnesium. Keep children off both until they're at least six or seven; then, if they ask for it, give them tea in the shape of a little milk and hot water and just a splurge of tea. Green tea would be even better, but if you're drinking Indian tea yourself, don't expect children to choose green. There's caffeine in many of the most popular soft drinks, too, including colas: read the labels carefully so that you know what to avoid.

burgers

The burgers served in popular chain-restaurants or sold from the supermarket deep-freeze are likely to be made from the cheapest source of factory-farmed meat, with a high content of saturated fat, and probably some chemical additives – colour, preservatives, flavourings – thrown in for good measure. Meeting the gang for burgers at the local burger-bar is one of those teenage rites of passage that you would be highly unwise to forbid. But otherwise, either buy readymade burgers from a trustworthy butcher, or make your own from good lean meat, or from grains and vegetables. There are plenty of recipes in Satisfying Suppers (see pages 164–187).

soft drinks

These drinks all have one thing in common: sweetness. Unless the drink is a 100 per cent fruit juice, its sweetness will be provided by either sugar or artificial sweeteners. As well as these, carbonated drinks are also likely to contain flavourings, colours and preservatives (see Additives, overleaf), carbon dioxide to provide the fizz, and phosphoric acid which can leach calcium out of bones and teeth. New research from Germany has also linked a high intake of phosphate-containing drinks with hyperactivity and other behaviour problems. Seventy per cent of fizzy drinks contain caffeine, which can quickly turn children who drink them often into addicts craving their next fizzy fix.

Juice-based drinks, squashes and -ades can look like a more healthy choice than other soft drinks. But look at the label: in many of them, the fruit content is actually tiny and colour, flavour and preservatives may all be supplied by additives. Even pure fruit juices are not the best choice for children if they are drunk in any quantity, as the fruit acids they contain can damage tooth enamel, while the natural sugars in fruit are still sugars, and you can have too much of them.

So if you give your children fruit juice, serve it undiluted only on very special occasions, such as Sunday morning breakfast with all the family; otherwise, dilute it at least half and half. When you're really thirsty, there's nothing like water.

sugar

Sugar turns up in the most surprising foods: there is quite a lot of it in a can of baked beans, a jar of peanut butter, a readymade pasta sauce, and even crisps. Food manufacturers love sugar because it is cheap, is an excellent preservative, and can help improve texture. In the USA, Canada, Australia and the UK, consumption of sugar is rising inexorably – not so much spooned out of the sugar-bowl at home as hidden in many foods and snacks eaten from babyhood upwards. Sometimes, it is called sugar on the label. More often you'll find it lurking under its other names – sucrose, maltose, dextrose, dextrin, glucose, or invert sugar which sounds somehow harmless. They're all sugars and your children don't need them in these quantities. See Carbohydrates (page 13) to remind yourself why.

artificial sweeteners

There have been many question marks over the safety of the artificial sweeteners saccharin and cyclamates. So most manufacturers now go for aspartame, the brand-name of which is NutraSweet. If your children eat flavoured yogurts, breakfast cereals, frozen desserts, refrigerated puddings or fruit spreads, if they drink any kind of soft drink including flavoured milk, or if they chew gum, they could be ingesting NutraSweet. It may also be added to foods and drinks as well as sugar: it is much cheaper. But the scientific history of this popular sweetener is not reassuring.

Regular intake of aspartame has been linked to headaches, brain tumours, seizure (as in epilepsy), and mood disorders. The manufacturer of NutraSweet claims that there is 'overwhelming scientific evidence' for its safety. In fact, of 166 studies into the safety of aspartame on human health, 74 had industry-related funding and all 74 gave it a clean bill; the remaining 92 were independently funded and only 12 failed to note some kind of adverse reaction.

A three-year study was begun at King's College in London in 1999, which should show whether the sweetener carries a risk of brain tumours.

Other studies suggest that artificial sweeteners trigger sensations of hunger in the brain that lead to over-eating and, therefore, obesity.

additives

Back in the 1960s, thousands of impossibly hyperactive children became controllable and near-normal when they were put on a diet which excluded numbers of additives commonly used in food, particularly colourings such as E102 (tartrazine). Some of these additives are no longer permitted in foodstuffs eaten by children, but many still are, numbers of which have been linked to health problems such as asthma and eczema in vulnerable children, or those with behavioural disorders such as hyperactivity (see page 206),

despite having passed safety tests. What has not yet been tested properly, is how damaging they can be in the endless combinations in which they are consumed – and, in the case of children, in the quantities. Most additives, most of the time, are used to give eye or taste appeal, or longer shelf life, to high-fat/high-sugar or high-salt foods that are not particularly healthy anyway. Yogurts aimed at children are likely to be specially high in sugar and in additives. If in doubt about E numbers, check in a good source (see Books to Read, page 216).

chocolate & sweets

To a child a bar of chocolate is a gift-wrapped chunk of sheer deliciousness. To the detached eye, it is a lot of unhealthy hardened fat, sugar, chemical additives, and some cocoa solids. Most sweets are made to the same unhealthy recipe, only more so. Continental dark chocolate with at least 70 per cent cocoa fat solids is a better choice

than most children's bars, especially the excellent organic versions. But it has a slightly bitter flavour, and is unlikely to appeal to young children. You will have to work out a strategy for limiting sweet and chocolate consumption that doesn't turn them into highly desirable foods, with all the extra appeal of forbidden fruit.

biscuits & cakes

Almost any home-made biscuit or cake you can produce is going to taste better than the wretched stuff on the supermarket shelves – mixes of highly refined flour, sugar, hardened fats, and flavourings.

crisps

Crisps are a delicious crunchy treat. But an occasional treat is what they should remain. Why? Firstly, they are more than one-third fat – even 'low-fat' crisps contain than 20 per cent fat – and an unhealthy highly saturated fat at that, which will help clog up young arteries. Secondly, they contain a staggering amount of salt – over 1 gram in an average packet. Thirdly, they often contain sugar and, if they are 'flavoured', they will contain artificial flavourings, too.

ice cream

Proper ice cream made with cream, sugar and perhaps fruit is delicious. It's pretty fattening stuff, but at least it can be said to be real food in some respects. Perhaps your best policy here is to serve real ice cream as part of a family meal for a treat, and to hope to persuade your children into spurning the ghastly ersatz stuff mostly on offer. Read the labels with them: hydrated fats, lots of sugar, air, water, powdered milk, and plenty of chemical additives, and that's about it.

breakfast cereals

We have been brainwashed into seeing the average packet of breakfast cereal as a nourishing, nutrient-packed food to give our children a great start to the day. Most cereals are far from this in reality: they have huge amounts of sugar by one or other of its names, a surprising amount of salt, and they're based on highly refined grains. A few cheap extra vitamins added will not compensate for such unhealthy eating. For plenty of better choices, see Big Breakfasts (pages 120–127).

meals for every age group

As children grow, so their nutritional needs develop. Here, the essential foods for each childhood stage, from baby to teenager, are profiled and danger foods noted. Menu plans offer great ideas for feeding children super meals every day of the week.

enjoying good food

Feeding children a generation or so ago was simpler than it is today.
Mothers prepared purées for babies, rather more exciting food for toddlers
and, after that, for much of the time, children ate with the family.
Ice cream, sweets, chocolate and crisps were treats, not everyday fare,
and there wasn't a burger bar in every high street.

Today, the feeding of our children has become a heavily mined battlefield, in which policies have to be carefully thought out and pursued, painful decisions made, and clever strategies devised. For the first two or three years, your children's diet is in your care. After that – from the first small tots' party for nursery-school friends – the world of commercial food marketing comes pushing in, and you will be up against it.

You will be up against little friends whose mothers allow them sweets, biscuits, soft drinks, crisps every day of their lives. You will be up against the irresistible lure of that children's Mecca which seems so grown-up to them, the local burger bar. You will be up against the relentless bombardment of commercials on the television your children watch, plugging junk food in every shape or form. You may very well be up against their school's unenlightened views on catering, the soft-drinks machine in the corridor and the burger-and-chips van in the playground. And finally, you'll be up against the urge of all children to conform, and not to be 'different'.

You will need to be firm. You'll have to say no much more often than you'd like. And you'll be treading a narrow path between a hard line which turns junk food into irresistible forbidden fruit, and the soft option of over-indulgence. It will undoubtedly be very, very tough. But you will be rewarded by healthy, vibrant children who are full of energy, with minds as active as their young bodies. You'll be rewarded by their growing realization of how much good health depends on what and how we eat. And you'll be rewarded by their enjoyment of real good food.

one stage at a time

In the following pages you'll find advice and tactics to deal with the problems and sort out the situations which may arise at the main stages of a child's development. There is also a special section for vegetarian children.

For each stage, there is listed half-a-dozen Superfoods especially appropriate for those years. And there are menu plans for Mondays to Fridays, for winter and summer, making great use of the recipes in this book. Since so many children take a packed lunch to school, the menus feature suggestions for every weekday, as well as ideas for simple lunches during half-term or the holidays. For more ideas, see Tasty Lunches.

Weekends should be a break from routine for everyone, when schedules tend to go out of the window and pre-planned menus are inappropriate. But hopefully, weekend eating should feature at least one relaxed family meal, when the children may be joined by their own friends, and for which you'll find plenty of ideas in the Recipes section.

healthy babies from day one

There is no better time than when a baby is planned for prospective parents to take a close look at lifestyle and eating habits. For healthy sperm, viable eggs and high fertility, optimum nutrition is needed and that means plenty of foods rich in beta-carotene, folic acid, vitamin E, zinc, protein, B vitamins and iron.

Both alcohol and caffeine are known to damage sperm and these should be kept to a minimum for three months before planned conception. Nicotine is harmful to sperm – sperm counts have declined by 50 per cent in the past 30 years – and also to developing babies so you should both quit smoking. But most important of all, you should both be eating as wide a variety of healthy, nutrient-packed foods as possible, a fact emphasized by another alarming statistic: almost half the women attending fertility clinics have been on some form of restrictive weight-loss diet in the previous 12 months – a sure sign that what you eat plays a major role in fertility.

safe eating for mum-to-be & growing baby

Although many experts advise a total ban on alcohol during pregnancy, others believe that two or three glasses of good red wine a week will not do you or the baby anything but good. Large amounts of caffeine should be avoided, however, as this substance can interfere with the absorption of iron and zinc from food.

Do not eat liver or liver pâté as they contain a lot of vitamin A, too much of which can cause birth defects. Avoid unpasteurized milk or cheese, and any soft or blue cheeses, as they may contain the listeria bug which is hazardous to the baby.

All red meats, including burgers, must be cooked thoroughly until there are no traces of pink in the middle; otherwise, there is a risk of toxoplasmosis and E.coli infection. Poultry must be cooked until the juices run clear and there is no trace of pink in the flesh, and eggs should be cooked until the yolk is hard to protect against salmonella. Wherever possible, this really is the time to choose organic foods to avoid unwanted antibiotics, neurotoxic chemicals and growth hormones.

Raspberry-leaf tea has been used by women for centuries as a tonic for the reproductive system. It should only be taken regularly in the last six weeks of pregnancy, when it will help to strengthen the long muscles of the uterus and assist with contractions and labour pains during labour.

pre-conception fitness for men

This pre-conception plan for men, to be started three months before you want to try for a baby, may sound cold and calculating, but it will dramatically increase the health and fertility of sperm, as well as being good for general fitness.

Stop smoking. There is growing evidence that cigarettes can reduce the level of male hormones, interfere with sperm development and even cause congenital defects in babies.

Stop drinking alcohol, or at least drastically reduce your intake. Alcohol can severely damage sperm, so make sure you have no more than two or three drinks a week in the three months leading up to conception.

Watch your weight. Obesity interferes with hormone balance and may cause infertility.

Take 500mg **vitamin C** daily to reduce the risk of sperm clumping together in bunches. One month before you start trying for a baby, increase your intake to 1 gram a day.

Make sure you are eating **plenty of fruit,** especially oranges, kiwifruit, and orange and dark green fruits and vegetables.

Boost your intake of **zinc,** a mineral essential for reproduction, by adding lots of shellfish, particularly oysters, and pumpkin seeds to your diet.

Now's the time to stop high-caffeine **coffee** and **cola** drinks; weak Indian or green tea is all right in small amounts.

It is now essential to try and eat only **organic meat,** to avoid the risk of added hormones.

eating healthily while pregnant

You are what you eat, and your baby is what you eat too, so ignore the friends, mother-in-law, grannies and busybodies who keep reminding you that you are 'eating for two'. You are not. You are eating for one and nourishing one and a bit.

Take good care of yourself and your diet because you will have extra nutritional needs. At the same time, don't become a food freak, don't become

obsessed by diet and don't worry about every bite you take. What you need is a simple commonsense approach that will make sure you have a healthy pregnancy, a healthy baby and the energy to look after it once it is born. This will also make sure you get back to your pre-pregnancy weight with as little fuss as possible, though this will take longer – and, indeed, should not be a priority – if you are breast-feeding as you will need plenty of extra calories.

There is another 'don't' that may seem obvious but is important. Don't diet to lose weight unless you are advised to by your doctor. Instead, take some extra exercise, so long as there is no medical reason why you should not.

Many women have problems with digestion during the last month or so of pregnancy, because the bulge gets in the way. It is more comfortable to eat little and often, but make sure that your total food intake does not go up.

six superfoods for men and women

Prawns High in protein, and a good source of zinc, calcium and iron, these are a delicious treat, but make the most of their low fat content by having them boiled or grilled – don't turn them into deep-fried scampi.

Herring A great source of vitamins A, B and D, they also supply plenty of much-needed iodine, selenium, phosphorus, potassium, iron and calcium. Most importantly during pregnancy, herring, like other oily fish, are a rich source of the essential fatty acids required for the baby's developing brain.

Brown rice Eat this for its B vitamins, potassium, iron, protein and fibre.

Broccoli A rich source of vitamins A and C, together with potassium and folic acid.

Citrus fruits These, and kiwifruit, are all super-rich in vitamin C; the citrus fruits also provide important bioflavonoids to maintain the health of the circulatory system.

Live yogurt Important for the extra calcium you need, yogurt also has all the beneficial probiotic bacteria which will keep your digestive system working efficiently so that you absorb maximum nutrients from your food. The bacteria also play an important part in stimulating your natural immune system, thus helping to protect against viral and bacterial infections.

eating plan for mums-to-be

As a mother-to-be, you need a minimum of 2,200 calories a day – more if you are physically active – and it is important that you get them from a good mixture of different foods. Your total food intake should increase by around 20 per cent, but your body's need for folic acid, vitamins B and C, calcium, zinc and magnesium go up by far more.

Vegetarians, and particularly vegans, may be at risk of vitamin B_{12} deficiency and any woman who has been trying to lose weight by drastic

dieting could be missing out on essential nutrients. If you are in either of these groups talk to your doctor about a vitamin and mineral supplement.

Eat lots of fresh fruit, vegetables and salads. Try to stick to wholegrain cereals. During pregnancy food passes through your intestines more slowly to make sure that your body can absorb all the nutrients in it in order to nourish the baby. Consequently, constipation is common, so drink lots of water to prevent it.

sources of particular nutrients

You should be getting around 60g (2oz) of **protein** a day. A chicken leg has about 30g (1oz) protein, 30g (1oz) cheese has about 7g (¼oz), 180g (6oz) cod 35g (just over 1oz), a two-egg omelette 15g (½oz), and 125g (4oz) cooked lentils 19g (just over ½oz).

Canned sardines with the bones, low-fat milk, yogurt and cheese, beans, cereals and nuts all provide extra **calcium,** and **essential fatty acids** are a bonus from the sardines.

Meat, chickpeas, leafy green vegetables, dried apricots, dates and raisins will give you extra **iron** and **folic acid.**

Carrots, spinach, oily fish, eggs, dairy products, and dark green, orange and yellow vegetables all provide **vitamin A** in safe amounts.

Green peppers, citrus fruits, kiwifruit and most vegetables, including potatoes, contain **vitamin C** and **bioflavonoids.**

Vitamin D is found in oily fish, eggs, and fish-liver oil, but it is also made by your body when you are out in the sunlight.

putting on weight

Weight gain during pregnancy is an important determinant of health for both mother and baby. The rate at which you gain weight varies during the nine months, with very little change occurring during the first 10 weeks. The healthy average during the second 10–12 weeks is about 250g (half a pound) a week, and from then on 500g or about one pound a week.

If you think you are putting on too much weight during your pregnancy, do not put yourself on any form of restricted diet. Instead, seek advice from your doctor.

breast-feeding & baby meals

The best possible start in life you can give your baby is breast-feeding. There is now overwhelming evidence that formula milks, even those based on the latest nutritional findings, can never rival mothers' milk as the perfect first food for babies.

Research carried out with premature babies, and published in the *British Medical Journal* in November 1998, suggests that nutrition during the earliest weeks of a baby's life has a critical impact on brain development as well as on general health in later life. Vital fats known as long-chain polyunsaturated fatty acids, including DHA and AA, present in mothers' milk but not routinely added to baby feeds, may be one reason for this.

Breast-feeding also helps babies develop stronger immune systems. Numbers of studies, in developed and developing countries, show that breast-fed babies have higher resistance to childhood infections, are less likely to become anaemic and, if breast-feeding is continued till they are at least four months old, are much less likely to develop those modern plagues of childhood, asthma and eczema. It might be years before scientists succeed in identifying all the complex protective substances in mothers' milk: a recent discovery was lactoferrin, present in colostrum, the first and richest breast milk, which supplies powerful immune-boosting factors for the newborn baby.

Breast-fed babies may also be less likely to grow up into overweight children: a study of 9,000 Bavarian children, published in the *British*

Medical Journal in July 1999, found that 4.5 per cent of the bottle-fed babies in the study had grown up into obese children, against 2.8 per cent of the breast-fed babies. This protective effect was directly linked, too, to the length of time the babies had been breast-fed: the longer the better.

There are other good reasons for breast-feeding. It is simpler than bottle-feeding, the milk does not need to be warmed in specially sterilized bottles and is always there in just the right quantities, and, most important, breast-feeding establishes an unique bond between mother and baby.

organic eating and mothers' milk

Sadly, for all its wonderful advantages, mothers' milk today is known to be contaminated with a number of pesticide residues and other toxic substances that nobody is happy to see in babies' food. Dioxins, toxic chemicals called PCBs, and traces of persistent pesticides such as DDT and lindane have all been found in human breast-milk at worrying levels, although they are seldom found in formulas. However, a comprehensive Dutch study in the mid-1990s could detect no negative effects of this exposure in breast-fed infants with measurable body-levels of these pollutants. And the positive advantages of breast-feeding were still present. While this means that the message is still that breast is best, breast-feeding mothers should eat 100 per cent organic if they possibly can.

Many of the problems that new mothers experience with breast-feeding can be resolved with a little expert help. Even if breast-feeding proves too difficult at birth and the mother chooses to bottle-feed, it is often possible to re-establish breast-feeding, with the help of a trained breast-feeding counsellor (see Resources, page 214).

But if the difficulties are insuperable, make sure you are giving your baby the best possible formula milk (see Resources, page 214).

foods to avoid while breast-feeding

When you are breast-feeding, much of what you eat or drink yourself is going to reach your baby through your milk. So if you or your partner have a family history of allergic problems such as hay fever or asthma, it would be a good idea to restrict your intake of or, if possible, omit altogether such well-known allergy-triggers as wheat and dairy products (see page 204). In a recent Scandinavian study of breast-fed babies suffering from colic, almost all the incidents of colic disappeared when their mothers stopped eating dairy products.

Highly spiced, chilli-laden 'hot' foods such as curries and 'Tex-Mex' food, lots of tea and coffee and alcohol in large quantities are other substances that could make your baby uncomfortable – or, in the case of caffeine, even keep him awake. Strong-tasting foods like onions and garlic may affect the taste of breast-milk and are perhaps best eaten in moderation by mothers who are breast-feeding their babies.

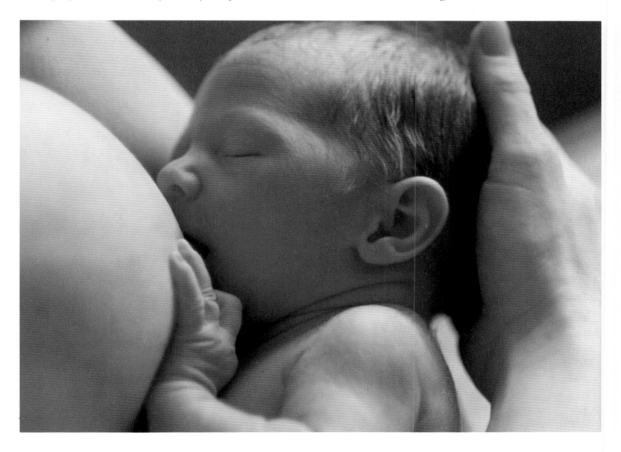

baby meals from 4-12 months

Whether your baby is breast-fed or bottle-fed, by the time he's around four months old he is probably ready to start experimenting with solid foods. Let him make the running. If he drops off to sleep soon after breast or bottle, and sleeps peacefully till the next feed, solid food can wait.

If, however, he's acting hungry long before feeding time, if he's still asking for more when the breast- or bottle-feed is over, it is time to start trying him on something more substantial – but only after his milk feed. Try introducing some little nibbles in a small soft plastic baby-feeding spoon from time to time. Little purées of fruit and vegetables are a good start. If he pushes them away after just a taste or so, don't persist. Give it a rest for a few days then try again. And remember that he's still getting all the nourishment he needs at this stage from breast or bottle.

But if he's hungry for more, give it to him. By the time your baby has been taking purées for two or three months, he will be quite used to eating and will be learning to chew or even bite with his gums, even if he cannot boast a single tooth. Now it is time to ease off the blender-made purées and start giving him food with more chewiness and texture to it: what the baby–food companies usually call Junior Foods. Food prepared by you can now be mashed with a fork instead of blended, and you can actually cook the same meal for yourself and your baby, but remember not to season the food during cooking and do not season the portion you give him.

It is in these early months of solid food that the first feeding problems may show up. Babies tend to pick on mealtimes as a good moment to assert their independence. Pushing away food lovingly prepared for them is one great way to do this. (It may also mean, of course, that they are not hungry just now, thank you.) Showing anger, frustration or disappointment is playing their game. The more you fuss and insist, the more their mouths will stay provokingly shut. Remain smilingly unmoved. After a little while, simply remove the rejected food. And don't replace it.

superfoods for babies

Broccoli should be steamed, or cooked in just a little water, until it is soft enough to mash and sieve. It is a good first food, but may be a little strong-tasting on its own, so try mixing it with sieved boiled potato or baby rice.

Turnip, like broccoli, should be steamed, or cooked in just a little water, until it is soft enough to mash or sieve. Along with other root vegetables, it blends well and is a good first food.

Avocado should be soft and ripe. Just mash it a little with a fork, or mix to a purée with breast or formula milk.

Carrots are a sweet and nutritious first food. As with broccoli and turnip, they can be steamed, or cooked in a little water, until they are soft enough to purée.

Spinach can be a teaspoonful from a packet of frozen chopped spinach, thawed and served at room temperature. Add it to a baby's diet from about six months old.

White fish is another nutritious food to add to a baby's diet from about six months. Give a tiny scoop of cod, plaice or hake, making sure it has absolutely no bones in it.

the eating plan

Babies are receptive to a wide range of tastes, including broccoli, cabbage and mild curry, between the ages of four and six months, when foods need to be puréed to a smooth and quite runny consistency. Even when their initial reaction is a pained or surprised look, a second or third taste of the food is often accepted.

This 'window' of developing taste-buds is brief, however, lasting no more than seven to eight weeks. By the time they are seven months old, most babies have developed strong preferences or dislikes, and babies this age are likely to spit out any novel food. If the only tastes a baby has known while the 'window' is still open are the bland sweet pap of most commercial baby foods, you'll have your work cut out for years to make him eat from a wide and nourishing range of foods.

For this reason, we have chosen the Superfoods (listed opposite, below) from the sharp end of the taste palate. Other foods you can be giving your baby from about six months are any fruit soft and ripe enough to be mashed, hard-boiled eggs, and any vegetable tender enough to mash when it is cooked. You could offer a spoonful of hummus – make sure it is unsalted – a little poached salmon or chicken, or some baked apple with a touch of ground cinnamon or nutmeg. You can introduce dairy foods like yogurt or cottage cheese, or stir grated cheese into soups or vegetables. You can offer the first cereals now, such as oatmeal soaked overnight in breast or formula milk, creamy rice, and millet porridge. And after six months – but no sooner – try him on wheat-based cereals (see Big Breakfasts, pages 120–127, for recipes).

When you introduce a new food, let two or three days go by before trying another; if digestive problems occur, you will know the likely cause.

By the age of 9–12 months your baby will have a few teeth, and some very strong views on what he's prepared to eat. He should still be getting the same amount of either breast milk or formula, but he'll be ready for three meals a day, with milk as his regular drink. He'll be cutting teeth and needing hard chewy foods to help him learn to bite: give him fingers of wholewheat toast baked in the oven, fingers of carrot, crisp apple or young turnip, and florets of broccoli or cauliflower. And he'll be ready for more sophisticated tastes, such as soups and stews made aromatic with herbs, fish puddings, a taste of your favourite pasta, savoury rice, a few forkfuls of roast lamb, garlicky roasted vegetables with couscous and cauliflower or broccoli cheese. Try to keep the menu as varied as possible (see overleaf).

foods to avoid

Any of the Danger Foods on pages 66–69 are inappropriate for babies. Some are especially perilous. Avoid sugar in any form other than the natural sugars present in fruit and vegetables, or your baby could be stuck with a sweet tooth for life. Avoid salt even when cooking vegetables, soups or other dishes you couldn't imagine eating unsalted: salt can actually be a killer for babies.

Studies have also shown that babies are far more at risk than adults from pesticide residues, and that cancer and damaged immune and nervous systems may result from regular exposure. This is why organic foods (see pages 22–3) are so important for babies.

Avoid nuts in any shape or form: nut allergies are becoming tragically common.

Be sparing with fruit juices. Their concentrated sugars make them undesirable unless they are diluted at least half and half with water. And water is something your baby should be developing a taste for, too, by this time.

Those little tins and jars of commercial baby-food can be life-saving for busy mothers; as far as possible, stick to the organic ranges, and check that they are not padded out with cheap low-nutrient fillers such as modified starch, and that they contain no added sugars of any kind. For excellent ranges see Resources, page 215.

menus for a 6-month-old baby

sunday

10am: Apple and Apricot Purée (see page 124), with a little yogurt.

2pm: Root Vegetable and Potato Purée (see page 136). Peeled and grated ripe pear.

6pm: Potato mashed with a little cottage cheese. Mashed banana.

monday

10am: The yolk of a hard-boiled egg with fingers of crustless wholemeal bread soaked in milk.

2pm: Turnip and carrot purée. Grated apple with a little orange juice.

6pm: Stewed apricots blended with yogurt.

tuesday

10am: Banana Porridge (see page 120).

2pm: Spinach purée with cottage cheese. A little mashed banana.

6pm: Carrot, broccoli and potato purée.

wednesday

10am: Banana mashed with a little yogurt and wheatgerm.

2pm: Roast Chicken Puréed with Vegetables (see page 167). Mashed fresh pear.

6pm: Millet muesli (see page 48) with a little mashed peach or nectarine.

thursday

10am: Proper Muesli (see page 120).

2pm: Root Vegetable and Potato Purée (see page 136). Skinned and grated ripe peach.

6pm: Stewed apple with yogurt. Fingers of wholemeal bread soaked in milk.

friday

10am: Banana mashed with yogurt and a little wheatgerm.

2pm: Broccoli, Green Bean and Sweet Potato Purée (see page 136). Puréed avocado with a few drops of lemon juice.

6pm: Proper Muesli (see page 120) with a little grated fresh apple.

saturday

10am: Yolk of hard-boiled egg with wholemeal rusks.

2pm: Fishy Feast (see page 139). Turnip and carrot purée.

6pm: Mashed banana with orange juice.

menus for an 18-month-old baby

sunday

breakfast: Scrambled egg with fingers of wholemeal bread and butter.

lunch: Cold roast chicken (see page 167) with braised carrots, new potatoes and broccoli. Fingers of fresh peach.

supper: Baked potato mashed with cottage cheese and spinach purée. Fresh apple.

monday

breakfast: Muesli with yogurt and grated apple.

lunch: Egg and Spinach Mornay (see page 198). Fresh fruit salad.

supper: Baked apple stuffed with raisins. Fingers of buttered wholemeal toast and sliced cheese.

tuesday

breakfast: Banana Porridge (see page 120).

lunch: Haddock Moussaka (see page 164) with puréed broccoli. Fingers of fresh pineapple.

supper: Beanburger (see page 184) with mashed potatoes. Fingers of celery and carrot.

wednesday

breakfast: Dried prunes and apricots soaked overnight, blended with a little yogurt.

lunch: Tomato and Cheese Pudding (see page 143) with puréed spinach.

supper: Split Pea and Rice Soup (see page 134). Fingers of wholemeal toast and butter. Sticks of carrot.

thursday

breakfast: Proper Muesli (see page 120) with yogurt and a sliced peach or pear.

lunch: Poached Chicken (see page 166). Steamed broccoli with a little butter and nutmeg. A peach.

supper: Minestrone with Rice and Tomatoes (see page 130). Oatcakes with a little cheese (see page 158).

friday

breakfast: Fruit salad of kiwifruit, apple and grapes, with Greek yogurt.

lunch: Riceburger (see page 183) with peas. A banana.

supper: Sticks of celery and carrot with cottage cheese. Apple crumble.

saturday

breakfast: Wholegrain cereal with goat's milk and raisins.

lunch: A baked potato with Roasted Vegetables (see page 174) with chopped tomato and cucumber salad.

supper: Irish Stew (see page 168). Apple purée with Greek yogurt.

hungry toddlers

Your baby is now a toddler with a mind of his own, alarming amounts of energy and a growing need to explore and test his world. To fuel all that activity, he needs plenty of good carbohydrates, found in grains like wheat, rice and oats; in pulses like beans and lentils; in starchy vegetables such as carrots and potatoes; and in fruit and milk.

Since this is also a period of active growth, toddlers need good-quality protein, too. But remember that this doesn't only mean meat, fish and eggs. Grains also contribute protein to the diet, and some grains are richer in protein than others: oats, millet and the ancient, newly revived grain amaranth, for instance (see page 51). Remember, too, that wholegrains are significantly higher in protein than those refined to produce white flour and white rice.

Once toddlers are eating their meals with the rest of the family they are also learning some of their first important lessons in social behaviour – among them that shouting, throwing their food about and trying other attention-getting tactics will be firmly dealt with.

As far as possible, they should be eating some of the same food as everyone else, even if only in mashed-up form. A taste of the pasta, a small serving of the vegetables, a couple of spoonfuls of stew can help make a toddler really feel one of the family. Watching other people enjoy foods will help toddlers accept them, too.

six superfoods

Millet This is the only grain that is a complete protein, rich in iron and other important minerals too. Millet is also very easily digested.

Beans A great energy food that also supplies protein. Baked beans in tomato sauce with fingers of wholemeal toast and a piece of fruit make great toddler food. But pick sugar-free beans (sometimes sweetened with a little apple juice).

Salmon Like other oily fish, salmon supplies fats vital to the nerves and brain, as well as quality protein.

Yogurt Natural live yogurt is rich in calcium, protein and some important B vitamins, and is much more easily digested than milk. The friendly bacteria supplied by live yogurt also aid digestion.

Kiwifruit Their sharp fresh taste is quite challenging for young taste-buds. Kiwifruit are especially rich in vitamin C, which remains in the fruit even after lengthy storage.

Cauliflower Like all cruciferous vegetables, this will help boost resistance and protect against respiratory problems.

the eating plan

This is the age when you can teach children the good eating habits that will stay with them for the rest of their lives: the habit of drinking water or milk to quench thirst rather than fruit juice or a can of fizzy drink; the habit of eating plenty of fruit – the best possible between-meals snack (and remember that bananas are not the only fruit); and the habit of enjoying a wide range of vegetables – lightly steamed, cooked in a minimum of water, or stir-fried, and seasoned with herbs or spices to enhance their flavour.

Toddlers should be eating proper meals now, to meet the nutritional demands of young growing bodies. They need a good breakfast to keep them going all morning, a protein-rich lunch – eggs, cottage cheese, fish, chicken, beans – and an end-of-the-day meal full of the carbohydrates that will help them sleep more soundly: rice, millet, a plate of muesli, a baked potato.

getting round the danger foods

Sugar is top of the list of Danger Foods for this age. A toddler's palate is easily satisfied with the natural sugars in fruits and vegetables unless he learns to crave the seductive sweetness of commercial yogurts aimed especially at children, 'fruit' drinks, breakfast cereals, cakes and biscuits, and sweets and chocolates.

Instead of ready-sweetened and flavoured fruit yogurts, grate a little apple or pear, mash a peach or nectarine, or chop kiwifruit or banana into creamy natural yogurt; try a little grated nutmeg or ground cinnamon on top. Instead of sweet biscuits, offer lightly buttered oatcakes or rye crispbread or rice cakes. And make cakes and biscuits, even the healthy, home-made kind, a treat for weekends only.

The other danger foods for children this age are soft drinks, canned or bottled. Don't have them in the house. For thirsty toddlers, the two best drinks are water and milk – choose whole, not skimmed, milk, and preferably organic.

summer weekday menu plan

monday

Breakfast
Some scrambled eggs served with fingers of wholemeal bread and butter. A glass of milk.

Lunch
Pasta with Avocado Sauce (see page 175). A salad of sliced tomatoes, cucumbers and shredded iceberg lettuce with a little mayonnaise. Fresh fruit.

Supper
Chicken in a Wrap (see page 178).
Yogurt with sliced peach or nectarine.

tuesday

Breakfast
Muesli with raisins and a sliced banana. Freshly pressed orange juice.

Lunch
A salad of tuna, avocado and tomato with a little mayonnaise and a crusty wholemeal roll and butter. A peach.

Supper
Onion-and-Squeakburger (see page 184), spinach. Sliced kiwifruit.

wednesday

Breakfast
Creamy yogurt with apple purée and raisins. Wholemeal toast with butter and honey.

Lunch
Cold roast chicken with Pisto (see page 144) and a small green salad. Fresh fruit.

Supper
Potato Cakes with Grilled Bacon (see page 171) and French beans. A fresh peach or nectarine.

thursday

Breakfast
Five-grain Kruska (see page 123) with yogurt and a sliced banana or some strawberries.

Lunch
Salmon Fish Cakes (see page 139) with steamed broccoli and new potatoes. A peach.

Supper
Sugar-free baked beans on wholemeal toast. Cucumber and tomato salad. Sliced fresh pear with a little yogurt.

friday

Breakfast
Soaked dried fruit with yogurt and a little honey.

Lunch
Poached Egg and Tomato (see page 126), with new potatoes. Fingers of carrot and celery. Fresh fruit.

Supper
Minestrone with Pesto (see page 130). Oatcakes with cream cheese. An apple.

winter weekday menu plan

monday

Breakfast
Freshly pressed orange juice. Porridge with milk or cream and a little honey.

Lunch
Spanish Omelette (see page 145). Celery and carrot sticks with Hummus (see page 156).

Supper
Pumpkin Soup (see page 133) with a crusty wholemeal roll and butter. Sliced banana with yogurt.

tuesday

Breakfast
A boiled egg with fingers of wholemeal toast. Freshly pressed orange juice.

Lunch
Chickpea Veggie Burgers (see page 182). Salad of iceberg lettuce, grated apple and carrot with mayonnaise. An apple.

Supper
Haddock Moussaka (see page 164).

wednesday

Breakfast
Lime-E-Shake (see page 124). Wholemeal toast and butter with sugar-free fruit spread.

Lunch
Spaghetti Bolognese (see page 177). Oatcakes, with sliced cheese and a few sticks of celery.

Supper
Irish Stew (see page 168) with steamed cauliflower. A pear.

thursday

Breakfast
Millet muesli (see page 48) with chopped banana and yogurt.

Lunch
Cauliflower and Broccoli Cheese (see page 171) and a baked potato. An apple.

Supper
Brown Rice with Roast Vegetables (see pages 173 and 174). Fresh fruit salad.

friday

Breakfast
Grapefruit segments. Proper Porridge (see page 122) with milk and a little honey.

Lunch
Sugar-free baked beans on wholemeal toast. Small mixed salad. An apple.

Supper
Leek and Watercress Soup (see page 131). A crusty wholemeal roll. Sticks of carrot and celery with Hummus (see page 156).

pre-school years

When they are four, children's energy needs increase dramatically. They're physically much more active, their developing brainpower and mental skills are demanding and their bodies are growing rapidly. The first requisite for them is good calories, derived from a well-balanced intake of foods that also supply adequate amounts of the other essential nutrients.

Boys of this age will need an average of around 1,700 calories a day and girls 1,550, and the major nutritional trap lies in wait for the unwary parent. Because children at this age can develop voracious appetites to fuel their calorie needs, it's all too easy to submit to 'pester power' and to let your youngsters get these calories from the worst possible food sources.

Packets of crisps, sweet biscuits, sticky buns, sweet drinks, sweets and chocolates are an instant and easy solution. But this type of diet of high-fat, high-sugar, high-salt convenience foods carries the following three great risks:

• Firstly, by filling children up, they displace healthy food items from the daily menu.

• Secondly, they deprive children of the life-time protection against heart disease, osteoporosis and many forms of cancer that is provided by the 'nutraceuticals' – natural chemical substances – found only in wholefoods.

• Thirdly, they encourage bad eating habits and foster addictions to salt and sugar which are likely to stay with a child for the rest of his life as well as turn him into one of today's generation of overweight children.

six superfoods

Bananas Whole, mashed, whizzed into a milkshake, baked – however they are eaten, they provide 100 calories of supernutrition, including potassium, vitamin B_6, folic acid and fibre.

Buckwheat Not in fact a cereal but a nut, this makes wonderful pancakes as 'holdalls' for many other foods. Buckwheat is rich in rutin, which protects the circulatory system and helps reduce the effects of over-consumption of wheat.

Chicken Free-range and organic, of course. Quick and easy to cook and perfect protein for children. Stir-fried with vegetables, wrapped in a buckwheat pancake, it is an ultimate superfood.

Grapes Virtually all children adore seedless grapes, which are strengthening, nourishing and bursting with energy.

Potatoes Another children's favourite, but save the chips as an occasional treat. Boiled, baked in their skins, roasted in olive oil or mashed, they are filling and supply good levels of fibre, B vitamins, minerals and vitamin C.

Wholemeal bread Definitely a taste to encourage as early as possible so that it becomes a child's automatic choice over white sliced pap. Another good source of healthy calories combined with B vitamins, protein and fibre.

the eating plan

By now your child is probably attending a playgroup or nursery school and is beginning to learn the social advantages of eating with others outside the family circle. This is a vital period for building on these social skills and on the ever-broadening taste and texture sensations which combine to produce the joy of eating.

As a toddler, your child has already learned to join in with the occasional family meal, and now this should be the norm rather than the special occasion. It isn't easy with busy lifestyles to have the whole family sit down together at any meal of the day, but at least try for regular family breakfasts, even if it does mean a slightly earlier start. The benefit will be worth the effort. Why not plan as well to reinstate the Sunday family lunch, a practice which is sadly declining in the UK and is almost non-existent in the USA.

Interestingly, in Europe, especially in the south, where children's diets tend to be much healthier, family meals are not confined to Christmas Day and Thanksgiving but are still an essential part of the pattern of family life.

the danger foods

The danger foods for four to five year olds are still the high-sugar snacks, breakfast cereals and soft drinks that you have been avoiding for your toddler. If you don't buy them they can't eat them – and they're not healthy at any age.

summer weekday menu plan

monday

Breakfast
Proper Muesli (see page 120).

Lunch
Fishy Feast (see page 139) with wholemeal bread and butter. A small bunch of seedless grapes.

Supper
Vegetable Couscous (see page 172). Mashed banana with yogurt and honey.

tuesday

Breakfast
Banana-to-Go breakfast in a mug (see page 124), with one slice of wholemeal toast and butter.

Lunch
Minestrone with Rice and Tomatoes (see page 130), with a wholemeal roll. Greek yogurt.

Supper
Rosti-topped Fish Pie (see page 167), with peas. Stewed apple with a little crème fraîche.

wednesday

Breakfast
French Toast (see page 126). A small apple, sliced.

Lunch
Savoury Egg (see page 153), with fingers of wholemeal toast for dipping. A banana.

Supper
Pasta Salad with Tuna (see page 147). A bunch of seedless grapes.

thursday

Breakfast
A poached egg on a slice of lightly buttered wholemeal toast. A tangerine.

Lunch
Granny Smith's Welsh Rarebit (see page 155). A small salad of chopped tomato and avocado.

Supper
Split Pea and Rice Soup (see page 134). Upside-down Pudding (see page 188).

friday

Breakfast
Fruitfast (see page 124), served with thick Greek yogurt and a little honey. A warm wholemeal roll and butter with organic jam (additive-free).

Lunch
Jacket potato filled with baked beans. Fresh berries with natural yogurt and a little honey.

Supper
Potato Cakes with Grilled Bacon (see page 171). (Note: if your youngster does not like smoked bacon, use unsmoked or thin strips of stir-fried ham or chicken breast instead.) Purée of fresh strawberries and mascarpone cheese.

winter weekday menu plan

monday

Breakfast
Plain Pancakes (see page 190, omit sugar), served wrapped around a ripe banana.

Lunch
Marinated Grilled Chicken (see page 138), with any green vegetable.

Dinner
Macaroni mixed with cooked diced carrot and broccoli, and a tomato sauce (see page 176). Small bowl of apple purée with custard.

tuesday

Breakfast
Barley Bannocks (see page 127), filled with a mixture of cottage cheese and seedless raisins.

Lunch
Spanish Omelette (see page 145), served with shredded iceberg lettuce, cucumber and a few cherry tomatoes.

Dinner
Real Fish Fingers (see page 166), with mashed potato and sweetcorn. Peeled sliced kiwifruit.

wednesday

Breakfast
Scrambled Egg with Tomatoes and Mushrooms (see page 125) on wholemeal toast.

Lunch
Cauliflower and Broccoli Cheese (see page 171). A ripe pear.

Dinner
Vegetable Couscous (see page 172) with a few tiny pieces of chicken fried together with the onion. A few slices of peeled fresh mango.

thursday

Breakfast
Real Fruity Yogurt (see page 123), with a hot wholemeal roll and a slice of Edam cheese.

Lunch
Pitta Plus (see page 149). A tangerine and a few grapes.

Dinner
Tuna Mash (see page 152), with carrots and French beans. A Blueberry Muffin (see page 162).

friday

Breakfast
Proper Porridge (see page 122), with one slice of wholemeal toast and butter.

Lunch
Indian Kidney Beans (see page 185).

Dinner
Poached Chicken (see page 166). Organic fruit yogurt.

off to school

Small bodies need good nourishment to get them through the school day. Children's brains are even hungrier than their bodies, voracious in their need for oxygen, for energy and for key nutrients, especially iron, magnesium and the B vitamins. If these demands are not met, children will find it a struggle to learn, remember and pay attention.

Hard to believe? Not for the teachers and pupils at 803 state schools in New York City. From 1979 to 1982 changes were made gradually to cafeteria menus in those schools. Out went soft drinks, sweet-vending machines, high-sugar snacks and artificial food colours. In came fresh fruit and salad, and wholewheat rolls, pasta and pizzas. Over the four years, the academic performance of two million pupils in those schools, assessed by the US California Achievement Test, rose from 11 per cent below the national average to 5 per cent above it. And the most dramatic improvements were seen in 'learning-disabled' children.

If the school your child is now attending hosts soft-drink and confectionery vending machines; if the lunchtime menu stars pies, puddings and chips with everything; if wholemeal bread, fresh fruit and salads are conspicuous by their absence – take your courage in both hands and organize a protest among like-minded parents.

six ★ superfoods

Apple This crunchy treat supplies energy, improves resistance, does wonders for the digestive system and nourishes nerves. Its skin is especially nutrient-rich.

Dried fruit Dates, figs, raisins, sultanas are nourishing and highly energizing, assist digestion and supply useful minerals like iron and calcium.

Oats Good brain-food and provide wonderful nourishment for the nervous system too. Porridge is ideal breakfast food for school-children.

Eggs Supply protein, iron, zinc and calcium, plus vitamin A to build resistance and vitamin E. Choose free-range or organic eggs.

Sardines Another great brain-food, because they are loaded with iron and zinc, plus lots of calcium. Persuade children to crunch up the bones.

Wholemeal bread Includes baps, pitta breads or crackers. A school-child's diet needs the protein, vitamins, minerals and fibre generously supplied by whole wheat.

the eating plan

If children eat a good nourishing breakfast, their school day is off to a flying start. But if breakfast is a snatched drink and a couple of biscuits or one of the sugar-laden 'healthy' breakfast cereals, yoyo-ing blood sugar levels (see Carbohydrates, page 00) will play havoc with concentration and alertness. This is because the brain needs 70 per cent of the body's blood-sugar supplies. By break-time kids will be desperate for a sugar-fix.

Many schools in the affluent West still provide a proper sit-down midday meal. If your child's school doesn't, pack a good lunchbox. Always include a piece of fruit, small cartons of a favourite salad with a plastic fork to eat them, tiny packets of nuts, if permitted, or dried fruit for snacking, perhaps a healthy muesli bar; and sandwiches, baps, or pitta pockets with some form of protein – eggs, fish, chicken – for filling.

It is a good idea to check if your child's school has guidelines about packed lunches. They may ban nuts or peanut butter, for instance, because of possible dangers to children allergic to them.

Most children come home tired and hungry from school. They need to relax, and have a drink and a bite to eat. In the summer, consider dips with a choice of crunchy vegetables or breadsticks to eat them with; or a fresh fruit salad or a fruit smoothie (yogurt blended with fresh fruit) in summer. In winter, offer a fruit purée and a muffin or a toasted tea cake as a special treat.

a good last meal of the day

Too much supper, including food that is too rich and eaten too late, can be a recipe for sleeplessness. Get children to nibble fresh carrot or celery sticks when they sit down and include a green vegetable in the menu. In winter, think of thick vegetable soups with garlic croûtons, in summer a simple salad. Fish cakes, good meat or vegetable burgers, baked potatoes with cottage cheese, or baked beans on toast are other ideas.

For drinks, choose whole organic milk – a glassful at breakfast and supper, water, or fruit juice diluted with plenty of water. Tea and coffee are inappropriate for children of this age.

The danger foods for this age group are crisps, often the currency of the playground, and soft drinks, which they may be encountering for the first time. Don't get cross when they demand these new treats – just make it plain that 'treats' are exactly what they are, and only to be enjoyed on special occasions.

summer weekday menu plan

monday

Breakfast
Wholegrain cereal with milk. A banana.

Lunch
Minestrone with Rice and Tomatoes (see page 130). Cucumber and cottage-cheese salad. A peach or nectarine.

Supper
Dips with crunchy vegetables (see page 149). Riceburger (see page 183) with French beans. Pieces of fresh fruit.

tuesday

Breakfast
Fruitfast (see page 124) with muesli.

Lunch
Tuna Eggs Mayonnaise (see page 196). Green salad with tomatoes and cucumber.

Supper
Sardines on toast. Pancakes (see page 190) rolled with a little sugar-free fruit spread.

wednesday

Breakfast
Poached Egg and Tomato (see page 126).

Lunch
Pizza Baguette (see page 154), with cucumber and lettuce salad. A peach or nectarine.

Supper
Sophie's Indonesian Vegetable Stew (see page 178). Yogurt with fresh fruit stirred into it.

thursday

Breakfast
Freshly pressed orange juice. Boiled egg with a slice of wholemeal toast and butter.

Lunch
Real Fish Fingers (see page 166) with boiled new potatoes. A salad of grated raw carrot, beetroot and slices of tomato with a little mayonnaise.

Supper
Brown Rice (see page 173) with cheese. Salad of watercress and chicory. Fresh fruit.

friday

Breakfast
Muesli with raisins, soaked overnight in apple juice, served with yogurt.

Lunch
Spanish Omelette (see page 145) with French beans. A peach or nectarine.

Supper
Pasta with Tomato and Red Pepper Sauce (see page 176). Salad of lettuce and cucumber. Greek yogurt with strawberries.

winter weekday menu plan

monday

Breakfast
Proper porridge (see page 122) with honey and a little cream.

Lunch
Bean Burger (see page 184) with Coleslaw (see page 198). An apple.

Supper
Real Fish Fingers (see page 166), Potato and Celeriac Mash (see page 180) and peas. Stewed pears with yogurt.

tuesday

Breakfast
Scrambled Egg with Tomatoes and Mushrooms (see page 125) and wholemeal toast.

Lunch
Quick Spinach Snack (see page 154). Oatcakes with butter and sticks of celery. An apple.

Supper
Baked potato with baked beans. Soaked prunes and apricots with yogurt.

wednesday

Breakfast
Proper Porridge (see page 122) with milk or cream. Wholemeal toast with butter and sugar-free fruit spread.

Lunch
South of France Omelette (see page 169). Wholemeal roll and butter. A pear.

Supper
Baked Savoy Cabbage Soup (see page 132). Sticks of celery and carrot with Hummus (see page 156). Stewed apple with yogurt.

thursday

Breakfast
Boiled egg with wholemeal toast and butter.

Lunch
Veggie Burger with Spinach Cheese Topping (see page 182). Coleslaw (see page 198).

Supper
Roast chicken with Potato and Celeriac Mash (see page 180). A baked apple stuffed with dried fruit.

friday

Breakfast
A tangerine. Wholegrain cereal, such as Five-grain Kruska (see page 123), with a dollop of yogurt and a sliced banana.

Lunch
Salmon Fish Cakes (see page 139), with puréed spinach. An apple.

Supper
Broccoli and Anchovy Pasta (see page 175). Rice cakes with cream cheese and celery sticks.

Lunchbox ideas

On school days, a proper lunch has to be replaced by a meal at school. These ideas for packed lunches ensure healthy food in the middle of the day.

• Hummus (see page 156), alfalfa sprouts and tomato wholemeal bread sandwiches. A small packet of raisins. A piece of fresh fruit.

• Tuna, cucumber and mayonnaise wholemeal bread sandwiches. A bunch of seedless grapes. A muesli bar.

• Cold chicken, lettuce and mayonnaise in a wholewheat roll. A packet of dried fruit. A banana.

• Wholemeal bread sandwiches filled with sardines mashed with a little mayonnaise and one or two lettuce leaves. A small container of Coleslaw (see page 198) – don't forget the fork! An apple.

• Tuna salad with sweetcorn, tomato and chopped parsley in a little container. A muesli bar. A piece of fresh fruit.

the years of growth

The period from nine to 13 is an indeterminate, in-between time
for youngsters. They are starting the transition from children to young
adults and beginning their passage through puberty. Although nutrition
is vital at every age, there are special needs during this period of
growth and development into maturity.

By now your children will be insisting on making
many more of their own food choices, and the
decisions they make can be crucial. What they eat
now has a profound effect on their day-to-day
quality of life and performance, but it is also a key
determining factor of their long-term health.

Good nutrition at this stage is a two-pronged
attack on many of the illnesses which are all too
often regarded as the inevitable consequences of
ageing. Firstly, by ensuring an abundant intake of
the protective nutrients that guard against heart
and circulatory disease, premature senility and
osteoporosis. Secondly, by avoiding dangerously
high consumption of damaging foods like
saturated animal fats, trans-fats, salt, sugar and all
the products of the commercial junk-food industry.

You won't achieve this balanced way of eating
by heavy-handedness or prohibition. The way to
instil good eating habits that will last your children
a lifetime is by setting a good example yourself,
encouraging an interest in food and getting
children into the kitchen. Take time to teach them
the simple basics of cooking, and make sure they
do their bit by involving them in food preparation,
laying the table and doing the dishes.

Most children of this age enjoy the creative
process of cooking and, as long as you teach
them properly, they are perfectly safe in the
kitchen with appropriate supervision.

six superfoods

Dates A healthy sweet and delicious treat which supplies plenty of much-needed iron with a good boost of potassium.

Oranges A fresh orange before any meal ups absorption of iron, calcium and other minerals from foods, thanks to its high vitamin C content.

Porridge No better start to the day, because of its iron, zinc, calcium and B vitamins.

Lentils A great source of protein which also supply iron and zinc.

Fish An excellent source of protein, but include oily as well as white fish to ensure sufficient intake of essential fatty acids.

Eggs Free-range or organic – the most natural convenience food of all. Cheap, quick, easy and full of protein and B vitamins.

the eating plan

During this period of rapid growth and development both boys and girls need a massive input of energy. Ideally, aim for six daily servings of starchy foods like rice, wholemeal bread, potatoes, pasta and wholegrain cereals; five portions of fruit and vegetables; and two portions each of dairy products and non-dairy proteins, animal or vegetable. The wider the selection of foodstuffs, the broader the spectrum of vitamins, minerals, trace elements and the other highly protective phytonutrients that your children will consume. It cannot be reiterated often enough that this is the vital time to establish healthy eating habits that will stay with your youngsters for life.

Try to keep your children to a minimum consumption of fried and high-sugar foods so they become occasional treats rather than their staple diet. The high-calorie, low-nutrient value of many convenience foods pushes aside the consumption of healthier nutrients. Studies in America show that some youngsters in this age group are getting in excess of 45 per cent of their calories from fat, making them prime candidates for heart disease and strokes in later life.

You must, however, beware of fanaticism which could turn children into total rebels who stuff themselves with junk at every opportunity when you're not watching, or you of risking malnutrition in your children by being obsessive about organic foods and wholegrain cereals. There are already parents so phobic about agrochemicals that they would rather their children went without fresh produce if organic isn't available.

danger foods for pre-teens

Salt, caffeine and canned cola drinks can all interfere with a child's absorption of calcium from the diet. High bran foods have the same effect and can also reduce the absorption of iron. For girls particularly, building up stores of iron is vital before their periods start.

summer weekday menu plan

monday

Breakfast

Sardines on Toast: mash sardines with a little vinegar, spread on a slice of wholemeal toast, cover with thin slices of tomato and heat under the grill. Serve with a dollop of ketchup. Serve a second slice of wholemeal toast with butter and honey.

Lunch

Hot Pancetta Savouries (see page 154), served with a mixed salad.

Supper

Zoë's Prawn and Vegetable Stir-fry (see page 164). Summer Pudding (see page 188).

tuesday

Breakfast

Proper Muesli (see page 120). Chunk of warm wholemeal French bread, with a piece of mild cheese.

Lunch

Fish Soup (see page 135). This may seem a lot of trouble for lunch, but simply reheat from a previous batch and omit the rouille and croûtons. Serve with crusty wholemeal rolls. Follow with sliced oranges sprinkled with chopped dates and natural yogurt.

Supper

Home-made chicken burger: combine minced chicken with finely chopped onion and raw egg; shape into thin burgers and cook under a hot grill until cooked right through. Serve on a bed of lettuce with tomatoes, ketchup, relish and oven chips. Creamy Fruit Tart (see page 186).

wednesday

Breakfast

Lime-E-Shake (see page 124), served with 2 slices wholemeal toast, butter and honey.

Lunch

Smoked Mackerel Quiche (see page 140), served with a tomato, watercress and cucumber salad.

Supper

Minestrone (see page 128), served with bread, cheese and an apple.

thursday

Breakfast

Salmon Fishcakes (see page 139). These are great served cold for breakfast within a day or two of making. Serve with thin slices of wholemeal bread and butter.

Lunch

Colcannon (see page 141). Sliced melon and sliced fresh orange.

Supper

Chicken Salad with Honey and Chilli (see page 138). Any fresh fruit.

friday

Breakfast

2 boiled eggs, served with 2 slices wholemeal toast and butter. Half a grapefruit.

Lunch

Bread and Tomato Salad (see page 147). 1 kiwifruit, peeled and chopped into a carton of natural yogurt.

Supper

Broccoli and Anchovy Pasta (see page 175). Fruit Dipped in Chocolate Sauce (see page 186).

winter weekday menu plan

monday

Breakfast
Proper Porridge (see page 122), with 2 slices wholemeal toast and butter. A banana.

Lunch
Spinach Soufflé (see page 152). Selection of presoaked dried fruits.

Supper
Herbed Kofta Kebabs (see page 169), with rice and peas. Upside-down Pudding (see page 188).

tuesday

Breakfast
Poached Egg and Tomato (see page 126) and crispy grilled bacon, with a slice of wholemeal toast.

Lunch
Fishcakes (see page 153), served with a large beefsteak tomato sliced thinly and drizzled with a little olive oil.

Supper
Pumpkin Soup (see page 133). Granny Smith's Welsh Rarebit (see page 155).

wednesday

Breakfast
Oatmeal Bannocks (see page 127); serve some with jam, some with cheese.

Lunch
Vegetable Curry with Dal (see page 181), served with a chapatti or pitta bread.

Supper
Marinated Grilled Chicken (see page 138), served with any grilled or steamed vegetables. Real Rice Pudding (see page 191).

thursday

Breakfast
Old-fashioned Kedgeree (see page 140): a substantial breakfast dish, ideal if this is a day for school sports.

Lunch
Pizza Baguette (see page 154). A ripe pear.

Supper
Irish Stew (see page 168), served with a mixture of puréed swede and parsnip. Fresh fruit.

friday

Breakfast
Baked beans on a helping of Bubble and Squeak (see page 174). Half a grapefruit or a fresh orange.

Lunch
Spanish Omelette (see page 145), served with a small green salad.

Supper
Any fresh fish fillet, grilled with tomatoes and served with boiled potatoes and any green vegetable. Blackberry and Apple Crumble (see page 189).

Lunchbox ideas

At this age, lunches at home are mainly for school holidays, so what goes into lunchboxes becomes very important. The suggestions here provide nutritious food that's great to eat.

• Hard-boiled egg. A tomato. A wholemeal buttered roll. A few dates. A carton of Greek yogurt.

• Pitta bread filled with a mixture of tuna, chopped apple, a little natural yogurt and a teaspoon of lemon juice. A thick slice of Green Tea Bread (see page 161).

• A small bottle or carton of fresh orange juice. A wholemeal sandwich with a filling of thinly sliced chicken breast and thinly sliced red pepper, spread with mayonnaise and sprinkled with torn basil leaves. Apricot Scone (see page 159).

• Selection of Stuffed Celery Sticks (see page 155). A tangerine. A packet of vegetable chips. A carton of natural yogurt.

• Two thin slices of Banana and Walnut Bread (see page 163), made into a sandwich with a slice of Edam cheese. A ripe pear, a packet of nuts and raisins, and a small bar of organic chocolate.

the turbulent teens

For today's children, the teen years can be both exciting and stressful. Settling down happily in a wider world, much of it centred on big school, with its crowd of new classmates and exams looming ever larger, requires the sort of self-confidence and energy that can be boosted enormously by good nutrition at home.

Out of school, there's a very competitive world, where looks and possessions can take on huge importance and, of course, there's the stress of puberty with its hormonal upheavals.

For all these reasons, children need the very best nourishment to help them deal with these challenges, and to meet the huge demands of puberty as well as growth. Sadly, it is for this age group particularly that junk food with all its anti-nutrients tends to become part of everyday life, and burgers, chips and a fizzy drink from a can constitute normal social eating. It is at this age that sound eating habits learned around the family table will really prove their value.

six superfoods

Oats Packed with enough B vitamins to make them first-class nourishment for nerves and exhaustion, oats are just the food for teenagers. They're also high in zinc (vital for active minds and clear skins), iron for stamina, calcium for healthy bones and magnesium for tranquillity.

Canned salmon An excellent source of the vital fats needed for brains, nerves and skin especially. Rich in bone-building calcium.

Watercress Slip a little watercress into salads, soups and sandwiches: it is rich in protective factors as well as useful minerals.

Sesame and sunflower seeds
Like nuts, these are excellent sources of protein. Eat them at the same time as vitamin C-rich foods for good absorption. These two seeds in particular are high in zinc, vital for puberty (see Eating Disorders, page 213).

Chicken Cold roast chicken is good grazing food for hungry teenagers who don't want to sit down and eat; low-fat, it supplies good protein, zinc and B vitamins.

Apples Keep a bowl of apples on the kitchen table for a super-healthy between-meals snack.

the eating plan

Much of the time, as the teenage years go by, your children will be eating and drinking away from home – lunching in the school cafeteria, socializing, going out on the town. It is your job to ensure that the meals they do eat at home make up for any deficiencies there may be in what they are eating elsewhere.

Breakfast, hopefully, will by now be established as a meal to which the family sits down. Make porridge in winter; in summer, serve wonderful muesli with sunflower and sesame seeds, soaked overnight, to which you add a little cream and a few berries at breakfast. Try, too, to make a point of having at least one evening a week that is sacrosanct for a family meal together. And as far as possible, weekend midday meals should be more occasions for relaxed eating at home.

healthy snacking

Many parents cannot be bothered to put up with constant invasion by strange teenagers dropping in for meals or snacks at all hours. But if your home is open house for your children's friends, not only will you see much more of them, you'll also have the pleasure of meeting those friends. And you'll have the chance to see that on these occasions, too, your children are eating food that is healthy as well as delicious.

Grazing seems to be an established habit of modern teenagers. If your fridge and store cupboard are junk-food-free, healthy snacking is what they'll be doing. See pages 182-4 for recipes for several burgers they could find in the freezer any time, along with wholemeal baps.

Tomato or Bolognese sauce from the freezer are the makings of a quick pasta; they should also be able to find at any time in the kitchen cupboard or fridge, cottage cheese and ordinary hard cheese, hummus, eggs, canned sardines and tuna, smoked mackerel, plain Greek yogurt and plenty of fruit.

the danger foods

Limitless crisps and fizzy drinks – the latter usually with artificial sweeteners, since many teenagers are on semi-permanent diets – are the danger foods most likely to prove irresistible to teenagers, because they are probably what the rest of the gang will be enjoying. Your children should know by now that these are treats that will have to come out of their own pocket money. They should also know that artificial sweeteners may be a serious health risk. In fact, by this time they should be savvy enough to read the small print on lists of ingredients without any urging from you.

summer weekday menu plan

monday

Breakfast
Muesli with sunflower and sesame seeds, soaked overnight in water, served with yogurt and a few raspberries or strawberries.

Lunch
Savoury Eggs (see page 153). Wholemeal roll and butter. Fresh fruit.

Supper
Cold roast chicken with new potatoes. Tomato and cucumber salad. Fresh fruit.

tuesday

Breakfast
Banana-to-Go (see page 124).

Lunch
Bean Burgers (see page 184) with a green salad. Fresh fruit.

Supper
Zoë's Prawn and Vegetable Stir-fry (see page 164). Stewed pears and yogurt.

wednesday

Breakfast
Scrambled Egg with Tomatoes and Mushrooms (see page 125). Wholemeal toast with butter.

Lunch
Minestrone (see page 128) with a crusty wholemeal roll. Salad of avocado, tomato and cottage cheese with chopped chives or fresh coriander.

Supper
Pasta with Avocado Sauce (see page 175). Spinach purée. Fresh fruit.

thursday

Breakfast
Five-grain Kruska (see page 123).

Lunch
Spanish Omelette (see page 145). Green salad. Fresh fruit.

Supper
Black Bean Chilli (see page 168), with French beans. Rice cakes with cheese. A pear.

friday

Breakfast
Boiled egg with wholemeal toast. A peach.

Lunch
Real Fish Fingers (see page 166) with some new potatoes and a green salad. Fresh fruit.

Supper
Veggie Burgers with Spinach Cheese Topping (see page 182). Braised fennel. Summer fruits with yogurt.

winter weekday menu plan

monday

Breakfast
Oatmeal Bannocks (see page 127); accompanied by apple purée.

Lunch
Brown Rice (see page 173) with chopped summer vegetables. Chicory and watercress salad.

Supper
Grilled chicken with mashed potato and braised leeks. Soaked dried fruit with yogurt.

tuesday

Breakfast
Fruitfast (see page 124) with Greek yogurt.

Lunch
Sardines on toast. Coleslaw (see page 198).

Supper
Celery, carrot and fennel sticks with Hummus (see page 156). Rabbit with Prunes (see page 166), served with a baked potato and spinach purée. A pudding (pages 186-191).

wednesday

Breakfast
Proper porridge (see page 122) cooked with raisins, served with milk or cream.

Lunch
Hot Pancetta Savouries (see page 154). Sticks of carrot and celery with cream cheese. An apple.

Supper
Salmon Fish Cakes (see page 139) with carrots and green beans. Baked apple stuffed with ground almonds.

thursday

Breakfast
Freshly pressed orange juice. Baked Eggs and Bacon (see page 125). Wholemeal toast.

Lunch
Granny Smith's Welsh Rarebit (see page 155). Chicory and watercress salad. A pear.

Supper
Pasta with Classic Bolognese Sauce (see page 177). Stir-fried cauliflower and broccoli.

friday

Breakfast
Wholewheat cereal with a sliced banana and yogurt.

Lunch
Savoury Eggs (see page 153). A green salad. Wholemeal roll and slices of cheese.

Supper
Beanburger (see page 184) with Broccoli with Spinach (see page 180). Pancakes (see page 190) filled with apple purée.

Lunchbox ideas
Despite the school canteen, there are many times – school day trips and sportsdays, for instance – when teens need a packed lunch. Here are some nutrient-filled suggestions.

• Peanut butter and banana wholemeal sandwiches.
A banana. A muesli bar.

• A carton of tuna, tomato and mayonnaise salad. A wholemeal roll with lettuce and cucumber. An apple.

• A wholemeal roll filled with cold chicken, tomato, lettuce and mayonnaise.
A small bar of dark organic chocolate. A packet of nuts and raisins.

• Wholemeal sandwiches with watercress, carrot, cucumber and mayonnaise filling. Cheese Pretzels (see page 157). An apple.

• A wholemeal roll filled with chicory and a sardine-and-mayonnaise mixture.
A banana. A slice of Carrot Cake (see page 163).

vegetarian children

Unless parents are vegetarian themselves, a child's decision to go vegetarian frequently causes panic and brings dire words of warning from the family doctor. In fact, being a good vegetarian can be much healthier than being a meat-eater – less heart disease, fewer strokes, less high blood pressure, less bowel cancer and less obesity.

While a simple vitamin and mineral supplement is often a good idea for children, many nutritionists think that it is essential for vegetarians. Buying the appropriate product for their age will make sure that children on a completely meat-free diet do not become deficient in vitamin B_{12} and iron.

Unfortunately, if your child simply gives up eating meat, fish and chicken and lives on little else apart from bread, cheese, eggs and junk food, you've got a recipe for disaster. Such children need to be persuaded to take a greater interest in eating more nutritious and healthy foods. One of the best ways of encouraging healthier eating for vegetarian children, and, in fact, of persuading virtually any child to eat some fresh produce, is getting them to grow their own.

Naturally, a garden is great and if you've got one give a corner to your children, but your kids can grow and eat their own produce in a backyard, on a terrace or balcony, or even in a window box. And once they have planted the seed, nurtured their crop and harvested the result they'll want to eat it.

six superfoods

Radishes These are one of the children's favourites because they grow so quickly. Sow small amounts regularly in a window box. Radishes are a great aid to digestion, and protect the liver.

Carrots These are easy if you've got good soil in the garden; otherwise plant them in tubs or window boxes. Bursting with beta-carotene for skin, eyesight and strong natural resistance.

French beans Use one of the dwarf bush varieties. These will grow well in a large window box but would probably be better in a large pot or half-barrel.

Cherry tomatoes Another all-time children's favourite, and the bush variety will grow brilliantly in a hanging basket. Rich in vitamin C and the unique cancer and heart disease protective nutrient lycopene.

Lettuce Your children will never turn their noses up at lettuce again once they've grown some for themselves. Grow the mixed 'cut and come again' varieties in a window box. The darker the colour lettuce you grow, the richer it is in nutrients.

Apples Give vegetarian or any other child one of the miniature apple varieties in a pot and he'll be itching to take the first ripe fruit to school in his packed lunch and show it off to his friends.

Vegetarian children need to get their protein from varied sources. While eggs and cheese are quick and easy, it is essential that you also feed them a mixture of cereals and pulses. Soya beans and their by-products like tofu, soya cheese and soya granules are an excellent protein source with the added benefits of the plant hormones that protect against cancer, heart disease and osteoporosis.

the eating plan

It's very important to be organized with a vegetarian diet, and for this reason pay particular attention to your store cupboard. Make sure you always have plenty of canned beans, lots of dried pasta, rice, lentils, chickpeas, nuts, seeds and dried fruits. With these available you can always rustle up a protein-rich sustaining meal, even if you haven't had time to get to the shops.

School meals can be a particular problem for vegetarians, as youngsters often end up with just a plate of chips and, if you're lucky, a small, uninteresting salad. The increasing availability of ethnic foods in schools has, however, made things easier, since dishes like vegetable curries, dal, vegetarian lasagnes and pizzas, and even vegeburgers are more often available.

During the winter, thick soups and root vegetable casseroles with beans and rice guarantee warming calories and body-building nutrients without relying on high fat cakes, puddings and other stodgy foods.

the danger foods
The major risk for vegetarians is that they stoke up their calorie needs with large amounts of cakes, biscuits and crisps. These all have poor nutritional value in relation to their high calorie content and easily lead to excessive weight gain. The other great danger is that in some young girls turning vegetarian may become a cover for eating disorders. It's all too easy to refuse food on the grounds of vegetarianism when the real reason could be anorexia nervosa (see pages 211-12).

summer weekday menu plan

monday

Breakfast
Proper Muesli (see page 120). A wholemeal roll with butter and either jam or honey.

Lunch
Roasted Vegetables (see page 174) with Brown Rice (see page 173). A fresh sliced peach.

Supper
Sophie's Indonesian Vegetable Stew (see page 178), served with basmati rice and a mixed salad. A favourite ice cream and fresh pineapple.

tuesday

Breakfast
Creamy Yogurt with Nuts and Honey (see page 123) (no nuts for the under fives). A slice of melon and a croissant.

Lunch
Potato and Celeriac Mash (see page 180). Fresh celery with cottage cheese.

Supper
Shepherdless pie: use TVP granules instead of mince and serve with courgette, cauliflower and baby broad beans. Fresh fruit and a small piece of cheese.

wednesday

Breakfast
Mushrooms and tomatoes on toast: put a handful of button mushrooms in a small saucepan with a tiny piece of butter and heat gently. As soon as liquid starts coming out of the mushrooms, cover and cook for 5 minutes. Add a small tin of chopped tomatoes, stir till warm and serve on a thick slice of wholemeal toast.

Lunch
Cauliflower and Broccoli Cheese (see page 171). Serving of any fresh berries with a tablespoon of fromage frais.

Supper
Vegeburger (see page 182) in a sesame bun with lettuce, tomato, ketchup and green relish. Serve with oven-baked sweet-potato chips: cut sweet potato into large chips, brush with olive oil and bake in a hot oven for about 30 minutes, or until cooked. Stewed summer fruits with custard.

thursday

Breakfast
Half a grapefruit. French Toast (see page 126).

Lunch
Pisto (see page 144).

Supper
Peppers Stuffed with Quinoa (see page 144): use organic peppers, if possible. Tofu yogurt with fresh fruit.

friday

Breakfast
Multi-grain Pancakes (see page 126). Bowl of fresh fruit salad with yogurt.

Lunch
A selection of different cheeses with wholemeal bread. A ripe nectarine and a few black grapes.

Supper
Minestrone with Pesto (see page 130). Summer Pudding (see page 188).

winter weekday menu plan

monday

Breakfast
Proper Porridge (see page 122), with one of the listed additions. Chunk of warm wholemeal bread with piece of mild cheese.

Lunch
South of France Omelette (see page 169).

Supper
High-protein Tofu Broth (see page 131). Blackberry and Apple Crumble (see page 189).

tuesday

Breakfast
Meat-free sausages brushed with olive oil and grilled with a large halved tomato.

Lunch
Black Bean Chilli (see page 168). Grapes.

Supper
Pasta with a mushroom and tomato sauce. Large mixed salad. Baked banana with honey.

wednesday

Breakfast
Scrambled Egg with Tomatoes and Mushrooms (see page 125) on wholemeal toast.

Lunch
Vegetable Samosas (see page 172), served with yogurt and mint, or tomato relish, and a small winter salad of celery, shredded lettuce and watercress.

Supper
Broccoli with Spinach (see page 180), served with dal (see Vegetable Curry with Dal, page 181). Upside-down Pudding (see page 188).

thursday

Breakfast
Wholegrain breakfast cereal with hot milk. 2 slices of wholemeal buttered toast. A banana.

Lunch
Creamy Celery Soup (see page 131), served with thick chunks of rough country bread.

Supper
Red Cabbage with Apple and Chestnuts (see page 181): omit the bacon and substitute vegetarian chicken or turkey slices). Baked apple stuffed with sultanas, raisins, chopped dates and honey.

friday

Breakfast
Cheese on toast: grate cheese, add a little milk, a dash of Worcester sauce and beat to a smooth cream; toast bread on one side, spread the cheese mixture on the other side and pop under a hot grill until bubbly. Serve with slices of apple.

Lunch
Broccoli with potatoes. A mixture of cashews, hazelnuts, walnuts, dried apricots and raisins.

Supper
Roasted Vegetables (see page 174), topped with some grated cheese and browned under the grill for 2 minutes before serving. Ginger Fruit Pudding (see page 189).

Lunchbox ideas
• Scoop out the middle of a chunk of French bread and fill with Roasted Vegetables (see page 174). A banana, nuts and raisins.

• A wholemeal bap spread with peanut butter, a mashed banana and a drizzle of honey. A couple of Shortbread Trees (see page 162). An apple.

• Selection of dips (see page 149) and a mixed bag of crudités, such as carrots, celery, peppers and cauliflower. A Blueberry Muffin (see page 162).

• A Thermos of Creamy Celery Soup (see page 131) with a few chunks of ciabatta bread. A thick slice of buttered Green Tea Bread (see page 161).

• Pot of Pasta Salad with Tuna (see page 147). A few Cheese Pretzels (see page 157). A small packet of dried apricots, raisins and sultanas. A bunch of seedless grapes.

family kitchen

Your kitchen is the natural focus of family life and the place where children learn vital lessons about food and eating well. Organize the kitchen and stock its cupboards carefully so that a good meal or healthy snack can always be rustled up, however short the notice or large the number of hungry young people.

what you need

With the right **pans, tools and gadgets** filling kitchen shelves and a well-planned choice of foods stocking **cupboards, fridge and freezer,** you'll be able easily to feed the family **healthily** and **enjoyably** at any time.

pans, tools & utensils

Saucepans
Buy the best you can afford – stainless steel will last a lifetime and is worth the investment. Fry vegetables for starting off soups and stews in the same pan you use to cook the dish, instead of using a separate pan – a useful time-saver. Avoid aluminium pans, which can be a health hazard. If you can't replace yours, do not use them to cook acidic foods such as fruit.

Non-stick saucepan
Essential for making sauces, scrambling eggs or heating milk.

Non-stick frying pans
If possible have two: a smaller one is good for making omelettes. Make sure you use non-stick utensils with them.

Wok
This is indispensable for stir-fry dishes, which are quick, tasty and very healthy. Classic Chinese steel woks are inexpensive, but you must follow the instructions for seasoning them. Or you may prefer to use a non-stick wok.

Hob-to-oven casseroles
These are useful for dishes that have to be started off on the hob, but can then be transferred to the oven.

Indispensables for the kitchen drawer

Vegetable peeler

Potato masher

Kitchen scissors
Must be tough enough to cope with bacon rind and to cut up pieces of chicken.

Small whisk

Garlic crusher

Knife sharpener

Mini stapler
A handy tool for resealing freezer packets.

Good can opener

Pasta server
A scoop with toothed sides for dishing out pasta, this also conveys boiled eggs from pan to eggcup without a spill.

Ovenproof dishes

Ovenproof china or earthenware dishes are useful for preparing gratins, vegetables and bakes.

Colanders

One of your colanders should be heatproof (steel or enamel), so it can double as a steamer with a saucepan lid on top.

Salad spinner

This allows even the busiest cook to have a perfectly dry, fresh green salad every day.

Sharp kitchen knives

It's useful to have three or four, including at least one with a serrated blade for slicing soft foods such as tomatoes.

Wooden chopping boards

In various sizes. Once a week, pour boiling water over them and give them a good scrub.

Spatulas, fish slices and slotted spoons

Have a metal set and a nylon set to use with non-stick pans.

Handled sieves

Wooden spoons

Have several, in different sizes. Don't put wooden spoons in the dishwasher if they are favourites.

Bowls

Various, in china or Pyrex, for mixing and storage.

Lidded glass or Perspex containers

For storing all kinds of food in the fridge, so you can see them.

Measuring jugs

You will find it helpful to have a small Pyrex jug for making sauces as well as a bigger plastic one.

Set of kitchen scales

Pepper mill

One of those items that it is worth spending a little more on. Test them and choose one that does a good grinding job.

Grater

The square kind with different-sized graters on each side is the most useful. Italian cylindrical cheese graters are quick to use.

Good gadgets

Food processor

Worth its weight in gold to the harassed cook. It's indispensable for mincing meat, making breadcrumbs, chopping and grating vegetables, puréeing, mixing batters, and many other processes.

Hand-held electric whisk

Much cheaper than a food processor and almost as useful.

Electric kettle

Make sure it has an automatic switch-off mechanism.

Electric toaster

Juice extractor

With a good juicer you can prepare in minutes a delicious mega-dose of fresh natural goodness – especially of the vital antioxidant vitamins (see Delicious Drinks, pages 192–195).

Mouli-legumes

This non-electrical French gadget allows you to blend and sieve at the same time, and produces soups with a much more interesting texture than made by a blender or a food processor.

Herb cutter

This comprises a shallow, wooden bowl with a handled, half-moon blade – an excellent device for chopping herbs swiftly and thoroughly, without crushing them to a purée.

the store cupboard

Canned foods

Italian plum tomatoes: *whole tomatoes are best, rather than chopped or sieved ones.*
Chickpeas.
Sugar-free baked beans.
A variety of canned beans including soya, borlotti, kidney and cannellini.
Tuna, sardines.

Oils

Extra-virgin olive oil and plain olive oil.
Lighter oils, such as groundnut oil or sunflower oil.
Sesame oil: *for wok cooking.*

Sauces and condiments

Shoyu, or a naturally fermented soy sauce.
Worcestershire sauce.
White-wine vinegar or cider vinegar.
Salt: *sea salt is incomparably superior in flavour to ordinary table salt.*
Low-salt stock cubes or vegetable bouillon powder.
Tomato purée in a tube.
Low- or no-sugar anchovy paste.

Organic jams without additives, and sugar-free fruit spread: *once opened, keep in the fridge.*
Good-quality pesto: *once opened, keep in the fridge.*

Grains and pasta

Wholewheat and unbleached white flour, plain and self-raising.
Rice – brown, pudding, long-grain and basmati: *have some quick-cook rice too for when you are pushed for time.*
Bulgur wheat.
Pasta – normal and some wholemeal: *make sure it is made from 100 per cent durum wheat, as other varieties can become flabby while cooking.*
Porridge oats.

Herbs

Fresh herbs can give a terrific boost to your cooking. Keep small pots of fresh herbs on the kitchen windowsill. Parsley: *best fresh, but freezes well.* Mint, chives and basil: *should always be used fresh.* Rosemary, sage, oregano, thyme and bay leaves: *ideally should be used fresh, but are also good dried.*

Dried herbs and spices can deteriorate quickly in storage. They are best kept in the dark, and should be regularly checked for use-by dates and replaced if necessary. Stale herbs and spices do nothing for your cooking.

Spices

Chilli powder or crushed, dried chillies.
Paprika.
Whole nutmeg.
Black peppercorns: *ready-ground pepper is a useful stand-by but the flavour is not as good.*
Whole cinnamon sticks and ground cinnamon.
Coriander and cumin, both ground: *renew them when they lose their aromas.*
Whole cloves.
Ground ginger and preserved ginger pieces in syrup: *one teaspoon or so of the syrup can spice up sauces and puddings.*
Turmeric.
A good ready-made curry powder, mild, medium or hot, according to your preference: *don't keep it for too long, since it loses its flavour rapidly.*

the vegetable rack and fruit bowl

Vegetables

Potatoes and onions: *store these in brown-paper, not plastic, bags away from light and heat. Be sure to use them before they start to sprout.*

Garlic: *store in a porous earthenware container to keep it in good condition.*
Avocados: *store in brown-paper bags for quick ripening, if they're still hard when you buy them.*

Fruit

Apples, Pears.
Bananas.
Kiwifruit.
Oranges, grapefruit.
Lemons.

the refrigerator

Cheese
Piece of good-quality Cheddar or other hard, mild cheese.
Piece of fresh Parmesan cheese, or ready-grated: *buy this from a reliable delicatessen.*
Fromage frais and cottage cheese.

Salads & vegetables
Iceberg lettuce: *keeps well, so is a good salad stand-by.*
Carrots.
Sun-dried tomatoes in olive oil: *once a luxury, these can now be bought quite inexpensively in many supermarkets. Use them up quickly as they don't keep well.*
A red and a green pepper.
Plenty of tomatoes.
Celery.
Spring onions.
Cucumber.

Miscellaneous
Milk.
Small carton of single cream.
Butter.
Natural live and Greek yogurt.
Eggs.
Smoked streaky bacon: *buy small amounts at a time and pay attention to the use-by dates.*
Whole lemon.
Fresh parsley.
Hummus, Tsatsiki, Taramasalata: *watch use-by dates.*
Good mayonnaise.
Tomato ketchup.
Good French mustard.
A mixture of relishes: *to accompany burgers (see pages 181–83).*
Fresh fruit juices and fizzy mineral water: *to replace commercial soft drinks.*

the freezer

Wholemeal sliced bread *for toasting.*
Wholewheat or granary rolls *for healthy burgers.*
Wholewheat pittas.
Home made garlic baguettes.
Breadcrumbs: *make these next time you have a few slices of stale bread.*
Spinach, puréed or in leaf form.
Sweetcorn, whole or kernels.
French beans.
Petits pois.
Broccoli.

Stew packets of mixed vegetables: *to form the basis of a quick nourishing soup.*
Stir-fry vegetables: *various combinations available.*
Fish fillets, or other cuts of firm white fish: *can be cooked from frozen.*
Packets of shrimps or prawns.
Fish stock: *to make all the difference to a quick fish soup.*
Readymade shortcrust and filo pastry.
Tomato and other pasta sauces.

Apple purée.
Simple vegetable purées for a young baby.
Summer fruits: *keep a mixture of blackcurrants, redcurrants, raspberries, blackberries, blueberries and bilberries.*
Butter.
The family's favourite ice cream.
Selection of herbs.
Whole or ground seeds: *sesame, sunflower and pumpkin seeds, pine nuts and peanuts; all can be used straight from the freezer.*

kitchen hygiene

Health statistics indicate that food poisoning is an increasingly serious problem in many Western countries. Although there are numerous points on the food chain at which infections can get in, the family kitchen cannot be absolved of all blame for the alarming rise in incidents of food-related illness.

For most healthy adults, a minor bout of food poisoning is an unpleasant inconvenience, but for small children particularly, or for anyone whose immune system is weakened by illness, an attack of salmonella – just one of the food-poisoning bugs currently at large– can have very serious consequences.

Throughout the food chain there are places where infection can occur. Intensive food production and the use of antibiotics in animal feed have created many resistant strains of bacteria; the huge expansion of food processing means more handling and greater risk of contamination; and the fast-food takeaway business is frequently dirty and unhygienic. Every time someone does something to the food you eat there is a risk of contamination – and this includes you cooking in your own kitchen.

Among common hazards in the kitchen are bacteria from uncooked chicken contaminating other food; gravy, stuffing, stews or mince left too long in a warm room or oven; soft, unpasteurized cheese and pâté becoming contaminated by listeria – pregnant women should avoid both; poultry and eggs being served undercooked; and shellfish eaten raw or undercooked.

For your children's sake, it is vital to observe the simple rules of hygiene in the kitchen. But do not be obsessive about cleanliness in general. In fact, recent studies have suggested that over-clean and germ-free homes, far from protecting children, may actually put them at risk of asthma and other allergic diseases. The reason for this is that their immune systems fail to reach full strength because they do not get enough practice at coping with bugs and germs.

basic hygiene for the kitchen

General

Dish cloths, kitchen scourers and dish mops can harbour bacteria. Wash them thoroughly in hot water after use and replace them regularly. For cleaning up surfaces after preparing fish or meat, always use disposable kitchen paper rather than a dish cloth.

While shopping

• Keep raw meat, poultry and seafood separately wrapped and apart from other food in your trolley.
• Do not take chilled or frozen food on a tour of the shopping centre. Use a proper cold bag, or buy such items last of all, and get them into your own fridge or freezer as soon as possible.

Storing food

- Keep cooked foods at the top of the fridge and raw meat, poultry and fish at the bottom.
- Never put cooked food on a plate or dish which previously held raw poultry, fish or meat.
- If your fridge does not have a built-in temperature gauge, buy a thermometer and make sure it is always between 0° and 5°C. Get another for your freezer and keep it below −18°C.
- Make sure you remove all stuffing from cooked chicken or turkey before storing it in the fridge. It is actually better to cook stuffing separately if you anticipate having leftovers.
- Cover cooked food and cool it as quickly as possible; refrigerate it within two hours.
- Put leftovers in several smaller containers for more rapid cooling in the fridge.
- Do not overfill your refrigerator: it is the circulating air inside that keeps your food at the right temperature and safe.

Preparing food

- Wash your hands with warm soapy water and dry them on kitchen paper before and between handling different foods.
- Wash all fruit, vegetables and salad ingredients, even pre-packed, pre-washed ones.
- Wash knives, chopping boards and counter tops with hot soapy water after use.
- Do not use the same knives and chopping boards for raw and cooked foods.
- Never allow pets on to kitchen work surfaces or to eat off plates or bowls used by the family.

Safe cooking

- Cook all poultry and burgers right through until there are no pink areas.
- Use a meat thermometer. Cook roasts and steaks to at least 145°C, whole chickens or turkey to 180°C, and burgers to 160°C. If you're eating out, break open children's burgers and do not let them eat them if they are still pink. It is safe to eat underdone steak or roasts – minimum 145°C – as any bacteria will be on the outside, which gets much hotter. When meat is minced any bacteria inside are spread throughout, so the temperature must reach at least 160°C to destroy them.
- Cook eggs until they are firm, not runny, unless you know they are organic, or free-range and free of salmonella. Some supermarkets now sell pasteurized eggs which can safely be used in home-made mayonnaise.
- Cook fish until it flakes easily with a fork and has turned just opaque.

Frozen and cook-chilled foods

- Unless labels on frozen packaged foods say the foods can be cooked from frozen, make sure they are thawed first. Always cook them for at least the time and at the temperature indicated on the packet. Frozen poultry should be left to defrost very slowly in the refrigerator. Never try to defrost poultry in hot water.
- Be very careful with microwaves. There may be 'cold spots' where bacteria are not killed. If your microwave does not have a turntable, switch it off and turn the dish by hand at least twice during cooking. If the instructions on a packet are not clear, or you do not know the wattage of your microwave oven, check with the manufacturer. Burgers, meat and poultry are safest cooked by conventional methods.
- Never re-freeze previously frozen food. Meat, poultry or fish in the supermarket may have been frozen before reaching the shop, and been thawed there. Counter labels should indicate this, so watch out for them when buying.
- Always defrost or marinate food in the fridge, never on the kitchen counter.

Reheating food

- When reheating soups, gravy and all sauces, be sure you bring them to the boil. Other leftovers should be reheated to a temperature of 165°C.
- Keep hot food above 63°C until it is served.
- Never reheat food more than once.

superfood recipes

Here are 160 easy-to-prepare, delicious and nutritious dishes, all making lavish use of the superfoods in this book. You will find recipes for every meal in a child's

day, from breakfast to supper, and for every age, from a baby's first solid foods and a hungry teenager's after-the-cinema snack to meals the whole family will enjoy.

about the recipes

All children are individuals, with their own tastes, appetites, likes and dislikes for food, as much as for everything else. Although every recipe in this book has been carefully planned to use the superfoods in ways that are both nutritious and great to eat, not every child is going to enjoy every one of them.

It is not helpful to try laying down absolute rules about what foods children will eat, and at what age. It is unrealistic to think that at 4 years and 11 months a child will not like real fish cakes and broccoli, yet four weeks later, at the age of 5, will devour them with relish.

Obviously, there are important guidelines for baby foods, weaning times and the introduction of solids, and for introducing foods that may potentially be allergens, all of which are included in this book. These excepted, why make your life difficult and your child's miserable by following totally arbitrary rules on what to feed and when?

Every recipe in this book is nutritious, delicious and healthy. With the exception of babies, for whom specially devised recipes are marked with a symbol (see the box, opposite), all children may happily eat any recipe in this book. If your child's taste is sophisticated and develops in advance of his years, then be happy that you can eat out in lovely places and not be embarrassed by a request for burger and chips from your 13-year-old.

Even in today's ethnically rich and diverse society, there are still well-meaning but ill-informed health professionals who throw up their hands in horror at the thought of feeding exotic dishes such as curry to small children – a culinary tradition throughout Asia for thousands of years. If a 5-year-old fancies a Vindaloo, let him have it.

What kids should not be offered on a regular basis is the ubiquitous and inevitably nutritionally-disastrous Children's Menu familiar in fast food chains, with their litany of burgers and chips, sausage and chips, chicken nuggets and chips, fish fingers and chips, followed by non-dairy ice cream and fruit pie with a coke on the side.

some feeding guidlines

There are a few simple guidelines to bear in mind when feeding children, and you will find them wherever they are relevant in this book. Here is a summary of the most important of them.

• Don't give nuts or anything containing them to children under 5.

• Stick to full-cream milk and other dairy products for under-5s, rather than semi-skimmed or low-fat, which do not contain the full complement of the essential fats children need.

• Vary the types of starch – rice, oats, millet, buckwheat, amaranth, spelt, quinoa – that you give your children. Don't feed them wheat more than four times a day.

• Feed your children a wide a range of foods as early as possible, and don't give up if a first attempt fails to please.

• Remember that all children, from babies upwards, are sociable creatures and enjoy their food most when they eat with the rest of the family.

time-saving tips in the kitchen

• Before you start on a recipe, read it through, and make sure that you have all the ingredients and any necessary equipment to hand.

• Have plenty of kitchen paper handy to blot meat, fish and vegetables dry after cleaning them, to drain excess fat from fried foods, to wipe out frying pans and to mop up spills.

• Clutter slows down cooking: tidy waste into the bin as you work.

• Make a supply of salad dressing and store it in a tightly sealed bottle – one with a porcelain cap is ideal – in a cool dark place. It will double as a marinade for chicken and fish.

• Here is how to have a dish to serve pasta in piping hot, without having to use the oven. Stand a colander in the serving dish in the sink. When the pasta is cooked, drain it into the colander, pick up the colander and deposit it on the saucepan to allow it to finish draining. Tip the hot pasta water out of the serving dish and wipe the dish dry.

• To skin tomatoes and peaches, put them in a bowl and cover with boiling water. Test the skin of one with the tip of a knife and when it is ready to slide off, empty the bowl.

• To skin a clove of garlic quickly, crush it under the blade of a knife.

• Keep three or four medicine-sized bottles containing olive oil, to which you can add a variety of surplus herbs and spices. This way you have ready-made flavoured oils to hand. Use garlic and chillies for a Mexican marinade, rosemary and tarragon for chicken dishes, dill for fish and oregano for a Mediterranean flavour.

• Keep a shopping list in a prominent place on which to note essential store-cupboard items that are running low, so that you can replace them before they run out.

freezing hints

Although most of the recipes in this book have been devised so that they may be quickly prepared, cooked and served, they may be frozen in the usual way, if their ingredients allow. The freezer is, in fact, one of your best time-saving assets in the kitchen. For instance:

• Freeze servings of baby food by cooling freshly made purées to room temperature and freezing them in sterilized ice-cube trays. When frozen, transfer the cubes to a freezer bag, label and date it and return it to the freezer. Use as required.

• Make large batches of favourite meat-free burgers (see pages 182-84 for recipes) and freeze them. Cool the prepared burgers in the fridge for 30 minutes then freeze in a freezer bag, separated by greaseproof paper. The burgers can be cooked direct from the freezer, allowing extra time to ensure they are cooked right through. Don't freeze meat burgers: unless they are properly defrosted and cooked right through, they could be a health hazard.

• Parsley, much used in the kitchen, freezes well. Finely chop a large quantity in the food processor and freeze it. You can then use a little at a time.

• Remove the crusts from wholemeal bread that is beginning to go stale and turn it into crumbs in the food processor. Store the crumbs in the freezer in a lidded carton and use them for rissoles and burgers, or for coating fish.

recipe points to remember

• All spoon measures are level unless otherwise stated. 1 tsp = 5ml, 1 tbsp = 15ml.

• Eggs are large.

• Follow either metric or imperial measurements, never mix the two.

• Baking times are a guide only, because ovens vary. Adjust oven temperatures for fan ovens.

This symbol appears by recipes suitable for giving to babies. The figures with the symbol indicate the age at which the baby may be first offered the food.

big breakfasts

Eating a **good breakfast** is the best way for children to **start** their day. The recipes here are all packed with **energy** and **good nutrition**. They look and taste good, too – the **perfect foundation** for a great day.

proper muesli

★ = superfood

Serves 2

This simple breakfast recipe is a wonderful source of energy, minerals and B vitamins.
• Prepare the muesli the night before, making it in individual bowls. For each serving of muesli, stir in enough fruit juice to moisten it well. Then stir in the yogurt and honey. Leave the bowls in the refrigerator overnight.
• In the morning, take the muesli out of the fridge as early as possible. Just before it is to be eaten, stir in fruit of your children's choice – grated apple or pear, sliced banana, a few strawberries, or a sliced peach. At the Bircher-Benner Clinic in Switzerland, where muesli originated, they add fresh blackberries and some thick cream.

2 tbsp organic unsweetened muesli
fruit juice, to moisten
★ **2 tbsp natural live yogurt**
2 tsp honey
★ **fresh fruit, to serve**

Illustrated right

banana porridge

Serves 1

6 months +

This porridge recipe provides an excellent intake of energy, minerals and B vitamins, and is easily adapted to suit small babies as well as older ones.
• For 8–9 month-old babies, or older, use oats straight from the packet and add the sultanas. For babies over 6 months, grind the oats to a fine meal, using a clean coffee grinder or a pestle and mortar.
• Put the oats and sultanas or oatmeal in a saucepan with 2–3 tablespoons of water, or breast or organic formula milk, or a mixture of the two. Bring gently to the boil, reduce the heat and simmer, stirring occasionally to prevent it sticking, until cooked. Mix the banana into the cooked porridge.

★ **1 tbsp organic porridge oats**
★ **1 tsp organic sultanas, washed (for older babies)**
water or milk, to mix (see method)
★ **½ ripe banana, mashed**

proper porridge

★ = superfood

Serves 2

As eaten by generations of Highlanders, porridge is traditionally made with oatmeal, rather than the whole flakes or rolled oats of today's cereal.

• Bring the water to the boil and sift in the oatmeal slowly, stirring all the time, until the water returns to the boil. Lower the heat, cover the pan, and let the oatmeal cook very gently for 10 minutes. Add the salt, stir again and cook for another 10 minutes.

• Add a sweetener before serving, if you like, but remember Highland heroes ate their porridge unsweetened, dipping each spoonful in thick cream.

• Serve with milk or cream, or, if you prefer, with soya or oat milk, or a nut milk made from almonds or hazelnuts.

500ml/16 fl oz water
★ 60g/2oz medium oatmeal
good pinch of salt
honey, maple syrup or dark brown cane sugar (optional)
★ milk or cream, to serve

other ideas for porridge

• With raisins, honey and cinnamon. Cook as above, omitting the salt. After 20 minutes, remove from the heat and stir in 2 teaspoons raisins, 1 teaspoon honey and a good pinch of cinnamon. Let stand, covered, for 5 minutes before serving.

• With fruit spread. Instead of sugar, syrup or honey, stir in a spoonful of one of the sugar-free fruit spreads, made with fruit juice concentrates instead of sugar.

• With apple and sultanas. Cook the oatmeal as above. After 20 minutes, stir in 1 tablespoon peeled and freshly grated apple and a sprinkle of sultanas.

• Overnight porridge. Heat a wide-mouthed vacuum flask by filling it with hot water then emptying it out. Put in 180g/6oz porridge oats, fill with boiling water, close and leave overnight. At breakfast, the porridge will be ready to eat and still hot. If it is too thick, thin with hot milk or water.

five-grain kruska

Serves 4

This healthy cereal dish, crammed with nutritional riches, appeared in the first *Superfoods* over 10 years ago. A real superfood for hungry, growing children, it was made famous in his own country by the great Swedish naturopath Are Waerland, and popularized in the USA by another famous Swedish naturopath, Paavo Airola. The grains should all be organically produced: a filling dish for breakfast or supper.

• Put the wholewheat grains and the millet, oats, rye and barley in a clean coffee grinder or food processor and process until coarsely ground. Put them in a flameproof casserole, pour in the water and leave to soak overnight.

• In the morning, preheat the oven to 150°C/300°F/gas 2. Bring the mixture in the casserole to the boil, add the wheatgerm or oatgerm and bran, and the raisins or sultanas.

• Transfer the casserole to the oven and bake for 30 minutes. The texture should be thick, but not gooey. If it is too thick, add a little more hot water. Serve the Kruska with hot or cold milk, or cream and a little honey, if liked.

★ 1 tbsp wholewheat grains
★ 1 tbsp whole millet
★ 1 tbsp whole oats
★ 1 tbsp whole rye
★ 1 tbsp whole barley
250ml/8 fl oz hot water
★ 1 tbsp wheatgerm or oatgerm
★ 1 tbsp wheat or oat bran
★ 2 tbsp raisins or sultanas
milk or cream, to serve
honey (optional)

creamy yogurt with nuts & honey

Serves 1

Stir the nuts and honey into the yogurt. Greek yogurt provides a nourishing, delicious and protein-packed start to the day.

★ 100g/3½oz Greek or thick-set natural live yogurt
★ 30g/1oz mixed chopped nuts
2 tsp honey

real fruity yogurt

Serves 2

Stir the fruit into the yogurt, for a fast and healthy breakfast.

★ 100g/3½oz Greek or thick-set natural live yogurt
★ 100g/3½oz whole raspberries, sliced strawberries, peaches or nectarines or other favourite fruit in season

breakfasts in a mug

★ = superfood

With the best will in the world, a proper leisurely sit-down breakfast isn't always possible. Here are two nourishing protein- and energy-rich breakfasts which can be quickly whipped up in your blender.

Serves 1

banana-to-go
Put the ingredients in a blender and whizz to a deliciously creamy froth.

★ 100g/3½oz natural live yogurt
★ 1 banana, sliced
2 tsp brewers' yeast
1 tsp runny honey

Serves 1

lime-e-shake
Put all the ingredients in a blender (including any citrus-fruit pith saved from the juicer). Blend together well.

★ juice of 2 oranges
juice of 1 lime
★ 1 banana, peeled
★ 300ml/½ pint milk
★ 150g/5 oz natural live yogurt
★ 2 heaped tbsp wheatgerm

apple & apricot purée

Serves 1

4-6 months

• Put the prepared fruits in a saucepan with enough water to cover. Bring to the boil, reduce the heat and simmer 8–10 minutes, until thoroughly cooked.
• Strain, reserving the cooking water. Purée the fruit, either in a blender or through a sieve. Mix it to a suitable consistency with the reserved water, cooled boiled water, breast milk or organic formula milk.

★ 1 organic apple, peeled, cored and chopped
★ 2 organic apricots, stones removed

fruitfast

Serves 4

• Wash the fruit thoroughly and drain it well. Put it in a bowl and pour over the boiling water. Add the orange peel and cinnamon stick, cover the bowl and leave to stand overnight.
• Next day, remove the orange peel and cinnamon stick from the fruit and discard. Put a dollop of thick yogurt on each bowlful before serving.

★ 500g/1lb mixed dried fruit – apricots, prunes, apples, pears, sultanas
1.2 litres/2 pints boiling water
★ a curl of orange peel
★ 7cm/3in piece cinnamon stick
★ thick natural yogurt, to serve

scrambled egg with tomatoes & mushrooms

Serves 1

• Line a grill pan with foil and heat it. Cut the tomato in half and brush both halves and the mushroom with oil. Put the tomato halves, cut side up and the mushroom, gill side up, in the grill pan and grill them until browned, turning the mushroom once during cooking.

• Meanwhile, whisk the egg and season it lightly. Put the butter in a small non-stick saucepan and melt it until hot. Add the egg and stir over a high heat until scrambled. Serve with the grilled tomato and mushroom, with wholemeal toast on the side.

★ **1 medium tomato**
1 large dark-gilled mushroom
★ **a little olive oil**
★ **1 egg**
salt and black pepper
★ **small knob of butter**
★ **wholemeal toast, to serve**

baked eggs & bacon

Serves 6

• Preheat the oven to 180°C/350°F/gas 4. Use all but 2 tablespoons of the butter to grease six ramekins, each about 150ml/¼ pint capacity. Put the buttered ramekins in a roasting tin.

• Heat the remaining butter in a small frying pan. Add the bacon pieces and fry them over a medium heat until lightly browned and crisp. Drain the bacon on kitchen paper, crush the pieces and sprinkle over the bases of the ramekins. Add the parsley and a little seasoning. Break an egg into each ramekin.

• Pour sufficient tap-hot water into the roasting tin to come halfway up the sides of the ramekins. Cover the tin with foil and bake in the oven for 16–18 minutes, or until the whites of the eggs are set and the yolks are creamy.

• Spoon some cream over each baked egg and serve immediately with fingers of buttered toast.

★ **60g/2oz butter**
★ **180g/6oz bacon, rinds removed and rashers chopped**
★ **180g/6oz fresh parsley, finely chopped**
salt and black pepper
★ **6 eggs**
★ **100ml/3½ fl oz whipping or double cream**
★ **wholemeal toast, to serve**

★ = superfood

poached egg & tomato

Serves 1

In this recipe, the unshelled egg is given an initial dip in boiling water. This sets the egg white slightly so it stays in one piece as it is poaching.

• Bring a small saucepan of water to a rolling boil. Put in the tomato. Put the unshelled egg in a slotted spoon and lower it into the boiling water for half a minute. Lift it out of the water, crack it open and slide the egg back into the water.

• Poach for 4 minutes, when the tomato and egg will both be cooked. Lift them out of the pan with a slotted spoon. Serve with buttered wholemeal toast.

★ 1 medium tomato
★ 1 egg
★ wholemeal toast, to serve

french toast

Serves 1

• Melt the butter in a frying pan. Dip the fingers of bread in the beaten egg. Put them in the frying pan and fry on both sides until golden.

• Remove the toasts from the pan, sprinkle with a little dark brown sugar and cinnamon and serve while still warm.

★ 30g/1oz butter
★ 1 thick slice wholemeal bread, cut into fingers
★ 1 egg, beaten
dark brown sugar, to sprinkle
★ cinnamon, to sprinkle

multi-grain pancakes

Makes 12–16

• Put the dry ingredients, baking powder, bicarbonate of soda and salt in a large bowl. Mix well together.

• In a separate bowl, whisk together the eggs, buttermilk, honey and melted butter. Add the wet ingredients to the dry ingredients and mix until just combined. (If you overmix the batter the pancakes will be tough; a few lumps are okay.) Gently stir in the toasted pecan pieces.

• Heat a griddle or shallow frying pan over medium-high heat until a drop of water sprinkled on it sizzles. Pour the batter in scant half cupfuls on to the pan and cook for 2–3 minutes, or until the bubbles that form around the outside edge pop. Flip each pancake and cook the other side until golden brown. Repeat with the remaining batter. The mixture should make 12–16 pancakes.

★ 400g/13oz dry ingredients, made up of a mixture of cornmeal, rolled oats, wholemeal flour, rye flour, wheat bran and flax seeds
1 tbsp baking powder
1½ tsp bicarbonate of soda
½ tsp salt
★ 3 eggs
★ 750ml/1¼ pints buttermilk
150g/5oz honey
★ 125g/4oz unsalted butter, melted and cooled
125g/4oz pecan pieces, toasted

barley bannocks

Makes approx. 6

These Scottish pancakes are traditionally cooked on an iron griddle. If you do not have one, use a shallow-sided frying pan or a crêpe pan instead.

• Sift the flour into a bowl. Make a well in the centre and break in the eggs. Add the melted butter. Beat the ingredients together, adding enough water to make a smooth batter. Set the batter aside to rest for 30 minutes.

• Heat a griddle or shallow frying pan to moderately hot. Pour a ladleful of the batter on to the heated pan, tilting it so the batter spreads to the edges. Cook for 2–3 minutes, then flip the bannock over and cook on the other side for another 2–3 minutes. Repeat until the mixture is finished. The mixture will make about six bannocks.

• When each bannock is cooked, place a filling in the centre, fold in four and eat it while still hot. Good fillings include apple purée; a purée of soaked dried prunes and apricots; a spoonful of berries, such as raspberries, blackberries or strawberries, stewed over a low heat for 2 minutes, until their juices run; yogurt with raisins; sliced bananas and yogurt; and blackberry jelly and Greek yogurt.

★ 125g/4oz barley flour (or beremeal)
★ 3 eggs
★ 30g/1oz butter, melted
water, to mix

oatmeal bannocks

Makes approx. 20

• Put the oatmeal, salt and sugar in a large bowl. Dissolve the syrup in the milk and add the mixture to the oatmeal. Cover and leave to soak overnight.

• Next day, preheat a griddle or shallow frying pan to fairly hot. Mix the eggs and bicarbonate of soda into the oatmeal. Mix in more milk, if necessary, to make a thickish, creamy batter.

• Drop the batter a tablespoonful at a time on to the hot pan – the batter should spread to 12–15 cm/5–6 in. Cook for 2–3 minutes, flip over and cook on the other side for 2–3 minutes.

• As you cook the bannocks, pile them on top of one another and wrap in a cloth to keep soft. The mixture should give about 20. Serve them hot, with butter and jam.

★ 375g/12oz fine oatmeal
1 tsp salt
1 tbsp sugar
1 tbsp golden syrup
★ 600ml/1 pint milk
★ 2 eggs, lightly beaten
1 tsp bicarbonate of soda

super soups

Making soups at home is a fun activity that children enjoy helping with. The results are wonderfully satisfying: hot or cold, thick and chunky or smooth and creamy, soups are full of goodness and easy to eat.

minestrone

Serves 6

This hearty Italian soup is a meal in itself, served with crusty bread, and some sticks of fresh carrot and celery to nibble while waiting for it. Minestrone tastes even better the day after it is made.

• Heat the olive oil in a heavy-based saucepan. Add the bacon and fry until it just begins to turn translucent. Remove from the pan and set aside. Add the garlic and onion to the pan and fry gently until soft. Return the bacon to the pan with the tomatoes.

• Pour in the hot stock, stir, then add the carrots, turnip, courgettes, celery and potatoes. Bring to the boil, cover the pan, lower the heat and simmer very gently for about 40 minutes, or until the vegetables are tender.

• Add the drained beans and frozen peas and heat through. Add the parsley and seasoning to taste. Serve the soup in warmed bowls, with the Parmesan served separately, to be added according to taste.

★ = superfood

★ 1 tbsp olive oil
★ 3 rashers streaky bacon, chopped
★ 1 clove garlic, finely chopped
★ 1 small onion, finely chopped
★ 200g/7oz canned chopped tomatoes
★ 1 litre/1¾ pints hot chicken or vegetable stock
★ 2 carrots, finely diced
★ 1 small turnip, finely diced
2 small courgettes, thinly sliced
★ 1 stick celery, sliced
★ 2 potatoes, diced
★ 425g/14oz canned cannellini beans, drained and rinsed
★ 60g/2oz frozen peas
★ 1 tbsp finely chopped fresh parsley
salt and black pepper
★ freshly grated Parmesan cheese, to serve

minestrone with pesto

★ = superfood

Serves 6

• Heat the oil in a heavy-based saucepan. Add the onion and garlic, reduce the heat to low, cover the pan and sweat the vegetables for a few minutes, until translucent. Add the leek, carrot, celery, potato, tomatoes and their juice, and the stock.

• Bring to the boil, reduce the heat and simmer for about 15 minutes, or until the vegetables are tender.

• Add the courgettes, cabbage and a pinch of oregano, and simmer until the cabbage is tender. Add the beans and heat through.

• Taste and adjust the seasoning, if necessary, stir in the pesto sauce, according to taste, and garnish with the torn basil leaves. Serve with the Parmesan cheese on the side.

★ 1 tbsp olive oil
★ 1 onion, chopped
★ 2 cloves garlic, chopped
★ 1 leek, sliced
★ 1 carrot, sliced
★ 2 sticks celery, sliced
★ 1 potato, sliced
★ 200g/7oz canned tomatoes
★ 1.5 litres/2½ pints chicken or vegetable stock
2 courgettes, sliced
★ a good slice out of a green cabbage, shredded
★ pinch of dried oregano
★ 425g/14oz canned cannellini beans, drained and rinsed
salt and black pepper
pesto sauce, to taste
★ fresh basil, to garnish
★ freshly grated Parmesan cheese, to serve

minestrone with rice & tomatoes

Serves 4

This is a filling summer soup, to be made when tomatoes are cheap and bursting with sunshine. If you use brown rice, allow an extra 20 minutes cooking time.

• Put the tomatoes, onion and celery in a heavy-based saucepan. Cover the pan and cook over a very low heat until the tomatoes are soft and pulpy.

• Pour the tomato mixture into a food processor or blender and process until smooth. Return the mixture to the pan, add the stock and bring to the boil. Add the rice. Cover the pan and cook over a very low heat for about 15 minutes, or until the rice is tender.

• Stir in the butter, add a little pepper, and either sprinkle with the chopped basil or stir in the pesto. Serve sprinkled with the grated Parmesan cheese.

★ 500g/1lb tomatoes, skinned and chopped
★ 1 small onion, roughly chopped
★ 1 stick celery, roughly chopped
1 litre/1¾ pints vegetable stock
★ 100g/3½oz long-grain rice
★ 30g/1oz butter
black pepper
★ bunch of fresh basil or 2 tsp pesto sauce
★ 2 tbsp freshly grated Parmesan cheese, to garnish

high-protein tofu broth

Serves 4

- Heat the stock in a heavy-based saucepan and add all the remaining ingredients, except the coriander. Bring to the boil, reduce the heat, cover the pan and simmer for about 10 minutes, or until all the vegetables are tender.
- Serve the broth immediately, sprinkled with the freshly chopped coriander.

Note: Tamari sauce, a Japanese variety of soy sauce, is available from health food stores.

450ml/¾ pint vegetable stock
★ 125g/4oz firm tofu, cubed
★ 1 large carrot, very thinly sliced
★ 2 spring onions, chopped
★ white part of 1 small leek, thinly sliced
★ 1 tbsp organic tamari sauce or dark soy sauce
black pepper
★ small bunch fresh coriander, chopped

leek & watercress soup

Serves 4

- Melt the butter in a heavy-based pan. Add the leek and cook gently until soft. Add the potatoes and stir them in the butter for 1–2 minutes. Add the water, bring to the boil, cover the pan and simmer for 10 minutes, or until the potatoes are cooked.
- Meanwhile, discard the thickest stems of the watercress, saving a couple of sprigs for garnish, and finely chop the rest. Add to the soup when the potatoes are almost done and simmer 1–2 minutes.
- Cool slightly then pour into a food processor or blender and process very lightly. Return to the pan and heat through, check the seasoning, swirl in the cream and garnish with the watercress sprigs.

★ 60g/2oz butter
★ 1 leek, trimmed and finely sliced
★ 2-3 potatoes, sliced
900ml/1½ pints water
★ 1 bunch watercress, thoroughly washed
salt and black pepper
★ 2 tbsp cream

creamy celery soup

Serves 4

- Chop the knobbly skin off the celeriac, slice the flesh and drop it into a bowl of water with the lemon juice or vinegar (to prevent the celeriac discolouring).
- Melt the butter in a heavy-based saucepan. Add the onion, sweat it for 1–2 minutes, then add the celery, drained celeriac and potato. Add the stock, bring to the boil, reduce the heat, cover and simmer for 25–30 minutes, or until the vegetables are tender.
- Pour the soup into a food processor or blender and process briefly, then return it to the pan or a serving bowl. Just before serving the soup, beat the egg yolk into the cream and whisk the mixture into the soup; do not reheat it. Sprinkle with the celery tops, or with chives or parsley before serving.

★ 1 small celeriac root
1 tbsp lemon juice or white wine vinegar
★ 30g/1oz butter
★ 1 onion, chopped
★ 4 sticks celery, sliced; feathery tops reserved for garnish
★ 1 small potato, diced
★ 900ml/1½ pints chicken or vegetable stock
★ 1 egg yolk
★ 3 tbsp double cream or crème fraîche
★ 1 tbsp chopped fresh chives or parsley, to garnish (optional)

beetroot & apple soup

★ = superfood

Serves 4

This brilliant red, sweet and slightly earthy soup first appeared in *The Superfoods Diet Book*. Serve it with plenty of crusty bread.

• Put the beetroot and onion in a food processor or blender. Add a cupful of the apple juice and process until you have a smooth purée. Stir in the rest of the apple juice and the lemon juice. Add a pinch of sea salt and black pepper.

• Chill the soup for 1–2 hours. Serve it in individual bowls, swirling in the cream just before serving.

★ 500g/1lb raw beetroot, grated
★ 1 small onion, finely chopped
★ 600ml/1 pint unsweetened apple juice
★ 1 tsp lemon juice
sea salt and black pepper
★ 150ml/¼ pint soured or single cream

baked savoy cabbage soup with melted cheese

Serves 6

This warming soup is more like a casserole and will fill a family of six for a weekend lunch. The best cheese to use is Italian fontina, but a medium Cheddar, havarti, Gruyère or Emmenthal would also be delicious.

• Preheat the oven to 200°C/400°F/gas 6. Heat 2 tablespoons of the olive oil in a large flameproof casserole. Add the garlic and fry gently until just soft. Remove the garlic with a slotted spoon and set aside. Cut the bread into slices 2.5cm/1in thick. Add the remaining oil to the casserole and heat until hot. Add the bread slices in batches and fry until light golden on each side. Remove and reserve.

• Heat the stock in a separate pan and add the cabbage. Bring to the boil, reduce the heat and simmer for about five minutes, or until the cabbage is just tender. Drain the cabbage, reserving the stock.

• To assemble the soup, lay some slices of fried bread across the bottom of the casserole. Sprinkle with some garlic, spoon over a layer of cabbage, dot over a few of the anchovies, then add a handful of the grated cheese, evenly spread. Continue with the same layering until everything is used, finishing with a layer of cheese. Spoon over all the reserved cabbage stock.

• Bake in the oven for about 30–40 minutes, or until a golden crust is formed. Serve in warmed shallow soup bowls, garnished with a little parsley.

★ 4 tbsp olive oil
★ 2 cloves garlic, thinly sliced
1 loaf stale ciabatta or French baguette (approx. 200g/7oz)
★ 1 litre/1¾ pints chicken stock
★ 1 Savoy cabbage, washed, de-stalked and finely shredded
★ 60g/2oz salted anchovies
★ 200g/7oz grated cheese
★ chopped fresh flat-leafed parsley, to garnish

pumpkin soup

Serves 6

• Remove the skin and seeds from the pumpkin, and cut the flesh into large cubes. Heat the oil in a heavy-based saucepan or flameproof casserole, add the potato and cook gently until golden but not brown. Add the onion and garlic, mixing them with the potato dice. Add the stock, then the pumpkin and the sage. Bring to the boil, reduce the heat, cover and simmer gently for 20–25 minutes, until the potatoes and pumpkin are both soft.

• Pour the mixture into a food processor or blender and process to a smooth cream. Return to the pan and heat through. Swirl in the crème fraîche and spoon the soup into bowls. Sprinkle the grated cheese on top, and serve the croûtons separately.

★ 1 pumpkin, weighing about 1 kg/2lb
★ 2 tbsp olive oil
★ 1 small potato, diced
★ 1 onion, chopped
★ 1 clove garlic
900ml/1½ pints vegetable stock
★ 4 fresh sage leaves, chopped
★ 150ml/¼ pint crème fraîche
★ 60g/2oz Gruyère cheese, grated
croûtons, to serve

split pea & rice soup

★ = superfood

Serves 4

• Rinse and drain the split peas. Put them in a heavy-based saucepan with the water. Bring to the boil, reduce the heat, cover and simmer for 1 hour.
• When the split peas are nearly cooked, heat the oil in another heavy-based saucepan or a flameproof casserole. Add the onions and garlic and stir-fry until softened but not browned. Add the cumin and stir-fry for a few minutes more.
• Drain the split peas and return them to their pan. Add the onion mixture, vegetable stock, lemon juice and cooked rice. Heat through and season with the pepper. Serve the soup in individual warmed bowls, garnished with the chopped coriander.

★ **250g/8oz split peas**
1 litre/1¾ pints water
★ **2 tbsp olive oil**
★ **2 large onions, chopped**
★ **1 clove garlic, crushed**
★ **1 tsp cumin seeds**
500ml/16 fl oz vegetable stock
★ **2 tsp lemon juice**
★ **handful of cooked brown rice**
black pepper
★ **chopped fresh coriander, to garnish**

cream of smoked haddock & potato soup

Serves 4

This delicious and substantial winter soup is a favourite on the menu of Zilli's restaurant in London. Try adding some parsnips to the ingredients here, cooking them with the potatoes. Their sweetness will give the soup a lovely flavour.
• Melt the butter in a heavy-based saucepan. Add the onion and cook for 2–3 minutes over a medium heat, until softened but not browned. Stir in the potatoes, reduce the heat and cover the pan tightly. Cook for 10 minutes, stirring frequently, until the potatoes are very tender. Add the haddock to the pan, then stir in the milk and bring to a simmer. Cook for 10–15 minutes until the fish is very tender.
• Pour the soup into a blender or food processor and process until completely smooth. Pour back into the pan, add half the parsley and reheat until bubbling. Taste and add seasoning, if necessary.
• Ladle the soup into four warmed bowls and sprinkle with the remaining parsley. Serve immediately with lots of crusty bread.

★ **90g/3oz unsalted butter**
★ **1 large onion, finely sliced**
★ **125g/4oz potatoes, diced**
★ **500g/1lb undyed smoked haddock fillet, skinned, boned and diced**
★ **1.2 litres/2 pints milk**
★ **6 tbsp chopped fresh flat-leafed parsley**
salt and white pepper

fish soup with rouille & croûtons

Serves 4

- Clean and skin the fish, being careful to remove all bones. Cut it into chunks and set aside.
- Heat the oil in a large saucepan. Add the onion, garlic and leeks and cook them over a gentle heat, stirring from time to time, until they are softened but not browned. Add the tomatoes, let them cook a little till their juices run, then add the oregano, a pinch of salt and a little black pepper. Add the fish, then pour over the stock or stock-and-water mixture. Cover the pan and cook gently for 15–20 minutes, or until the fish is cooked through.
- Meanwhile, make the rouille and croûtons. For the rouille, put the mayonnaise into a bowl, and stir in the tomato purée, crushed garlic and chilli powder. For the croûtons, bake the slices of French bread in a moderately hot oven (200°C/400°F/gas 6) for 20 minutes, then cut them into cubes.
- When the fish is cooked, pour the contents of the pan into a food processor and blend to a smooth purée. Return the soup to the pan and stir in the crème fraîche. Heat the soup through and serve it sprinkled with chopped parsley, with the rouille and croûtons in separate bowls.

★ 675g/1lb 7oz white fish
★ 2 tbsp sunflower oil
★ 1 onion, chopped
★ 2 cloves garlic
★ white part of 2 leeks, sliced
★ 3–4 large juicy tomatoes, chopped
★ pinch of dried oregano
salt and black pepper
★ 1.2 litres/2 pints fish stock or half stock and half water
★ 1 tbsp crème fraîche
★ handful of parsley, finely chopped

For the rouille:
4 tbsp mayonnaise
★ good squeeze of tomato purée
★ 2 cloves garlic, crushed
good pinch of chilli powder

For the croûtons:
4 slices French bread

tasty lunches

At lunchtime, children need **nourishing** food to keep their activity and **concentration levels** high for the rest of the day. Here is a great-to-eat choice, from baby purées to food to **satisfy** hungry schoolchildren.

root vegetable & potato purée

★ = superfood

Serves 1

4-6 months

You need approximately equal amounts of each vegetable (organic, if possible) for this purée.
• Put the vegetables in a saucepan. Add enough water to cover. Cover the pan, bring to the boil, reduce the heat and simmer gently for about 10 minutes, or until the vegetables are cooked.
• Strain the vegetables, reserving the water. Purée the vegetables, either in a food processor or through a sieve. Mix the purée to a suitable consistency with some of the reserved water, or with cooled boiled water, breast milk or organic formula milk.

¼ swede, cut into chunks
1 small parsnip, cut into chunks
★ 1 small potato, peeled and chopped

broccoli, green bean & sweet potato purée

Serves 1

5-6 months

By the time your baby is 5–6 months old, you can start to introduce green vegetables – ideally, organic.
• Put the chopped sweet potato in a saucepan with enough water to cover. Bring to the boil, reduce the heat and simmer for 5 minutes. Add the broccoli and beans and cook for another 5–6 minutes, until the vegetables are soft.
• Strain the vegetables, reserving the water. Purée the vegetables in a food processor or through a sieve. Mix the purée to a suitable consistency with a little of the reserved water, or with cooled boiled water, breast milk or organic formula milk.

★ ½ sweet potato, peeled and cut into chunks
★ 3–4 broccoli florets, chopped
★ a few French or runner beans, strings removed and chopped

Illustrated right

chicken salad with honey & chilli

★ = superfood

Serves 4–6

• Beat the egg white and cornflour together in a bowl. Add the chicken pieces and one garlic clove, stirring them so they are well coated in the egg white. In a separate bowl, mix together the honey, vinegar, soy sauce and mustard, until dissolved. Set aside. Arrange two radicchio leaves on each plate.

• Heat a wok or frying pan and add the oil. When the oil smokes, add the chicken pieces and stir-fry until golden. Remove the chicken from the pan with a slotted spoon and set aside. Add the peanuts to the pan, stir-frying them until golden. Remove from the pan and set aside. Add the chillies (if using), remaining garlic clove and spring onions to the pan. Stir-fry for 1 minute. Put the chicken and nuts back in the pan, add the honey and vinegar mixture and let the sauce bubble a little and reduce.

• Spoon the chicken and sauce over the lettuce and scatter with the tomato halves, and with the coriander and parsley. Serve immediately.

★ 1 egg white
★ 1 tbsp cornflour
★ 4 chicken breasts, skinned, boned and cut into 5cm/2in pieces
★ 2 garlic cloves, crushed
2 tbsp runny honey
2 tbsp rice vinegar
★ 2 tbsp soy sauce
1 tsp mustard
★ 8 cup-shaped radicchio lettuce leaves
★ 4 tbsp olive oil
★ 125g/4oz unsalted peanuts (omit for small children)
★ 1-2 tiny dried red chillies (1 or omit for younger children)
★ 12 spring onions, trimmed and cut diagonally
★ 12 cherry tomatoes, halved
★ coriander sprigs
★ flat-leafed parsley sprigs

marinated grilled chicken

Serves 4

Serve these delicious chicken pieces with grilled or steamed vegetables and a garlic mayonnaise.

• Score the chicken breasts two or three times with a sharp knife and place in a baking dish. Mix together the remaining ingredients and pour over the chicken. Chill for at least 2 hours.

• Take the chicken pieces out of the marinade. Lay the herb sprigs over them and either grill under a hot grill for 8–10 minutes on each side, or bake in a moderately hot oven (200°C/400°F/gas 6) for 20–25 minutes, or until no pink shows. Baste the chicken pieces occasionally with the marinade. The chicken is cooked when the juices run clear when the pieces are pierced with a skewer.

★ 4 chicken breasts
★ juice of 1 lemon
★ 4 sprigs rosemary
★ 4 sprigs thyme
★ 2 cloves garlic, roughly chopped
★ 2 tbsp soy sauce
1 tbsp honey
sea salt and black pepper

fishy feast

Serves 2

This recipe makes enough to feed a hungry toddler and the grown-up who is helping him to eat.

• Put the milk into a small saucepan with the herb and lemon zest. Bring to the boil, reduce the heat and add the fish and potato slices. Simmer for 3–4 minutes, until the fish is cooked. Remove the fish from the pan with a slotted spoon, leaving the potatoes still cooking.

• Skin and flake the fish, being careful to remove all bones. Put the fish into a small buttered casserole. When the potato is cooked, take the pan off the heat and remove and discard the lemon zest. Mash the potato into the milk with a fork and spoon it on top of the fish in the casserole. Sprinkle the wheatgerm over the top, dot with butter and brown under a grill.

★ 300ml/½ pint milk
★ 1 tbsp chopped fresh mint or parsley
★ a curl of lemon zest
★ 100g/3½oz smoked haddock
★ 2 potatoes, peeled and thinly sliced
★ small knob of butter
★ 2 tsp wheatgerm

salmon fish cakes

Makes 4

• Cook the potatoes until soft. Drain, return to the pan they were cooked in and heat for a few seconds to dry off any residual water. Mash the potatoes with the butter, spring onions and parsley.

• Break the salmon up into small pieces with a fork and mix it into the mashed potato. Add seasoning to taste. If the mixture seems too thick, stir in a little milk. Shape the mixture into four cakes.

• Heat the oil in a frying pan. Add the fish cakes and cook them for a few minutes on each side, until they are brown and crispy. Remove them with a slotted spoon and drain on kitchen paper. The fish cakes are delicious served hot or cold.

★ 500g/1lb potatoes, peeled and quartered
★ 125g/4oz butter
★ 2 spring onions, finely chopped
★ generous handful of fresh parsley, finely chopped
★ 750g/1½lb canned salmon, drained
salt and black pepper
★ 150ml/¼ pint olive oil

old-fashioned kedgeree

★ = superfood

Serves 4

Use natural (undyed) smoked haddock or cod for this dish. Salmon, smoked salmon and/or prawns are also very good additions, especially if you are serving this for a child's main meal of the day.

• Rinse the rice well and drain it well. Put it in a saucepan and pour in the boiling water. Bring the water to a simmer, cover the pan and cook the rice gently for 35 minutes. Drain, if necessary, and gently fork the rice up to separate the grains.

• While the rice is cooking, cook the fish. Place it in a shallow pan and pour in enough milk to cover. Bring slowly to the boil, then turn off the heat and cover the pan. Do not disturb it for 10 minutes, by which time the fish should be just cooked but still succulent. Lift the fish from the pan with a slotted spoon and skin and flake it, making sure all the bones are removed.

• Stir the fish and the remaining ingredients gently into the warm rice, reserving a few pieces of egg for garnish. The diced butter should melt into it. Taste and adjust the seasoning, if necessary. Serve the kedgeree garnished with the reserved egg and with extra chopped parsley, if liked.

- ★ **250g/8oz whole-grain long-grain rice**
- **1.2 litres/2 pints lightly salted boiling water**
- ★ **250g/8oz cooked flaked fish**
- ★ **milk, to cover**
- ★ **4 hard-boiled eggs, chopped**
- ★ **30g/1oz butter, diced**
- **1 tsp mild curry powder**
- ★ **1 tbsp chopped fresh parsley**
- ★ **generous squeeze of lemon juice**
- **sea salt and black pepper**
- ★ **2 tbsp cream (optional)**

smoked mackerel quiche

Serves 4

• Heat the oven to 200°C/400°F/gas 6. Roll out the pastry on a lightly floured surface and use to line a 20cm (8in) flan tin.

• Spread the flaked mackerel over the pastry. Scatter the well-drained sweetcorn over the mackerel. Whisk the egg lightly in a bowl and add the cream, milk and seasoning. Whisk again lightly to mix and pour over the mackerel and sweetcorn.

• Bake in the oven for about 30 minutes, or until the filling has risen and is golden brown on top.

- **400g/13oz shortcrust pastry, thawed if frozen**
- ★ **2 smoked mackerel fillets, each about 250g/8oz, flaked**
- ★ **325g/11oz canned sweetcorn, drained and rinsed**
- ★ **1 egg**
- ★ **150ml/¼ pint whipping cream**
- ★ **150ml/¼ pint milk**
- **pinch salt and black pepper**

colcannon

Serves 6

This traditional Irish country dish is comfort food for the coldest days of winter.

- Cook the cabbage in boiling water until tender. Drain and chop it finely and set it aside. Boil the potatoes, carrot and turnip together in water until tender, then drain them. In a separate pan, simmer the leek and milk together until the leek is tender.
- Add the nutmeg and a little pepper to the potato mixture. Pour the leeks and milk into the potato mixture. Mash all the vegetables well together, adding more milk, if necessary, to make a firm, smooth mash. Add the chopped cabbage and the butter and mash a little more. Pile the mixture into a heatproof dish, rake the top with a fork, and put under a hot grill to brown.

★ 250g/8oz white cabbage, halved and cored
★ 500g/1lb potatoes, sliced
★ 1 small carrot, diced
★ 1 small turnip, diced
★ 1 small leek, well washed and thinly sliced
★ 125ml/4fl oz milk, plus extra for mashing
★ a pinch of nutmeg
a little black pepper
★ 90g/3oz unsalted butter, diced

vegetable nests with crunchy cheese topping

Serves 4

- First, make the topping. Put the breadcrumbs, flour, seasoning, basil, cornflakes and grated cheese into a bowl and rub in the butter. Set aside.
- Heat the oil in a large, heavy-based saucepan and add the carrots, courgettes and parsnip. Fry the vegetables for a few minutes, turning, until golden on all sides.
- Stir in the flour and pour on the vegetable stock. Bring to a simmer, stirring all the time. Stir in the broccoli and cauliflower florets. Simmer very gently for about 15 minutes, until the vegetables are tender. Add the parsley, a little seasoning to taste and the crème fraîche.
- Transfer the vegetables to an ovenproof dish. Sprinkle on the topping and bake in a moderately hot oven (190°C/375°F/gas 5) for 30 minutes, or until golden on top.

★ 2 tbsp olive oil
★ 2 carrots, cut into matchsticks
2 courgettes, cut into matchsticks
1 parsnip, cut into matchsticks
1 tbsp plain flour
300ml/½ pint vegetable stock
★ 125g/4oz broccoli florets
★ 125g/4oz cauliflower florets
★ 1 tbsp chopped parsley
salt and black pepper
★ 2 tbsp crème fraîche

For the topping:
2 slices brown bread, crumbed
★ 60g/2oz wholemeal flour
salt and black pepper
★ 1 tsp dried basil
★ 60g/2oz cornflakes
★ 2 tbsp Parmesan or Cheddar cheese, finely grated
★ 60g/2oz butter

pesto & tomato tarts

★ = superfood

Makes 6

• Preheat the oven to 200°C/400°F/gas 6. Roll out the puff pastry on a lightly floured surface to a thickness of 5mm/¼in. Cut out six rounds, each about 15cm/6in, using a small bowl or saucer as a guide. Crimp the edges of the rounds with a knife and prick all over with a fork. Put them on a lightly floured baking sheet and bake for 5 minutes. Take the baking tray out of the oven.

• Spread a smooth layer of passata over each pastry round. Lay the cherry tomato halves, flat side down, over the passata. Season with salt and pepper and dot generously with pesto. Drizzle over a little olive oil and return the baking tray to the oven. Bake for a further 10 minutes, until the pastry is golden. Serve the tartlets garnished with basil leaves. They are delicious hot or cold.

Illustrated left

375g/12oz puff pastry, thawed if frozen
★ 300 ml/½ pint passata (sieved tomatoes)
★ 180g/6oz cherry tomatoes, halved
100g/3½oz pesto sauce
sea salt and black pepper
★ olive oil, to drizzle
★ fresh basil, to garnish

tomato & cheese pudding

Serves 4

• Preheat the oven to 190°C/375°F/gas 5. Lightly grease a 1.8 litre/3 pint-capacity gratin dish.

• Cut the tomatoes into slices about 5mm/¼in thick, cutting away the central cores when you come across them. Lay half the sliced tomatoes in an even layer in the dish. In a bowl, toss together the breadcrumbs, grated cheese and a generous amount of seasoning. Sprinkle half this mixture over the tomatoes, cover with the remaining tomato slices, then the rest of the breadcrumb mixture.

• Put the pieces of butter over the top and transfer the dish to the oven. Bake for about 40 minutes, or until bubbling juices are clearly visible and the top is browned. Serve the pudding hot.

★ 1kg/2lb fresh tomatoes
★ 60g/2oz wholemeal breadcrumbs, made from day-old bread
★ 60g/2oz Parmesan cheese, freshly grated
salt and black pepper
★ 30g/1oz butter, diced

peppers stuffed with quinoa

★ = superfood

Serves 4

• Wash the quinoa in several changes of water and drain it in a sieve. Put the drained quinoa in a small heavy-based saucepan. Pour in the measured water, bring to the boil, reduce the heat, cover and cook over the lowest possible heat for 20 minutes. Remove from the heat and leave covered in a warm place for 15 minutes.

• Preheat the oven to 200°C/400°F/gas 6. Heat the oil in a frying pan. Add the onion and garlic and fry gently for a few minutes, until softened but not browned. Add the quinoa, currants, pine nuts, lemon juice, herbes de provence, a pinch of salt and a little black pepper. Stir the ingredients together.

• Cut the tops off the peppers and set them aside. Core and deseed the peppers carefully. Divide the quinoa mixture among the four peppers and put the tops on them. Pack the peppers into an ovenproof dish just big enough to hold them, and brush them with oil. Stir the tomato purée into 150ml/¼ pint water and pour in around the peppers.

• Bake in the oven for about 45 minutes, until the peppers are cooked but not too soft. If the dish dries out, add a little more hot water. Serve with tomato sauce and a green salad.

★ **180g/6oz quinoa**
525ml/17fl oz water
★ **2 tbsp olive oil, plus extra for brushing**
★ **1 onion, chopped**
★ **2 cloves garlic, crushed**
★ **1 tbsp currants**
★ **1 tbsp pine nuts**
★ **1 tsp lemon juice**
pinch of herbes de provence
salt and black pepper
★ **4 large red peppers**
★ **1 tbsp tomato purée**

pisto

Serves 4

This is the Spanish version of those aromatic dishes of stewed vegetables found all round the Mediterranean. Eat it on its own, with grilled meat, fish or chicken, or with a beaten egg stirred in and cooked for a few minutes more.

• Heat the oil in a heavy-based saucepan. Add the onion, pepper and garlic and fry gently until just soft. Add the aubergine and fry for a few minutes more, turning several times. Add the tomatoes with all their juices, the potato, courgette, a pinch of salt and a good grinding of pepper.

• Reduce the heat, cover the pan and cook for 20–25 minutes. Remove the lid and, if there is still a lot of liquid left, cook more briskly, uncovered, for a few minutes. Sprinkle with the herbs and serve.

★ **3 tbsp olive oil**
★ **1 onion, chopped**
★ **1 large red, green or yellow pepper, cored, deseeded and cut into strips**
★ **1 clove garlic, crushed**
1 aubergine, diced
★ **4 tomatoes, skinned and chopped**
★ **1 potato, diced**
1 courgette, sliced
salt and black pepper
★ **plenty of chopped fresh herbs, such as parsley, chives and basil**

spanish omelette

Serves 4

You can make this omelette with almost any leftover vegetable; broccoli, peas, asparagus, and French beans are all good. Make it in a small frying pan, as it will come out too thin if made in a large one.

• Heat the olive oil in the frying pan. Add the potato and fry over a moderate heat until just golden. Add the onion and continue cooking gently until soft but not browned. Add the peppers and cook gently for 3–4 minutes, until just soft.

• Add the eggs, season lightly, and turn the heat right down – the omelette should cook very slowly. Once it has started to set, give the pan an occasional shake and do nothing else until the edge of the omelette begins to curl away from the pan.

• When reasonably firm but still moist on top – after about 10 minutes – put the pan under a very hot grill until the surface of the omelette starts to turn golden brown. Serve hot or cold.

★ 2 tbsp olive oil
★ 1 large potato, diced
★ 1 onion, chopped
★ ½ red pepper, cored, deseeded and chopped
★ ½ green pepper, cored, deseeded and chopped
★ 4 eggs, lightly beaten
sea salt and black pepper

fennel with lemon & mixed herbs

Serves 2–3

This herby fennel is good with fish. The recipe is also a good way of cooking leeks.

• Cut the base and top off the fennel, leaving the white bulbous part. Slice across into fairly thin slices. Melt the butter in a large frying pan. Add the fennel and fry it gently for 10–15 minutes, until it is tender and starting to brown slightly. You may have to add a little more butter during cooking. Transfer the cooked fennel to a serving dish.

• Add another knob of butter to the pan. When it has melted add the mixed herbs and lemon juice and swirl the sizzling mixture around the pan. Pour it over the fennel and serve.

1 large bulb fennel
★ 30g/1oz butter
★ 1 tsp dried mixed herbs
★ juice of ½ lemon

broccoli stir-fried with ginger & garlic

★ = superfood

Serves 4

• Cut the thick stalks off the broccoli and peel and slice them. Break the heads into small florets. Heat the vegetable oil in a frying pan or wok until hot.
• When the oil is hot, put the ginger into the pan and stir once. Add the broccoli, salt and garlic. Stir-fry vigorously for 1 minute, or until the broccoli turns bright green. Add the stock. Cover the pan and cook over a high heat for about 1½ minutes. Remove the pan from the heat. Add the sesame oil and stir to mix. Serve immediately.

★ **1–2 large heads of broccoli**
★ **2½ tbsp vegetable oil**
★ **2 thin slices fresh root ginger**
1½ tsp salt
★ **3 cloves garlic, lightly crushed**
3 tbsp vegetable stock
★ **1 tsp sesame oil**

broccoli with potatoes

Serves 4

• Peel the potatoes and cut them into chunky dice the same size as the broccoli florets. Heat the oil over a medium heat in a large non-stick frying pan.
• When the oil is hot, put in the asafetida and, a second later, the mustard seeds. As soon as the mustard seeds begin to pop – a matter of seconds – add the green chilli and the curry leaves. Stir once, then add the potatoes. Stir-fry for about 4 minutes, or until the potatoes are very lightly browned.
• Sprinkle in a good pinch of salt and toss to mix. Add the broccoli and amchar masala. Stir-fry for 1–2 minutes, or until the broccoli is heated through. Remove the chilli and serve immediately.

★ **250g/8oz waxy potatoes, boiled, drained and cooled**
★ **3 tbsp groundnut oil**
large pinch of asafoetida
½ tsp brown or yellow mustard seeds
★ **1 fresh green chilli, tip cut off**
10 fresh curry leaves
salt
★ **375g/12oz broccoli florets, blanched**
1 tsp amchar masala

tuna & bean salad

Serves 4

• Put the cannellini beans in a bowl. Add the tomatoes, cucumber and spring onions, and mix them all well together.
• Mix the oil, lemon juice, salt and pepper together and stir into the salad. Fork the tuna into the salad. Arrange the hard-boiled egg halves on top, and sprinkle over the finely chopped herbs.

★ **400g/13oz canned cannellini beans, drained and rinsed**
★ **3 tomatoes, skinned and finely chopped**
½ cucumber, peeled and diced
★ **6 spring onions, sliced**
★ **60ml/2fl oz extra-virgin olive oil**
★ **2 tsp lemon juice**
sea salt and black pepper
★ **200g/7oz canned tuna, drained and flaked**
★ **2 hard-boiled eggs, halved**
★ **a small bunch of parsley and basil, finely chopped**

bread & tomato salad

Serves 4

Use ripe plum tomatoes when they're at their best and most flavoursome. This salad only works with coarse home-made wholemeal bread or good country bread and is really good when both the tomatoes and bread are organic.

• Heat the oil in a large, deep frying pan. Add the cubes of bread and the garlic. Fry, stirring continuously, until the bread becomes crisp. Drain the bread cubes on kitchen paper.

• Put the bread cubes into a bowl, add the chopped tomatoes, lemon juice, the basil, a pinch of salt and plenty of freshly milled black pepper. Toss all the ingredients together well and serve.

★ 3 tbsp extra-virgin olive oil

4 thick slices of bread, crusts removed and cut into 2.5cm/1in cubes

★ 2 cloves garlic, chopped

★ 6 ripe plum tomatoes, chopped

★ 1 tbsp fresh lemon juice

★ 2 tbsp fresh basil, torn in pieces

salt and black pepper

pasta salad with tuna

Serves 4

• Bring a large pan of water to the boil, add a dash of vegetable oil and 1–2 teaspoons of ordinary salt, then add the pasta.

• While the pasta is cooking, mix the olive oil, lemon juice, mustard, sea salt and pepper together to make a dressing.

• When the pasta is just tender – it should have a little bite to it – drain it well, and put it into a serving bowl. Pour over the dressing and toss together. Gently mix in the tomatoes, spring onions and tuna, then sprinkle over the parsley.

★ dash of vegetable oil

salt

★ 250g/8oz spiral pasta

★ 2 tbsp extra-virgin olive oil

★ 2 tsp lemon juice

1 tsp Dijon mustard

sea salt and black pepper

★ 3–4 ripe tomatoes, skinned and chopped

★ 6 spring onions, sliced

★ 200g/7oz canned tuna, drained and flaked

★ 1 tbsp chopped fresh parsley

buckwheat crêpes

★ = superfood

Makes 12

The best way to eat these crêpes is to put some filling (see below for ideas) on each one, roll it up and enjoy it while it is still warm.

• Stir the melted butter into the milk. Put the flours and salt together in a mixing bowl or into a food-processor bowl. Whisking all the time, pour in the milk-and-butter mixture and then drop in the eggs one at a time, until everything is blended well. Allow the mixture to rest in the refrigerator for at least 30 minutes.

• Brush an 18cm/7in crêpe pan with a little oil. Set it over a medium heat. When the oil is smoking, pour a ladleful of batter into the pan and tilt it around until it is evenly spread. When the underside is golden, turn the crêpe over and cook on the other side for a minute or two.

• Slide the crêpe out of the pan on to kitchen paper on a warm plate and keep warm while you make the rest of the crêpes. You will need to re-oil the pan between each crêpe. The mixture should make about 12 crêpes.

★ 2 tbsp melted butter
★ 450ml/¾ pint milk
★ 125g/4oz buckwheat flour
125g/4oz plain flour, sifted
½ tsp salt
★ 4 eggs
★ vegetable oil, for frying

filling mixtures for crêpes

• Apple slices, walnuts and raisins, sprinkled with a little cinnamon and brown sugar, and served with fromage frais or Greek yogurt.

• Creamy, mild goat's cheese and honey, or strawberries and blueberries, with a little sugar and freshly squeezed lemon juice.

• Savoury fillings such as baked beans, sautéed mushrooms, grilled tomatoes, grated cheese, or ratatouille – the list is endless.

pitta plus

Serves 4

• Lightly grill the pitta breads on one side and split them while still warm. Mix the shredded radishes with the onion and watercress. Add the tuna and toss it into the radish mixture. Stuff the pitta breads with the mixture.
• Serve with ramekins of mayonnaise on the side. For a tapenade-flavoured mayonnaise, add finely chopped black olives, capers, a couple of anchovy fillets and a squeeze of lemon to the mayonnaise.

★ **4 large wholemeal or sesame pitta breads**
1 bunch radishes, very finely shredded
★ **1 small red onion, very finely sliced**
★ **1 bunch watercress, washed and sprigs separated**
★ **200g/7oz canned tuna in oil, drained and flaked**
mayonnaise, to serve

four dips

Serve these dips with wholemeal breadsticks or hot pitta bread, and with raw vegetables, such as sticks of carrot, chunks of cucumber, radishes, cherry tomatoes, sticks of celery and cauliflower florets.

avocado dip

Serves 4

Prepare the tomato and spring onion in advance, if liked. Just before you are ready to eat the dip, halve, stone and peel the avocados, and mash the flesh to a soft mush. Add the lime juice, tomato, spring onions and a little salt and pepper.

★ **1 small tomato, finely chopped**
★ **2 spring onions, finely chopped**
★ **2 ripe avocados**
★ **juice of 1 lime**
salt and black pepper

tomato & yogurt dip

Serves 4

Put the yogurt into a bowl and stir in the tomatoes, oil and herbs – choose from basil, mint, parsley or chives, or a mixture. Add seasoning to taste.

★ **200g/7oz thick, creamy yogurt**
★ **2 ripe, red tomatoes, skinned and finely chopped**
★ **2 tsp extra-virgin olive oil**
★ **1 tbsp chopped fresh herbs**

cream-cheese dip

Serves 4

Combine the cream cheese, yogurt and olive oil in a bowl, mixing well until smooth. Add the remaining ingredients, stir thoroughly, chill and serve.

★ **200g/7oz low-fat cream cheese**
★ **2 tbsp natural live yogurt**
★ **1 tsp extra-virgin olive oil**
★ **1 tbsp chopped red onion**
★ **2 tsp finely snipped chives**
black pepper

smoky dip

Serves 4

Put the trout fillet and cottage cheese in a food processor and blend briefly. Add the lime juice and a little pepper and blend again. Turn into a bowl and serve sprinkled with the red pepper.

★ **1 smoked trout fillet, flaked**
★ **150g/5oz cottage cheese**
★ **juice of ½ lime**
black pepper
2 tsp finely chopped red pepper

snacks & teas

Quickly produced snacks and tempting teas are just what children need to boost energy as their busy day at home, nursery or school slows down. There is a great selection of both to choose from here.

quick & easy wholemeal bread

**Makes 1
1kg/2lb loaf**

Many variations of this wonderful loaf, originally developed during World War II, can be made by mixing different flours: try 250g/8oz white, rye, or buckwheat flour and 500g/1lb wholemeal flour. You can also use chopped walnuts, pumpkin seeds, pine nuts or poppy seeds.

• Preheat the oven to 200°C/400°F/gas 6. Lightly oil a 1kg/2lb loaf tin and keep it warm.

• Mix the flour and yeast together in a mixing bowl. Dissolve the oil, sugar or honey, molasses and salt in the water. Make a well in the centre of the flour, pour in the water and add the sunflower seeds (if using). Mix all the ingredients together with a wooden spoon, then knead energetically for 3–4 minutes, until the dough comes together in a ball without sticking to the sides of the bowl. Add a little flour if the dough seems too sticky, or water if it is dry and crumbly.

• Put the dough into the warm tin, cover with a clean, damp teacloth and leave to rise in a warm place for 30–40 minutes, or until the dough has risen to near the top of the tin.

• Transfer the tin to the oven and bake in the centre of the oven for 35–40 minutes. The bread will be ready if it sounds hollow when you tap the bottom of the tin. If it doesn't, bake it for another five minutes. Cool in the tin on a wire rack.

★ = superfood

★ **750g/1½lbs stoneground wholemeal bread flour**

6g/¼oz sachet easy-blend dried yeast

★ **2 tsp extra-virgin olive oil**

1 tsp molasses, barbados sugar or honey

½ tsp salt

600ml/1 pint lukewarm water

★ **1 tbsp sunflower seeds (optional)**

salmon surprise

★ = superfood

Serves 1–2

6-9 months

• Melt the butter in a small non-stick saucepan. Add the onion and cook it over a low heat until it is softened but not browned. Sprinkle the flour over the onion, stirring it in, and add the milk to make a creamy sauce – you may need a little more milk.
• Cook the sauce very gently for about 10 minutes, stirring it occasionally.
• While the sauce is cooking, skin the fish, carefully removing all the bones. Add the fish to the sauce and cook for another 3–4 minutes, or until the fish is tender. Mash the sauce and fish well together.

★ small knob of butter
★ ½ small onion, finely chopped
★ ½ tsp wholemeal flour
★ 2 tbsp milk
★ about 60g/2oz salmon fillet

tuna mash

Serves 1–2

6-9 months

• Put the potato slices into a saucepan and add enough milk to cover. Add the onion. Bring to the boil, lower the heat and cook gently until the potatoes are cooked and the milk has been almost soaked up. Lightly grease a small heatproof casserole.
• Mash the potatoes, stirring in the butter, then stir in the tuna. Turn into the casserole, sprinkle the wheatgerm on top, and brown under a hot grill.

★ 3–6 new (depending on size) or 2 medium potatoes, thinly sliced
★ milk, to cover
★ ½ small onion, grated
★ small knob of butter
★ 3 tbsp canned tuna, carefully skinned and boned
★ 1 tbsp wheatgerm

spinach soufflé

Serves 2

6-9 months

This recipe, like the two above, makes enough to give mother and baby an enoyable tea or light meal.
• Preheat the oven to 190°C/375°F/gas 5. Lightly butter a small casserole or two cocottes or ramekins.
• Chop the spinach finely, then mix it with the cottage cheese. Beat the egg yolks lightly and stir them and the grated cheese into the spinach.
• Whisk the egg whites to soft peaks and fold them into the spinach mixture. Pile the lot into the prepared dishes. Bake in the oven for 35–40 minutes – a little less if you are using individual ramekins.

★ butter, for greasing
★ 125g/4oz cooked spinach, drained
★ 4 tbsp cottage cheese
★ 2 eggs, separated
★ 60g/2oz grated cheese

fish cakes

Makes 4

- Cook the potatoes in boiling water until soft. Drain, return to the pan and heat for a few seconds to dry off any residual water.
- Put the stock in a saucepan. Add the fish, bring to the boil, reduce the heat and poach gently for 10 minutes. Drain the fish and flake it very carefully to remove any bones or remaining skin. Mash the potatoes with the butter, chives and a little salt and white pepper. Mix in the flaked fish. Shape the mixture into four cakes.
- Heat the oil in a shallow frying pan and cook the cakes for a few minutes on each side, until brown and crispy. Remove with a slotted spoon and put on kitchen paper to drain. The fish cakes are delicious served either hot or cold.

★ 500g/1lb potatoes , peeled and quartered
900ml/1½ pints vegetable stock
★ 375g/12oz salmon fillet, skinned
★ 375g/12oz cod fillet, skinned
★ 125g/4oz butter
★ 1 tbsp chopped chives
salt and white pepper
★ 150ml/¼ pint olive oil

savoury egg

Serves 1

- Preheat the oven to 220°C/425°F/gas 7. Butter a small ramekin.
- Put the chives, grated cheese and milk into the ramekin. Crack in the egg carefully, so as not to break the yolk. Stand the ramekin in a small roasting tin and pour in boiling water to come halfway up the side. Bake in the oven for 15–20 minutes, until the egg is set.

★ butter, for greasing
★ chopped chives
★ 1 tsp grated cheese
★ 2 tsp milk
★ 1 egg

mushrooms on toast with crumbly cheese

Serves 2

- Melt the butter in a frying pan. Add the onion, garlic and mushroom slices and fry them gently until softened. While they are cooking, grill the bacon rashers until crisp.
- Divide the mushrooms between the two slices of the toast and top with the cheese. Put under a hot grill and grill until the cheese melts. Serve with the crisy bacon slices on top.

★ 30g/1oz butter
★ ¼ medium onion, chopped
★ 1 clove garlic, chopped
4 large flat mushrooms, organic if possible, sliced
★ 8 rashers lean unsmoked back bacon
★ 2 slices coarse wholemeal bread, toasted
★ 60g/2oz Cheshire cheese, sliced

quick spinach snack

★ = superfood

Serves 2

It's not always easy to get children to eat spinach, but cooked like this and served as the Italians do – warm rather than hot – you'll be surprised how much they enjoy it, especially if you use superb-tasting organic spinach.

• Heat the oil in a small saucepan. Add the garlic and cook gently for 5 minutes, without browning it. Add the pine nuts and cook for another 5 minutes.

• Put the spinach in a large saucepan with no extra water, cover the pan, and cook until thoroughly wilted. Leave to cool for a few moments then add the warm oil, garlic and pine nuts and the lemon juice. Stir well and arrange on the bread.

★ 4 tbsp olive oil
★ 500g/1lb baby spinach leaves, washed
★ 2 cloves garlic, sliced
★ juice of 1 lemon
★ small handful pine nuts
★ 2 thick slices wholemeal bread

hot pancetta savouries

Serves 2–4

• Dry-fry the pancetta in a frying pan until crisp. Drain on kitchen paper. When cool, mix it with the grated cheese.

• Spread the slices of bread with butter on one side only. With the buttered sides facing down, spread the pancetta mixture over two slices. Dot with a few basil leaves and press the remaining slices of bread on top, buttered sides uppermost.

• Heat the oil in a frying pan. Add the sandwiches and fry gently for a couple of minutes on each side, or until the cheese is melted and the bread is golden and crisp. Cut the sandwiches into triangles while still hot and serve immediately.

★ 60g/2oz pancetta, chopped
★ 60g/2oz mozzarella cheese, grated
4 slices wholemeal bread
★ 30g/1oz butter, softened
★ few basil leaves
★ 1 tbsp olive oil

pizza baguettes

Serves 4

Flavoured baguettes, such as those with onion, multigrains and sun-dried tomato, would all be good in this recipe.

• Preheat the oven to 180°C/350°F/gas 4. Mix the tomatoes, garlic and basil together and heat gently in a saucepan. Split the baguettes and spread the tomato mixture on the cut surfaces. Drizzle with a little olive oil, if liked. Sprinkle with grated cheese.

• Bake in the oven for about 10 minutes, or until the cheese has melted and the bread is hot and crisp.

★ 400g/13oz canned chopped tomatoes; or the same weight of fresh tomatoes, skinned and chopped
★ 1 clove garlic, crushed
★ fresh basil leaves
4 baguettes, or the equivalent in lengths of other slim bread
★ olive oil (optional)
★ 4 tbsp grated Cheddar cheese

granny smith's welsh rarebit

Serves 4

Welsh Rarebit is NOT a piece of processed cheese put on a piece of toast and melted under a grill. Here is a more authentic version.

• Toast the bread and butter it, using about two-thirds of the butter. Keep the toast warm while you make the topping.

• Put the cheese in a heavy-based saucepan and add the crème fraîche and mustard powder. Heat slowly, stirring, until the cheese has melted and the mixture has become a thick cream.

• Melt the remaining butter in a frying pan. Add the apple wedges and fry them gently. Spread the cheese mixture on the slices of toast and brown under a hot grill. Serve each slice of toast with four wedges of apple.

★ 4 medium-thick slices wholemeal bread
★ 90g/3oz unsalted butter
★ 250g/8oz mature Cheddar cheese, grated
★ 4 tbsp crème fraîche
½ tsp mustard powder
★ 2 large Granny Smith apples, peeled, cored and each cut into 8 wedges

stuffed celery sticks

Serves 2–4

With these ingredients you can give children greens to eat in a way they will enjoy. Simply stuff celery sticks with the following mixtures:

• Cottage cheese with chives: many supermarkets sell this ready-made.

• Grated carrots and seedless raisins tossed in a little oil and lemon juice.

• Grated carrots and shredded watercress mixed into cream cheese.

★ 4–6 sticks celery, trimmed and strings removed
★ cottage cheese with chives
★ carrots, grated
★ seedless raisins
★ vegetable or olive oil
★ lemon juice
★ watercress
★ cream cheese

hummus

★ = superfood

Serves 4–6

Hummus is very good served with lots of raw vegetables, such as chicory leaves, sticks of red pepper, raw carrots or celery. It is also great served with hot pitta bread, black olives and whole baked garlic cloves.

• Put all the ingredients, except the olive oil, in a food processor or blender. Switch the food processor on and add the olive oil in a steady stream until you have a smooth consistency. The hummus can be thinned with a little of the chickpea canning or cooking liquid, or made more creamy with extra olive oil.

★ 400g/13oz canned chickpeas, drained, or same weight of freshly cooked chickpeas, drained (reserve some of the canning or cooking liquid)

★ juice of 1 lemon

★ 2 cloves garlic, peeled

★ 2 tbsp tahini (pulped sesame seeds)

salt and black pepper

★ 125ml/4 fl oz olive oil

★ 1 tsp freshly ground cumin

sandwich fillings

Here are some splendid fillings for sandwiches, using many of the book's superfoods. Make the sandwiches from wholemeal bread, wholemeal pitta pockets, wholemeal baps, or ciabatta rolls.

• Hummus (see above), alfalfa sprouts, chopped tomatoes and fresh basil or coriander.

• Peanut butter, bananas and a little honey.

• Watercress, finely grated carrot, thinly sliced cucumber and mayonnaise.

• Tuna, thinly chopped celery and red pepper with mayonnaise.

• Shredded chicken, lettuce, chopped tomato, a few bean sprouts and a few basil leaves, all tossed in a little dressing made with extra virgin olive oil, lemon juice, a pinch of sea salt and black pepper. Pile this mixture into pitta pockets.

• Well-drained canned salmon, sliced spring onions, a little chopped fresh parsley, and mayonnaise with half a ripe avocado and a squeeze of fresh lemon juice beaten into it.

• Mashed sardines with paper-thin slices of cucumber and chopped chives.

• Finely chopped apple mixed into smooth peanut butter.

• Cream cheese with shredded lettuce and chopped walnuts.

cheese pretzels

Makes about 20

• Dissolve the yeast and sugar in the warm water. Put the flour, grated cheese and salt in a food-processor bowl or a mixing bowl. Pour in the water and yeast and mix thoroughly, either with the dough hooks of the food processor or by hand.

• Knead the dough in your machine or on a lightly floured surface for 5–10 minutes, until really smooth and elastic. Cover with a damp cloth and leave to rise in a warm place until doubled in size; this should take about 1 hour.

• Punch down the dough and knead it again briefly. Divide it into about 20 pieces and roll into strands. Form the pretzels by looping the strands and twisting over the ends. Lay on baking sheets. Leave to rise again for about 20–30 minutes. Meanwhile, preheat the oven to 200°C/400°F/gas 6.

• Brush the risen dough with the egg and sprinkle the seeds over. Bake in the oven for 20 minutes, until shiny and golden. Cool on wire racks.

6g/¼oz sachet dried yeast

1 tsp sugar

300ml/½ pint warm water

500g/1lb plain flour

★ 180g/6oz Cheddar cheese, grated

pinch of salt

★ 1 egg, beaten

★ sesame seeds and poppy seeds, mixed, to sprinkle

mighty muesli munchies

★ = superfood

Makes 12

• Preheat the oven to 180°C/350°F/gas 4. Lightly grease a 33 x 25cm/13 x 10in shallow baking tin.
• Mix the muesli and spices together in a large bowl. Put the honey, sugar and butter in a small saucepan and heat slowly until the sugar has dissolved. Pour the mixture into the muesli and mix together thoroughly.
• Put half of the muesli mixture in the prepared tin. Mix the bananas, dates and lemon juice together and spread on top of the muesli mixture. Top with the rest of the muesli mixture, smoothing it over.
• Bake in the preheated oven for 25–30 minutes, or until golden. Leave to cool in the tin. Then cut the mixture lengthways down the middle and divide each half into six substantial bars.

300g/10oz unsweetened muesli (preferably without nuts)
★ pinch of nutmeg
★ 1 tsp ground cinnamon
60g/2oz runny honey
125g/4oz brown cane sugar
★ 125g/4oz butter
★ 3 ripe bananas, thinly sliced
★ 180g/6oz fresh or semi-dried dates, stoned and chopped
★ juice of 1 lemon

doris grant's oatcakes

Makes 16

The oatmeal must be absolutely fresh to make these oatcakes successfully. This recipe is based on one by the wartime nutritionist and cook, Doris Grant.
• Preheat the oven to 180°C/350°F/gas 4. Put the oatmeal in a bowl. Put the butter and salt in another small bowl and pour the boiling water over them. Add this mixture to the oatmeal and mix well. Leave to stand for 5 minutes.
• Turn the dough on to a well-floured board and form into two balls. Roll each ball into a circle and cut into eight wedge-shaped pieces. Roll each wedge out to a nice firm, thin shape.
• Place on a very lightly greased baking sheet and bake in the oven for 8–10 minutes, or until light golden at the edges. Cool the oatcakes on a wire rack and store them in an airtight container.

★ 150g/5oz medium oatmeal
1 tsp unsalted butter
good pinch of sea salt
125ml/4fl oz boiling water

moist apple bread

**Makes 1
1kg/2lb loaf**

• Preheat the oven to 180°C/350°F/gas 4. Lightly grease and line a 1kg/2lb loaf tin.
• Mix together the flour, sugar, baking powder and spices in a large mixing bowl. In a separate bowl, mix together the butter, cold tea and beaten egg. Beat the mixture into the dry ingredients, stirring until smooth. Fold in the apples, sultanas and nuts.
• Pour into the prepared tin and bake in the oven for 1 hour, or until the cake is well-risen and not wet in the middle when tested with a skewer.

★ **180g/6oz wholemeal flour**
125g/4oz soft brown sugar
1 tsp baking powder
★ **1 tsp cinnamon**
★ ½ tsp ground cloves
★ ¼ tsp grated nutmeg
★ **125g/4oz butter, melted**
150ml/¼ pint cold tea
★ **1 egg, beaten**
★ **180g/6oz apples, skins on and grated**
★75g/2½oz sultanas
★ 75g/2½oz walnuts or pecans, roughly chopped

apricot scones

Makes 16

• Preheat the oven to 180°C/350°F/gas 4. Lightly grease a baking sheet, or cover it with a piece of baking parchment cut to size.
• Sift the flour and baking powder into a mixing bowl, returning the bran in the sieve to the bowl. Rub in the butter with your fingertips and mix in the sugar. (Alternatively, process the flour, baking powder, butter and sugar together in a food processor.) Add the apricots, sultanas and sunflower seeds and stir in. Mix in enough milk and water to bind the mixture without making it wet.
• Roll the dough out on a lightly floured surface to a thickness of about 4cm/1¾in. Use scone cutters to cut out eight 6cm/2½in and eight 7cm/3in rounds.
• Place the rounds on the prepared baking tray and bake in the oven for about 15 minutes, or until golden on top. Eat the scones warm, split and buttered. Leftovers can be split and toasted.

★ **500g/1lb wholemeal self-raising flour**
2 tsp baking powder
★ **90g/3oz butter or margarine, diced**
60g/2oz dark soft brown sugar
★ **125g/4oz ready-to-eat dried apricots, washed, dried and cut into sultana-size pieces**
★ **60g/2oz sultanas, washed and dried**
★ **60g/2oz sunflower seeds**
★ **300ml/½ pint milk and water mixed**

hot cross buns

Makes 12

These buns are just as delicious for breakfast as for tea. Try them split and toasted.

• Mix 125g/4oz of the flour with the caster sugar. Sprinkle the mixture over the yeast in a mixing bowl and stir in the milk and water. Leave the mixture in a warm place for 20–30 minutes, until it is frothy.

• Meanwhile, mix the remaining flour with the mixed spice and salt. Add the brown sugar, currants and mixed peel. Stir the melted butter and beaten egg into the frothy yeast mixture. Gradually fold in the flour mixture and mix to a smooth dough.

• Knead the dough on a lightly floured surface until it is smooth and elastic. Divide the dough into 12 pieces and shape them into flattish round little buns. Make two slashes to form a cross on top of each one. Set the buns well apart on a greased and floured baking sheet and leave to rise again in a warm place for about 30 minutes, or until they have doubled in size.

• While the dough is rising, preheat the oven to 190°C/375°F/gas 5. Bake the buns in the oven for 15–20 minutes, until golden on top.

★ 500g/1 lb wholemeal flour
1 tsp caster sugar
1 tbsp active dried yeast
★ 150ml/¼ pint lukewarm milk
★ 60ml/2fl oz hand-hot water
1 tsp mixed spice
1 tsp fine salt
60g/2oz soft light brown sugar
★ 30g/1oz currants
30g/1oz mixed peel
★ 60g/2oz butter, melted
★ 1 egg, beaten

green tea bread

**Makes 1
1kg/2lb loaf**

• Put the dried fruit in a large bowl and stir in the tea and sugar. Cover and set aside to soak overnight.

• Next day, preheat the oven to 180°C/350°F/gas 4. Lightly grease a 1kg/2lb loaf tin.

• Add the remaining ingredients to the dried-fruit mixture and beat well. Pour into the prepared loaf tin, pushing the mixture into the corners of the tin.

• Transfer to the preheated oven and bake for 1 hour 15 minutes, or until a skewer inserted into the centre of the bread comes out clean. Turn out of the tin and leave to cool on a wire rack.

★ 375g/12oz seedless raisins and sultanas, mixed
300ml/½ pint green tea (or your favourite tea)
180g/6oz soft brown sugar
★ 250g/8oz wholemeal self-raising flour
★ 1 egg
1 tsp mixed spice
★ grated zest of 1 lemon
★ 90g/3oz mixed chopped almonds, walnuts and hazelnuts

blueberry muffins

★ = superfood

Makes 12

• Preheat the oven to 180°C/350°F/gas 4. Put 12 paper muffin cases into a muffin tin.
• Sift the flours, baking powder and mixed spice into a mixing bowl, putting the bran in the sieve back into the bowl. Beat together the milk, butter, egg, lemon juice and sugar in a bowl or wide jug. Make a well in the centre of the flour mixture and pour in half the milk mixture. Gently fold it in, then add the rest and stir it in. Fold in the blueberries.
• Spoon the mixture into the muffin cases. Bake in the oven for about 20 minutes, until well-risen and golden on top. Take the muffins out of the tin and leave on a wire rack to cool.

100g/3½oz self-raising flour
★ **60g/2oz wholemeal flour**
1 tsp baking powder
1 tsp mixed spice
★ **125ml/4fl oz milk**
★ **60g/2oz butter, melted**
★ **1 large egg**
★ **2 tsp lemon juice**
90g/3oz soft brown sugar
★ **90g/3oz fresh blueberries**

shortbread trees

Makes 12

• Preheat the oven to 150°C/300°F/gas 2. Put the butter, sugar, flour and rice flour or cornflour in a mixing bowl and rub together with your fingertips. Then work the mixture together with your hands into a smooth dough.
• Put the dough on a work surface lightly dusted with icing sugar and roll out to a thickness of about 1cm/½in. Cut out 12 'trees' – tall triangles with tree trunks are easy shapes. Press the nuts vertically into the tree shapes to achieve a spiky effect.
• Place the trees on a baking sheet and bake for 30 minutes. Cool them on a wire rack and, when completely cold, store in an airtight tin.

★ **125g/4oz butter, softened**
60g/2oz golden caster sugar
★ **125g/4oz wholemeal flour**
★ **60g/2oz rice flour or cornflour**
★ **60g/2oz pine nuts or slivered almonds**

carrot cake

**Makes 1
18cm/7in cake**

• Preheat the oven to 180°C/350°F/gas 4. Grease and line an 18cm/7in cake tin.
• Beat the eggs and sugar together to a creamy mix. Add the remaining ingredients and mix to a batter. Spoon into the prepared tin.
• Bake in the preheated oven for 20–25 minutes, until well-risen and nicely brown on top. A skewer inserted into the middle of the cake should come out clean when it is completely baked.

★ **2 eggs**
100g/3½oz raw brown sugar
★ **180g/6oz carrots, grated**
★ **90ml/2½fl oz light vegetable oil**
★ **100g/3½oz wholemeal self-raising flour**
★ **1 tsp ground cinnamon**
★ **½ tsp ground nutmeg**
★ **60g/2oz raisins**
★ **60g/2oz chopped walnuts**

banana & walnut bread

**Makes 1
1kg/2lb loaf**

• Preheat the oven to 180°C/350°F/gas 4. Line a 1kg/2lb loaf tin with greased greaseproof paper or baking parchment.

• Cream the cottage cheese and sugar together until well blended. Gradually beat in the eggs. Add the chopped nuts and bananas and mix well. Add the flour, mixing it in well. Spoon the mixture into the prepared tin, pressing it into the corners.

• Bake in the oven for 40–45 minutes, or until a skewer inserted into the centre of the bread comes out clean. Cool on a wire rack and serve in lightly buttered slices.

★ 250g/8oz cottage cheese, pressed through a sieve
125g/4oz soft brown sugar
★ 3 eggs, beaten
★ 60g/2oz chopped walnuts
★ 2 bananas, mashed
★ 250g/8oz wholemeal self-raising flour

banana & almond muffins

Makes 12

• Heat the oven to 200°C/400°F/gas 6. Lightly grease a 12-cup muffin tin.

• Put the flour, baking powder, baking soda and salt in a large mixing bowl and mix well together. Mix the eggs, bananas, sugar, oil, buttermilk and vanilla extract in a separate bowl and then pour them into the dry ingredients. Mix them together until just combined. (Be careful not to overmix or the muffins will be tough.) Fold in the almonds. Fill each muffin cup to the rim with batter.

• Bake for 25–30 minutes, until firm to the touch and golden on top. Cool the muffins for 2–3 minutes and serve them warm or at room temperature.

180g/6oz plain flour
1½ tsp baking powder
1½ tsp baking soda
½ tsp salt
★ 2 eggs
★ 6 large ripe bananas, thoroughly mashed
250g/8oz dark brown sugar
★ 90ml/2½fl oz sunflower oil
★ 90ml/2½fl oz buttermilk
½ tsp vanilla extract
★ 100g/3½oz almonds, toasted and chopped

satisfying suppers

The last meal of the day is a great opportunity to give children nutrition-packed food that you and they can **prepare together** quickly and easily and that can be eaten in a **relaxed atmosphere**.

★ = superfood

haddock moussaka

Serves 2

• Preheat the oven to 190°C/375°F/gas 5. Lightly butter a shallow ovenproof dish.
• Slice the fish into very small pieces, checking very carefully for the tiniest bones and removing them. Put the fish in the dish and sprinkle with the lemon juice. Cook the courgettes for just a minute in boiling water then drain, pat dry and place on top of the fish. Beat the egg and milk together, add the nutmeg and dill and pour over the fish and courgettes. Sprinkle the wheatgerm on top.
• Put the dish in a small roasting tin and pour in cold water to come halfway up the side of the dish. Bake in the oven for 45 minutes, or until the top is golden brown.

★ **butter, for greasing**
★ **180g/6oz undyed haddock fillets, skinned**
★ **1 tsp lemon juice**
2 small courgettes, thinly sliced
★ **1 egg**
★ **150ml/¼ pint warm milk**
★ **pinch of nutmeg**
a little fresh dill
★ **1 tbsp wheatgerm**

zoë's prawn & vegetable stir-fry

Serves 4

Teenager Zoë has been an enthusiastic cook since she was nine. This is one of her favourite recipes.
• Heat the oil in a frying pan. Add the prawns and garlic, stir-fry for 2 minutes, then remove with a slotted spoon and set aside. Put the pepper, carrot, green beans and sweetcorn in the pan and stir-fry for 2–3 minutes. Pour the stock into the pan, bring to the boil, lower the heat and simmer for about 10 minutes, until the vegetables are tender.
• Meanwhile, cook the noodles according to the packet instructions and drain. Return the garlic and prawns to the pan, add the noodles and stir in the chilli and soy sauces.

Illustrated right

★ **3 tbsp olive oil**
★ **250g/8oz cooked prawns, thawed if frozen, drained and blotted dry**
★ **1 clove garlic, chopped**
★ **1 red pepper, deseeded and chopped**
★ **1 large carrot, finely diced**
★ **a handful of green beans, chopped**
★ **125g/4oz sweetcorn kernels**
550ml/18fl oz vegetable stock
200g/7oz egg noodles
1 tsp sweet chilli sauce
dash of soy sauce

poached chicken

Serves 4

Let baby join in this meal by puréeing a little chicken breast meat with some of the vegetables.
• Put the butter and oil in a heavy-based saucepan or flameproof casserole and heat until the butter is melted. Put the chicken in the pan and brown it on all sides. Add the water or stock, leeks, onion, carrots and bouquet garni and bring to the boil.
• Reduce the heat, cover the pan, and simmer gently for 45–60 minutes, or until the chicken is cooked through and tender. Add the potatoes after 25 minutes' cooking time.

★ = superfood

★ knob of butter
★ 1 tbsp olive oil
★ 1 medium-sized chicken
300ml/½ pint water or vegetable stock
★ white part of 2 leeks
★ 1 large onion, chopped
★ 2 carrots, sliced
★ bouquet garni (sprig of thyme, a bayleaf and a sprig of parsley)
★ 2 large potatoes, peeled and cut into chunks

rabbit with prunes

Serves 4

This is a popular Tuscan dish, in which sweet and juicy prunes are a nice match with rabbit, which can be a bit on the dry side. Young children may prefer it made with chicken.
• Heat the oil in an heatproof casserole. Add the onions and fry over a medium heat until soft. Remove from the casserole with a slotted spoon. Roll the rabbit joints in the flour, put them in the casserole and brown in the hot oil, adding a little more oil, if necessary.
• When the rabbit pieces are browned all over, add the onions, wine, prunes, thyme, bay leaf and seasoning. Bring to the boil, cover the pan, reduce the heat and simmer for about an hour, or until the rabbit is cooked through and is tender.

★ 2 tbsp olive oil
★ 2 onions, chopped
★ 1 rabbit, jointed and chopped
★ 1 tbsp wholemeal flour
150ml/¼ pint red wine
★ 12 prunes, well washed
★ few sprigs of thyme
1 bay leaf
salt and black pepper

real fish fingers

Serves 1

• Cut the fish into fingers, feeling carefully for any bones which may have been left after filleting. Dip the fish fingers first in the matzo meal, then in the egg. Heat the vegetable oil in a frying pan, add the fish and shallow-fry for 2–3 minutes on each side.

★ 125g/4oz white fish fillets
2–3 tbsp matzo meal
★ 1 egg, beaten
vegetable oil, for frying

roast chicken puréed with vegetables

Makes 1–2 portions

6-9 months

This highly nutritious baby meal is best made with all organic foods. Make sure the roast chicken is completely cooked through: when pierced with a skewer the juices from the thickest part of the thigh must run clear, not pink. The peas and sweetcorn can be either fresh or frozen, but not canned.

• Cut off any skin from the piece of chicken breast and chop the meat quite finely. Set aside. Cook the pumpkin, peas and sweetcorn in unsalted water until soft. Drain the vegetables, keeping some of the vegetable water in case you need to thin down the purée a little. Purée the chicken meat and vegetables together in a mouli, using the coarse disk.

★ **small piece skinless breast meat from a roasted chicken**

★ **60g/2oz pumpkin flesh, cubed**

1 tbsp peas, fresh or frozen

★ **1 tbsp sweetcorn kernels, fresh or frozen**

rosti-topped fish pie

Serves 4

• Preheat the oven to 200°C/400°F/gas 6. Put the fish in a saucepan and pour over the milk. Bring to a simmer and cover the pan. Turn off the heat and leave to stand for 10 minutes. The fish will be just cooked but still succulent.

• Meanwhile, peel the skins from the par-boiled potatoes and coarsely grate them. Strain the milk from the fish into a jug. Flake the fish, discarding all skin and the bones.

• Melt 30g/1oz of the butter in a small saucepan and stir in the flour. Gradually stir in the milk from the fish over a low heat, so that the sauce thickens slowly. Simmer the sauce, stirring, until it is smooth.

• Stir the flaked fish, chopped eggs and parsley into the sauce. Season with pepper and a little salt. Add a little grated nutmeg. Spoon the mixture into an ovenproof dish.

• Melt the remaining butter, toss the grated potatoes in it and spoon them on top of the pie. Bake in the oven for 15–20 minutes, until the potatoes are crisp and golden on the top.

★ **250g/8oz white fish**

★ **250g/8oz natural smoked fish**

★ **600ml/1 pint milk**

★ **500g/1lb waxy potatoes, par-boiled in their skins**

★ **60g/2oz butter**

30g/1oz plain flour

★ **2 hard-boiled eggs, peeled and chopped**

★ **2 tbsp chopped fresh parsley**

sea salt and black pepper

★ **nutmeg**

★ = superfood

irish stew

Serves 2

There should be plenty of delicious stew here for a hungry grown-up and a toddler.
- Trim as much excess fat as possible off the lamb. Put the meat in a small flameproof casserole or a heavy-based saucepan. Cover it with the onions, and top with the potato slices. Add the thyme and pour in the vegetable stock.
- Bring to the boil, reduce the heat to very low, cover the pan and cook for at least 1½ hours. By this time the potatoes and onions should have melted into a delicious savoury mush, and the lamb will be very tender.
- Pick the meat off the bones (if using lamb chops) and mash it into the vegetables.

★ 3 lamb chops or 375g/12oz stewing lamb
★ 2 small onions, thinly sliced
★ 2 potatoes, thickly sliced
★ sprig of fresh thyme
5 tbsp vegetable stock

black bean chilli

Serves 6

Omitting the lamb from this recipe turns it into a good vegetarian dish.
- Heat some olive oil in a large, heavy-based saucepan or flameproof casserole. Add the carrots, celery and garlic and stir-fry until the vegetables are turning a little golden. Add the chillies, ground cumin and ground coriander. Fry for a few more minutes. Add the minced lamb and stir-fry until the meat is browned all over.
- Pour the tomatoes and drained beans into the pan and season well. Cover the pan and simmer for about 45 minutes, or until the beans are melting and tender. Check the pan occasionally and stir the contents. If the mixture seems to be getting dry, add a little stock or water to moisten it. Add seasoning to taste and the fresh coriander towards the end of the cooking time, to preserve its colour and flavour.
- Serve the chilli in bowls with a dollop of sour cream, some guacamole and lots of warm tortillas or corn bread to soak up the juices.

olive oil, for frying
★ 2 carrots, very finely diced
★ 2 sticks celery, very finely diced
★ 6 cloves garlic, finely chopped
★ 1–2 red chillies, finely chopped
★ 2 tsp ground cumin
★ 2 tsp ground coriander
★ 500g/1lb lean minced lamb
★ 800g/1lb 10oz canned plum tomatoes
★ 500g/1lb black beans, soaked overnight in plenty of cold water, and drained
sea salt and black pepper
★ bunch of fresh coriander, chopped
sour cream, guacamole and tortillas or corn bread, to serve

herbed kofta kebabs

Serves 4

Soak eight wooden skewers or satay sticks in water for an hour before making these kebabs.

• Put the lamb in a large bowl and mix in the spices and herbs. Season well with salt and pepper. Heat the olive oil in a frying pan. Add the onion and garlic and fry until soft. Stir into the lamb mixture and mix everything together really well.

• Take a little of the lamb mixture and shape it into an oval in your hands. Thread the oval on to a wooden skewer and continue with the process until all the lamb mixture is used up. Cook the kebabs under a hot grill for 5 minutes on each side, or char-grill or barbecue them.

• Serve with natural yogurt with a little freshly chopped mint added. Couscous or bulgur wheat salad would go very well with the kebabs.

★ 250g/8oz lean minced lamb
★ 1 tsp ground coriander
★ 1 tsp ground cumin
★ 2 tsp chopped fresh mint, plus extra to serve
★ 2 tsp chopped fresh coriander
★ 2 tsp chopped fresh parsley
sea salt and black pepper
★ 1 tbsp olive oil
★ 1 red onion, finely chopped
★ 1 clove garlic, minced
natural live yogurt, to serve

south of france omelette

Serves 4

For the more adventurous breakfast eaters, this is a very satisfying and tasty omelette that children enjoy for any meal, perhaps with the accompaniment of a few little potatoes roasted in their skins. You can be experimental with the vegetables – it would be a very good way of using up a few spoonfuls of leftover ratatouille or some roasted vegetables.

• Heat 1 tablespoon of the oil in a frying pan. Add the tomatoes, aubergine and garlic and fry them until they are cooked through and almost a purée.

• Break the eggs into a bowl and add the fresh herbs and seasoning. Beat the eggs with a fork until just blended and stir in half the vegetable mixture.

• Heat the remaining olive oil in a frying pan. Pour the egg mixture evenly into the pan. Cook until the underneath is firm and golden brown and the omelette is ready to lift and fold over. Spoon the rest of the vegetable mixture into the middle of the folded-over omelette. Slide the omelette on to a warm plate and serve at once.

★ 2 tbsp olive oil
★ 2 ripe tomatoes, diced
★ 1 small aubergine, diced
★ 2 cloves garlic, finely chopped
★ 8 eggs
★ 2 tsp chopped fresh parsley
★ 2 tsp chopped fresh chives
2 tsp chopped fresh chervil
salt and pepper

cauliflower & broccoli cheese

★ = superfood

Serves 4

• Preheat the oven to 180°C/350°F/gas 4. Butter a gratin dish thoroughly.
• Put the cauliflower and broccoli florets in a saucepan, add the milk and cook until just tender. Drain, reserving the milk, and put the vegetables in the gratin dish.
• Melt the butter in a small non-stick saucepan. Stir in the flour, 1 tablespoon of the cheese, the mustard and seasoning to taste. Stir in the hot milk, a little at a time, until you have a smooth creamy sauce.
• Heat through and pour over the cauliflower and broccoli. Scatter the remaining cheese on top and bake in the oven for 15–20 minutes. For a nice browned surface, finish the dish under a hot grill.

★ 1 small cauliflower, broken into small florets
★ 1 small head of broccoli, broken into small florets
★ 500ml/16fl oz milk
★ 60g/2oz butter
★ 1 tbsp wholemeal flour
★ 60g/2oz grated hard cheese, such as mature Cheddar
1 tsp Dijon mustard
salt and black pepper

potato cakes with grilled bacon

Serves 4

This is an excellent way to use up boiled or mashed potatoes without going to any extra trouble. The dough should be squeezed from hand to hand until it looks smooth and unbreakable.
• Mash the warm potatoes thoroughly with the butter and salt and pepper. Work in the flour. Taking about 2 tablespoons of the mixture at a time, make eight potato cakes, using some extra flour on the surface and squeezing and patting the dough into flat rounds that are nice and smooth in texture.
• Heat a little olive oil in a frying pan, add the potato cakes and fry them until crisp and golden on each side. While the potato cakes are cooking, grill the bacon and drain it on kitchen paper.
• Serve the potato cakes with the bacon and with grilled tomato halves, if your children like them.

Illustrated left

★ 500g/1lb cooked potatoes
★ good knob of butter
salt and pepper
★ 2 tbsp wholemeal flour, plus extra for coating
★ olive oil, for frying
★ 8 rashers smoked lean bacon
★ grilled tomato halves, to serve (optional)

vegetable couscous

★ = superfood

Serves 2

If a child insists on having meat with this, fry a few small pieces of chicken with the onion.

• Heat a little olive oil in a frying pan. Add the onion and fry until golden. Add the carrots, courgette, red pepper and ground cumin and continue to fry for a few minutes.

• Add the tomatoes, a little salt and the coriander leaves. Simmer for about 10 minutes, or until the vegetables are cooked and nicely tender. Add the chickpeas and heat through.

• While the vegetables are cooking, steam the couscous, according to packet instructions. Serve the vegetables and steamed couscous together.

★ **olive oil, for frying**
★ **1 onion, finely chopped**
★ **2 carrots, halved lengthways and sliced**
1 small courgette, halved lengthways and sliced
★ **½ red pepper, deseeded and chopped**
★ **1 tsp (or more to taste) ground cumin**
★ **2 tomatoes, skinned and diced**
salt
★ **1–2 tbsp fresh coriander leaves**
★ **400g/13oz canned chickpeas, drained**
★ **150g/5oz couscous**

vegetable samosas

Makes approx. 16

• Boil the potato cubes in lightly salted water for about 10 minutes, or until soft. Drain well. In a separate pan bring enough water to the boil to just cover the chopped vegetables and cook them until tender but still crisp. Drain well.

• Put the vegetables and potatoes into a bowl. Add the curry powder or paste, cheese and salt and pepper. Mix everything really well together. Preheat the oven to 190°C/375°F/gas 5.

• Melt the olive oil and butter in a small saucepan. Lay out one sheet of filo pastry and brush it with the melted butter and oil. Lay another sheet on top and brush again. Now cut the pastry lengthways into strips about 7cm/3in wide. Put a heaped teaspoonful of filling at one end of a strip. Fold the pastry diagonally across so that it makes a triangle. Keep folding over along the length of the strip until your triangle is completed. Brush the outside with butter and roll the samosa in poppy or black sesame seeds. Repeat with all your pastry and filling. You should get about 16.

• Put the samosas on a baking sheet and bake in the oven for 15–20 minutes, until golden. Serve the samosas while they are still warm.

2 potatoes, cut into cubes
★ **125g/4oz finely chopped vegetables – use combinations of favourite vegetables, such as carrots, beans, peas, spinach, sweetcorn, cauliflower and parsnips**
1 tsp mild curry powder or paste
★ **2 tbsp cream cheese or cottage cheese**
salt and black pepper
★ **1 tbsp olive oil**
★ **30g/1oz butter, melted**
8 sheets filo pastry
★ **poppy seeds or black sesame seeds**

brown rice four ways

Serves 4

Brown rice is sustaining comfort food for a simple meal. Once cooked, it can be served in many ways, not just the four suggested below.

• Preheat the oven to 160°C/325°F/gas 3. Wash the rice thoroughly in several changes of water, then drain well. Put it in an ovenproof casserole and cover with water to the depth of a thumbnail above the surface of the rice. Cover tightly, put in the oven and bake for about 40 minutes. If the rice is still a little soggy after this time, put it back in the oven for a few minutes without the cover.

To make a delicious meal of the cooked rice, try the following ideas – or adapt them to your own and your children's liking:

• Serve with a knob of butter, some grated cheese and a little chopped fresh mint stirred into it.

• Serve it with Roasted Vegetables (see page 174).

• Make it into a salad. Add a couple of tablespoons of extra-virgin olive oil, a teaspoon of lemon juice, a pinch of sea salt, freshly ground black pepper, a finely chopped garlic clove and any of the following: in summer, chopped ripe red tomatoes, cucumber, spring onions, avocado and fresh basil; in winter, small chunks of celery, fennel, raisins, sunflower seeds or pine nuts tossed in a little oil and with chopped fresh parsley or coriander sprinkled over.

• Serve it with apple purée and a little cinnamon. Classic French food for anyone who has been unwell or suffered a digestive upset, this is also a perfect meal-in-itself supper.

★ **250g/8oz brown rice**
water (see method)

roasted vegetables

Serves 4

Served these vegetables with plain brown rice (see page 173), couscous, or bulgur for an appetizing and colourful supper. The vegetables are also a delicious accompaniment to the Sunday roast, grilled fish or meat, or to a simple omelette.

• Preheat the oven to 200°C/400°F/gas 6. Arrange all the vegetables and garlic in a shallow roasting tin. Add the olive oil and push all the vegetables around till they are well-coated with the oil. Sprinkle with a little salt and pepper.

• Roast in the oven for about 40 minutes, giving them a stir once or twice. They should be tender, and just starting to turn golden-brown. Serve sprinkled with the chopped fresh herbs.

★ 1 red pepper, cored, deseeded and cut into chunks
★ 1 yellow pepper, cored, deseeded and cut into chunks
★ 2 onions, quartered
2 medium or 4 small courgettes, thickly sliced
★ 8 cherry tomatoes
★ 4 cloves garlic
★ 4 tbsp olive oil
salt and black pepper
★ bunch of fresh coriander, basil or parsley

bubble & squeak

Serves 4

Traditionally, this is made with leftover cooked cabbage and potatoes, but you can use up Brussels sprouts, peas and broccoli this way too: fry-ups are always popular! The one cardinal rule is that there should be more potatoes than greens.

• Break up the cooked potatoes with a fork, add a little milk and the butter and roughly mash. Add the shredded cooked greens to the potato and mix together. Shape the mixture into one big cake or four smaller patties and dust with seasoned flour.

• Heat the olive oil in a frying pan. Add the cakes of bubble and squeak, press down firmly, and fry on both sides till golden brown.

★ 500g/1lb cooked potatoes
★ milk, for mashing
★ knob of butter
★ 300g/10oz shredded and cooked cabbage
seasoned flour, for dusting
★ 2-3 tbsp olive oil

broccoli & anchovy pasta

Serves 4

• Bring a large saucepan of lightly salted boiling water, to which you have added a dash of vegetable oil, to the boil. Add the broccoli florets and cook until just tender. Drain, reserving the cooking water.

• Add more water to the broccoli cooking water, if necessary, as pasta needs plenty of water to cook in. Bring the water back to the boil, add the pasta and cook it until it is tender, but still a little firm – or 'al dente', as the Italians describe it.

• While the pasta is cooking, heat the oil in a frying pan. Add the garlic and fry until just translucent. Add the anchovies or anchovy paste and the broccoli florets, turn all together in the oil and add freshly ground black pepper. Keep hot until the pasta is cooked. Drain the pasta, return it to its pan, add the broccoli sauce and toss well. Stir in the cheese and serve piping hot.

★ 1 medium head broccoli, broken into small florets
★ 375g/12oz pasta shapes, such as orecchiette, spaghettini or conchigli
★ 5 tbsp olive oil
★ 2 cloves garlic, finely chopped
★ 3–4 anchovy fillets, finely chopped or 1 good squeeze of anchovy paste
black pepper
★ 3 tbsp freshly grated Parmesan cheese

pasta with avocado sauce

Serves 4

In this delectable simple pasta dish the taste depends on the freshness and quality of the ingredients. With its creamy delicate texture, this is a pasta which even young children will enjoy.

• Scoop out the flesh of the two avocados – which should be perfectly ripe, deep yellow and unblemished – into the bowl in which you will serve the pasta. Mash to a cream. Add the lemon juice and mash again. Add the crushed garlic and stir in. Add the seasoning to taste, followed by the olive oil and mash thoroughly to a creamy sauce.

• Cook the pasta in plenty of boiling water. When it is nearly cooked, add a tablespoon or so of the pasta cooking water to the sauce and mix in thoroughly. When the pasta is cooked – it should be tender, but still slightly firm – drain it well. Tip it on top of the sauce and toss very thoroughly to combine before serving.

Note: you can use more or less lemon juice, garlic or olive oil according to family taste.

★ 2 ripe avocados
★ juice of 1 lemon
★ 1 fat garlic clove, crushed
salt and black pepper
★ 1 tbsp olive oil
★ 375g/12oz dried pasta, preferably tagliatelle

pasta sauces

★ = superfood

Pasta is wholesome fast food that the right sauces can turn into delicious and healthy feasts. On these pages you will find some great, easy-to-prepare sauces that work well with all the huge variety of pasta shapes, fresh and dried, available today. When cooking pasta for a main meal, allow approximately 500g/1lb to serve four.

raw tomato sauce

Serves 4

• Put the tomato quarters in a food processor with the basil, parsley, garlic and seasoning and process into a thick sauce. Put the sauce in the dish in which you will serve the pasta.
• Cook your chosen pasta until it is al dente (see page 175). Drain it well and tip it on top of the sauce. Stir together very quickly and sprinkle over the grated Parmesan cheese, if using. Serve at once.

★ 375g/12oz ripe fresh tomatoes, skinned and quartered
★ 8–10 basil leaves
★ handful of fresh parsley
★ 2 garlic cloves, lightly crushed
salt and black pepper
★ freshly grated Parmesan cheese (optional)

raw tomato & red pepper sauce

Serves 4

• Put the tomato quarters in a food processor with the pepper(s), parsley, grated Parmesan cheese and 2–3 tablespoons of the olive oil. Process to a thick sauce, adding more olive oil through the top of the processor as needed.
• Cook your chosen pasta (see page 175) and drain well. Add the sauce and stir it through. Serve at once.

★ 150g/5oz ripe fresh tomatoes, skinned and quartered
★ 1 large red pepper, or 1 small red and 1 small yellow pepper, cored, deseeded and quartered
★ 1 tbsp fresh parsley
★ 2 tbsp freshly grated Parmesan cheese
★ 4–5 tbsp olive oil

mozzarella, tomato & parmesan sauce

Serves 4

• A couple of hours before you plan to eat, skin and finely chop the tomatoes. Put them in a bowl with the olive oil, basil leaves, oregano and grated Parmesan. Leave to macerate for 2 hours.
• Put the cubes of mozzarella into the dish in which you plan to serve the pasta.
• Cook your chosen pasta until it is al dente (see page 175). Drain it well and tip it on top of the mozzarella cubes, stirring very quickly so that the melting cheese disperses throughout the pasta.
• Add the tomato mixture, stir again, and serve.

★ 375g/12oz ripe fresh tomatoes
★ 6 tbsp olive oil
★ handful of fresh basil leaves, roughly torn
★ sprig of fresh oregano
★ 3 tbsp freshly grated Parmesan cheese
★ 150g/5oz mozzarella cheese, cubed

tomato & anchovy sauce

Serves 4

Older children will enjoy this Italian classic. But the first time you make it, add just a touch of anchovy – perhaps a blob of anchovy paste from a tube. The sauce can be made in advance and reheated to serve with your chosen pasta.

• Heat the oil in a small saucepan, add the garlic and cook gently for 2–3 minutes. Add the tomatoes, olives and oregano. Simmer very gently for a few minutes then add the chopped anchovies. Cook a few minutes longer, until the anchovies have softened and blended with the sauce.

• Add the parsley and a twist or two of pepper. The anchovies will give the sauce all the salt it needs.

★ 100ml/3½fl oz olive oil
★ 3 cloves garlic, finely chopped
★ 200g/7oz canned chopped tomatoes
60g/2oz soft pitted black olives, chopped
pinch of dried oregano
3–4 anchovy fillets, well rinsed, dried and finely chopped
★ 2 tbsp finely chopped fresh parsley
black pepper

ham & mushroom sauce

Serves 4

• Melt the butter in a small saucepan, add the onion and garlic and cook until softened. Add the mushrooms and let them colour a little. Add the ham and fry gently until it has taken on a little colour. Add the wine, nutmeg and seasoning.

• Simmer over a very low heat for 5–10 minutes, adding a little boiling water if the sauce gets too dry.

• Cook your chosen pasta till it is al dente (see page 175), drain well and stir in the sauce. Serve at once.

★ 60g/2oz butter
★ 1 onion, finely chopped
★ 1 clove garlic, finely chopped
90g/3oz fresh mushrooms, finely sliced
★ 125g/4oz cooked ham, cubed
125ml/4fl oz white wine
★ pinch of grated nutmeg
salt and black pepper

classic bolognese sauce

Serves 4

• Melt the butter with the oil in a saucepan. Add the vegetables and soften them in the fat. Add the minced beef and fry gently until the meat begins to take colour. Add the wine and cook until most of it has been absorbed. Add the tomatoes and herbs, turn the heat up and boil for a couple of minutes.

• Turn the heat down and simmer gently for about an hour, adding a little stock from time to time if the sauce looks too dry: it should be dense but runny.

• Traditionally, this sauce is eaten with tagliatelle. Cook the pasta (see page 175) and drain it well. Stir in the sauce. Serve with the grated Parmesan handed round separately.

★ 60g/2oz butter
★ 1 tbsp olive oil
★ 1 onion, finely chopped
★ 1 carrot, grated
★ 1 stick celery, finely chopped
★ 200g/7oz lean minced beef
125ml/4fl oz red wine
★ 200g/7oz canned chopped tomatoes
★ 1 tbsp chopped fresh parsley
★ sprig of fresh or a pinch of dried thyme
★ 1 bay leaf
a little vegetable stock
salt and black pepper
★ 4 tbsp freshly grated Parmesan cheese

★ = superfood

sophie's indonesian vegetable stew

Serves 2

Four-year-old Sophie Toledo has been eating spicy savoury food like this ever since she graduated from little fruit and vegetable purées: proof that bland doesn't have to be best where babies and toddlers are concerned. The lime leaf gives this dish its lovely special flavour: it can be bought in shops selling Thai or Indonesian foods.

• Heat a little sunflower oil in a frying pan. Add the tofu dice and fry until golden. Drain and set aside. Add a little more oil to the pan, if necessary, and fry the onion and garlic in it until softened. Add the lime leaf, cabbage, pepper, carrots and beans and fry for 3-4 minutes. Add the coconut milk, salt to taste and tofu and let the mixture simmer until the vegetables are tender. Add the sweetcorn and heat through. The dish should be soup-like in consistency. Eat it with basmati rice.

★ **sunflower oil, for frying**
★ **125g/4oz firm tofu, diced**
★ **1 onion, chopped**
★ **1 clove garlic, chopped**
1 lime leaf
★ **small wedge white cabbage, chopped**
★ **½ red pepper, deseeded and chopped**
★ **2 carrots, sliced**
★ **10 butter beans**
2–3 cups coconut milk
salt
★ **150g/5oz fresh or frozen sweetcorn kernels, drained**
basmati rice, to serve

chicken in a wrap

Serves 4

Put all the ingredients, except the flour for coating and the olive oil, in a large bowl. Mix very thoroughly together and set aside for a few minutes to let the flavours amalgamate. Shape the mixture into four burgers. Toss each burger lightly in the seasoned flour to coat.

• Heat a little olive oil in a frying pan and fry the burgers for 3–4 minutes on each side, until cooked well through. Alternatively, the burgers can be brushed with oil and grilled or baked in a moderately hot oven, turning them once.

• Serve in soft tortillas, with mayonnaise, shreds of crisp lettuce and slices of avocado. As a variation, put the brgers in warm wholemeal baps and substitute soured cream for the mayonnaise.

★ **500g/1lb chicken meat, skinned, boned and finely chopped or minced**
★ **1 tbsp dark soy sauce or tamari sauce**
★ **1 tsp grated fresh root ginger**
★ **1 clove garlic, crushed**
★ **1 tbsp finely chopped fresh coriander**
½ tsp sea salt
black pepper
★ **seasoned wholemeal flour, to coat**
★ **olive oil, for frying**
4 soft tortillas, mayonnaise, lettuce and avocado, to serve

Illustrated right

potato & celeriac mash

Serves 4

Serve this tasty mash with burgers, sausages, roast chicken or fish dishes.

• Add the lemon juice or vinegar to a large saucepanful of water. Bring the pan to the boil. Slice the knobbly skin off the celeriac, cut the celeriac into chunks and drop them into the boiling water.

• Add the potato chunks to the pan. Bring back to the boil, reduce the heat and simmer for 15–20 minutes, until both vegetables are tender. Drain, reserving the cooking liquid.

• Return the vegetables to the pan and mash them, adding the butter and as much of the reserved liquid as you need to make a creamy purée. (This can be done in a food processor, but be very careful not to over-process or the potatoes will turn to glue.)

• Heat the oil in a small pan. Add the chopped onion and fry very gently until just turned gold, then stir into the mash with the hot oil from the pan.

★ 1 tbsp lemon juice or white wine vinegar

★ 1 large celeriac

★ 4–5 potatoes, cut into chunks

★ large knob butter

★ 2 tbsp olive oil

★ 1 small onion, very finely chopped

black pepper

broccoli with spinach

Serves 4

Even people who dislike broccoli may enjoy this spicy savoury way of cooking it, taken from Madhur Jaffrey's book *World Vegetarian* (Ebury Press). For all but the most grown-up children, leave out the chilli and use just a touch of ginger. You could leave out the salt, too. It is delicious cold.

• Bring a large saucepan of water to the boil. Add the spinach and broccoli florets, bring back to the boil and boil rapidly for 3–4 minutes, or until both the spinach and broccoli are tender. Drain into a colander, saving the cooking water for another use. Run cold water over the greens, and let them drain before chopping them finely.

• Heat the oil in a large non-stick frying pan or wok set over a medium-high heat. When hot, put in the onion, garlic, ginger and chilli. Stir-fry until the onion pieces turn brown at the edges. Add the cumin. Stir once, then quickly put in the broccoli and spinach into the pan. Stir once or twice and turn the heat to medium. Cook gently, stirring, until the vegetables are just heated through.

★ 375g/12oz spinach, well washed and trimmed

★ 375g/12oz broccoli florets, cut to leave a little of the stems

★ 4 tbsp olive oil

★ 30g/1oz finely chopped onion

★ 1 clove garlic, very finely chopped

★ 2 thin slices fresh root ginger, peeled and very finely chopped

★ ½–1 fresh red chilli, seeded (optional) and very finely chopped

★ 4 tsp ground cumin

vegetable curry with dal

Serves 4

• First, make the dal. Put the mung beans in a heavy pan, add the water, bring to the boil, reduce the heat and simmer very gently, skimming off the froth. When the froth has all gone, stir in the turmeric, partly cover the pan and simmer gently for about 1 hour, until the beans are soft. Drain the beans, add salt to taste and turn the dal into a serving dish. Heat the oil in a small frying pan, add the cumin seeds and let them sizzle for a couple of minutes. Add the chilli and garlic and let it soften but not brown. Tip the mixture into the mung beans and stir well. Serve the dal garnished with coriander.
• While the dal is cooking, prepare the vegetables. Break broccoli or cauliflower into very small florets, peel and dice potatoes or carrots into quite small pieces. Blanch in boiling water for 1 minute.
• Heat the oil in a wok or deep frying pan. Add the curry powder, stir for 1 minute, then add the onion and garlic, and stir-fry for 1 more minute. Add the vegetables and stir-fry for 5–10 minutes, until they soften. Add the chickpeas, lemon juice, coriander, apple and creamed coconut. Heat through for 2–3 minutes. Serve with the dal.

★ 750g/1½lbs mixed vegetables, such as broccoli, cauliflower, potatoes, carrots, french beans
★ 3 tbsp groundnut oil
2 tsp medium curry powder
★ 1 onion, chopped
★ 3 cloves garlic, chopped
★ 200g/7oz canned chickpeas, drained and rinsed
★ juice of 1 lemon
★ fresh coriander, chopped
★ 1 eating apple, peeled and chopped
30g/1oz creamed coconut

For the dal:
★ 180g/6oz mung beans, picked over, washed and drained
1 litre/1¾ pints water
½ tsp turmeric
a good pinch of salt
2 tbsp vegetable oil
★ 1 tsp cumin seeds
★ chilli powder or flakes, to taste
★ 2 cloves garlic
★ fresh coriander, to garnish

red cabbage with apple & chestnuts

Serves 4

• Cut away the outer leaves of the cabbage and the hard white core. Shred the cabbage finely.
• Make a slit across the fat side of each chestnut and put them in a pan of water. Bring to the boil and boil for 10 minutes. Take the chestnuts out of the water one by one and peel and skin them. Break them up roughly and set aside.
• Melt the butter in a large saucepan. Put in the bacon and cabbage. Cover the pan and cook over a medium heat, turning it all over from time to time.
• When the cabbage is beginning to soften, add the apple to the pan, then the vinegar and sugar. Cook the mixture for about 45 minutes, longer if you prefer the cabbage softer. Add the chestnuts at the end, giving them time to warm through. Season to taste before serving.

★ ½ large red cabbage
★ 250g/8oz chestnuts
★ 30g/1oz butter
★ 2 thick slices streaky bacon, chopped
★ 1 large dessert apple, such as Cox's, peeled, cored and grated
1–2 tbsp wine vinegar
2–3 tsp soft brown sugar
salt and black pepper

chickpea veggie burgers

★ = superfood

Makes 6 large or 8 medium burgers

- Put the split peas and chickpeas in a food processor and process until very finely chopped, but not reduced to a mush. Heat the oil in a heavy-based pan, add the chopped onion and fry gently until soft and golden.
- Put the processed split peas, chickpeas, celery, apple, ground almonds, sunflower seeds, and fried onion in a large bowl. Mix everything well together and season with salt and pepper.
- Shape the mixture into six or eight burgers, pressing them firmly into shape. Dip them first in the beaten egg, then in the breadcrumbs.
- Heat a little sunflower oil in a frying pan and fry the burgers gently for about 7 minutes on each side, until cooked well through. Serve the burgers in wholemeal baps with watercress or lettuce, and a spoonful of mayonnaise.

★ **250g/8oz canned yellow split peas, drained and rinsed**
★ **500g/1lb canned chickpeas, drained and rinsed**
★ **2 tbsp olive oil**
★ **1 large onion, finely chopped**
★ **3–4 tender inner sticks celery, finely chopped**
★ **1 crisp eating apple, finely chopped**
★ **60g/2oz ground almonds**
★ **1 tbsp sunflower seeds**
sea salt and black pepper
★ **1 small egg, beaten**
fresh or dried wholemeal breadcrumbs, to coat
★ **sunflower oil, for frying**
baps, watercress or lettuce, and mayonnaise, to serve

veggie burgers with spinach cheese topping

Makes 6

- Heat the sunflower oil in a frying pan. Add the onion and fry until soft. Add the garlic and mushrooms. Cook, stirring occasionally, until the juices have evaporated and the vegetables are getting crisp and golden. Take the pan off the heat and mix in all the remaining ingredients, except the egg, and season to taste. Mix in the beaten egg.
- Shape the mixture into six burgers, pressing each one firmly into a round. Toss them in wholemeal flour to coat. Heat a little vegetable oil in a frying pan and fry the burgers for 3–4 minutes on each side, or until cooked well through. Alternatively, the burgers can be brushed with vegetable oil and grilled or baked in a moderately hot oven.
- Top each cooked burger with a few lightly cooked spinach leaves, and lay a slice of cheese on top of the spinach. Pop under a hot grill until melting and crisp.
- Serve the burgers in wholemeal baps with added mayonnaise, and a few onion rings, if liked.

★ **2 tbsp sunflower oil**
★ **1 red onion, finely chopped**
★ **2 cloves garlic, crushed**
250g/8oz mushrooms, finely chopped
★ **125g/4oz almonds, chopped**
★ **125g/4oz cooked brown rice or soaked bulgur**
★ **180g/6oz carrots, grated**
1 tbsp vegetable bouillon powder
★ **handful fresh parsley, chopped**
★ **1 tbsp dark soy sauce**
sea salt and black pepper
★ **1 egg, beaten**
★ **wholemeal flour, to coat**
★ **vegetable oil, for frying**

For the topping:
★ **lightly cooked spinach leaves**
★ **slices of cheese**
wholemeal baps and mayonnaise, to serve

nut burgers

Makes 4

• Put the nuts and breadcrumbs in a food processor or blender and process until quite fine.

• Heat the olive oil in a heavy-based saucepan, add the onion and fry gently until soft and golden.

• Off the heat, pour the hot stock into the pan then add the nut mixture, herbs and seasoning to taste. Mix all the ingredients well together, adding a little more stock if the mixture looks on the dry side.

• Shape the mixture into four burgers and dip them into the wholemeal flour to coat lightly. Heat a little oil in a frying pan and shallow-fry the burgers for 3–5 minutes on each side, until golden brown.

• Serve the burgers, which are delicious either hot or cold, in wholemeal rolls with a little mayonnaise and shredded lettuce or watercress.

★ 250g/8oz mixed nuts, such as walnuts, hazelnuts, cashews and peanuts

125g/4oz wholemeal breadcrumbs

★ 1 tbsp olive oil

★ 1 onion, very finely chopped

300ml/½ pint hot vegetable stock, made with vegetable bouillon powder

★ 1 tbsp chopped fresh parsley

★ 2–3 fresh sage leaves, torn in small pieces

sea salt and black pepper

★ wholemeal flour, to coat

★ vegetable oil, for frying

wholemeal rolls, mayonnaise and lettuce or watercress, to serve

rice burgers

Makes 4

• Wash the rice thoroughly and drain it. Bring the bouillon to the boil in a large saucepan. Add the rice, reduce the heat, cover the pan and cook over a very low heat for about 30 minutes, until all the bouillon is absorbed and the rice is tender.

• While the rice is cooking, put the bread and peanuts in a food processor or blender and process them to crumbs.

• Heat the oil in a large frying pan. Add the onion and fry gently until soft and golden. Reduce the heat and add the parsnip and carrot, stir and fry gently for a few minutes. Add the soy sauce and yeast extract and stir them well in. Add the breadcrumbs and peanut mixture and stir in. Season to taste.

• Tip the fried-onion mixture into a mixing bowl. Add the cooked rice and mix everything well together. Allow the mixture to cool a little, then turn it out on to a floured board. Shape into four fairly thick burgers and chill in the refrigerator for an hour or so, or overnight.

• Dip the burgers in beaten egg, then coat them with breadcrumbs. Heat a little vegetable oil in a frying pan and fry the burgers for 5–7 minutes on each side, until crisp and brown.

★ brown basmati rice, measured up to the 125ml/4fl oz level in a measuring jug

300ml/½ pint vegetable bouillon, measured in the same jug as the rice

1 slice wholemeal bread

★ 60g/2oz dry-roasted peanuts

★ 2 tbsp olive oil

★ 1 onion, finely chopped

1 parsnip (hard core removed), finely grated

★ 1 carrot, finely grated

★ good splash soy sauce

½ tsp yeast extract

salt and black pepper

★ 1 egg, beaten

dry breadcrumbs, to coat

★ vegetable oil, for frying

bean burgers

★ = superfood

Makes 6

- Heat the oil in a large frying pan. Add the onion and fry over a medium heat until soft and golden. Add the carrots, potato and mashed beans and continue to cook for about 7 minutes, stirring from time to time, until the vegetables have cooked a little. Add the tomato purée, ketchup, garlic, herbs, soy sauce, and seasoning, and mix well, mashing everything together to a sticky paste.
- Turn the mixture out on to a floured board and, with floured hands, shape into 6 burgers. Chill in the refrigerator for an hour or two to firm up. Dip the burgers in the beaten egg, then in the breadcrumbs.
- Heat a little olive oil in a frying pan, and fry the burgers over medium heat for about 5 minutes on each side. Serve in wholemeal baps with chutney, onion rings and lettuce.

★ 2 tbsp olive oil
★ 1 large onion, finely chopped
★ 2 carrots, finely grated
★ 1 potato, finely grated
★ 250g/8oz canned red kidney beans, drained, rinsed and mashed
★ 1 tbsp tomato purée
★ 1 tbsp tomato ketchup
★ 1 clove garlic, finely chopped
pinch of herbes de provence
★ 1 tsp soy sauce
pinch of salt
black pepper
★ 1 egg, beaten
★ 2 tbsp dried wholemeal breadcrumbs

onion-&-squeak burgers

Makes 6

- Wash and cook the spring onions in boiling water till soft. Drain and chop. Mix the eggs, nutmeg, breadcrumbs, mashed potato and seasoning together thoroughly. Mix in the spring onions. Shape the mixture into six burgers.
- Heat a little oil in a large frying pan. Add the burgers and fry for 3–5 minutes on each side, until golden brown. Serve with iceberg lettuce, raw onion rings, slices of tomato and a favourite relish.

★ 12 spring onions
★ 2 eggs, lightly beaten
★ good pinch grated nutmeg
2 slices wholemeal bread, crusts removed, and crumbed
★ 375g/12oz cold mashed potato
sea salt and black pepper
★ sunflower oil, for frying

radar burgers

Makes 4 large or 6 medium burgers

- Heat a little oil in a frying pan. Add the onion and fry gently until soft. Put the beef, carrot, breadcrumbs and herbs in a bowl. Add the onions and mix well. Shape the mixture into four or six burgers.
- Dust the burgers lightly with flour. Fry them in the pan in which you fried the onions, adding a little more oil, if necessary, for 3–4 minutes on each side.
- The burgers are delicious hot or cold. Serve them on their own with a salad, or in a traditional bun with raw onion, crunchy iceberg lettuce and ketchup.

★ vegetable oil, for frying
★ 1 large onion, finely chopped
★ 375g/12oz chuck steak or shin of beef, all fat removed, minced
★ 250g/8oz carrot, finely grated
1 tbsp wholemeal breadcrumbs
★ 1 tbsp chopped fresh mint
★ 1 tbsp chopped fresh parsley
flour, for dusting

indian kidney beans

Serves 2

This delicious dish is fabulous served with basmati rice. It can, of course, be made with dried beans, but they must be soaked overnight and boiled hard for 10 minutes then cooked more gently for another 20 before you can use them – too much fuss, perhaps, for most working parents!

• Melt the butter in a heavy-based frying pan. Add the onions and fry gently until golden. Add the garlic and pepper and fry over a medium heat until the pepper is cooked. Make sure the garlic does not turn too dark. Add the beans with half their liquid, the coriander, garam masala and salt. Cover the pan and cook for about five minutes.

★ 3 tbsp butter
★ 1 onion, chopped
★ 1 clove garlic, chopped
★ 1 green pepper, deseeded and chopped
★ 400g/13oz canned red kidney beans
★ 1–2 tbsp chopped fresh coriander
1 tsp garam masala
salt

oliver's pizza

Makes 2

These pizzas can be open-frozen before wrapping and storing in the freezer. Cook them from frozen, allowing about 7 minutes' extra cooking time.

• To make the bases, put the flours, salt and yeast in a warmed, dry bowl and mix well. Make a well in the centre, add the water and olive oil and mix to a dough. On a lightly floured surface knead the dough for 3 minutes, or until it feels firm and springy. Put the dough in a clean, warmed bowl, cover with clingfilm or a clean tea towel and leave to rise in a warm place for up to 2 hours, until well-risen.

• Meanwhile, make a tomato sauce for the topping. Heat the oil in a saucepan, add the onion and garlic and fry over a gentle heat till soft and translucent. Add the tomatoes, and the marjoram or oregano, crushing the tomatoes roughly with the back of a wooden spoon. Cook until the sauce has thickened and reduced a little.

• Preheat the oven to 190°C/375°F/gas 5. Take the dough from the bowl and divide it in two. Roll out each piece of dough to a 30cm/12in circle. Put in two oiled pizza tins and brush the surfaces with oil. Cover with slices of mozzarella, then some tomato sauce. Sprinkle grated cheese over the top. Bake the pizzas in the oven for about 20 minutes.

For the pizza bases:
250g/8oz strong white flour
★ 250g/8oz wholemeal flour
2 tsp salt
2 x 6g/¼oz sachets dried yeast
300ml/½ pint tepid water
(1 part boiling to 2 parts cold)
4 tbsp olive oil

For the topping:
★ 2 tbsp olive oil
★ 1 onion, finely chopped
★ 1 clove garlic, crushed
★ 250g/8oz canned tomatoes
★ fresh marjoram or good pinch of dried oregano
★ 100g/3½oz mozzarella or other firm soft cheese, sliced
★ 2 tbsp grated cheddar or other hard cheese

puddings

Children need no persuading to eat sweet things. Choose any of the tempting puddings here and you will be giving your youngsters nutritious food that they will eat with pleasure.

fruit dipped in chocolate sauce

★ = superfood

Serves 4

Choose your children's favourite fruit for this fondue – apples, pears, grapes, strawberries, peaches, tangerine segments, chunks of pineapple, bananas, melon – and use organic chocolate, if possible. Have plenty of wooden skewers handy for dipping the fruit into the chocolate.

• Cut large fruits into chunks, if appropriate, and put all the fruit in a bowl or on a large platter.

• Break the chocolate into pieces and put it in a bowl set over a pan of hot, but not boiling water. Leave it to melt. Keep hot in a fondue pot or over a tea light while the children are dipping fruit into it.

★ **fresh fruit, washed and chilled for 2–3 hours**

250–300g/8–10oz dark chocolate (minimum 70% cocoa solids)

Illustrated right

creamy fruit tart

Serves 6

• Heat the oven to 220°C/425°F/gas 7. Lightly grease a 25 x 33cm/10 x 13in loose-bottomed flan tin. Wash, dry, halve and stone the fruit.

• Roll out the pastry on a lightly floured surface and use to line the flan tin. Lay the prepared fruit lightly on the pastry, cut sides down.

• Beat the eggs in a bowl, add the crème fraîche and sugar and beat together until smooth. Pour the mixture over the fruit. Sprinkle extra sugar on top.

• Bake in the oven for about 30 minutes, or until the top is lightly golden.

★ **8 large ripe plums, apricots, greengages or small peaches**

250g/8oz puff pastry, thawed if frozen

★ **2 eggs**

★ **200ml/7fl oz crème fraîche**

2 tbsp vanilla golden caster sugar, plus extra for sprinkling

summer pudding

Serves 4

Classic Summer Pudding is made with white bread and much more white sugar than this. But the pudding works just as well with wholemeal bread, and the lovely fruity taste comes through much more sharply when it is not overwhelmed by sugar. You may find you like even less. Make the pudding at least six hours before it is going to be eaten.

• Wash the fruit, pull the currants off their stalks with a fork, and put all the fruit in a large saucepan together with the sugar. Set the pan over a very low heat for 2–3 minutes, until the sugar melts and the juices begin to run. Set aside.

• Use five slices of the bread to line a 1kg/2lb pudding basin, making sure there are no gaps which could spoil the pudding's appearance. Add the fruit, reserving a good half-cup of the juice. Roof over the pudding with the remaining slice of bread, then put a plate on top with a weight on it to press it down into the basin. Chill the pudding for at least 6 hours.

• To serve, up-end the basin over a pretty china dish so that the pudding slides on to the middle of it. Pour over the reserved juice and serve, on its own or with a little crème fraîche or Greek yogurt.

★ = superfood

- ★ 375g/12oz raspberries
- ★ 180g/6oz red currants
- ★ 60g/2oz blackcurrants
- 60g/2oz soft brown sugar
- ★ 6 thin slices wholemeal bread, crusts removed
- ★ crème fraîche or Greek yogurt, to serve

upside-down pudding

Serves 4

• Heat the oven to 180°C/350°F/gas 4. Lightly grease a 23cm/9in cake tin.

• Cream together 125g/4oz butter and the caster sugar. Beat in the eggs, one at a time, until the mixture is light and fluffy. Fold in the flour.

• Melt the remaining butter and pour it all over the bottom of the prepared tin. Sprinkle on the brown sugar evenly. Arrange the fruits neatly in an attractive flower-like pattern in the tin, decorating the pattern with the cherries. Try not to leave gaps.

• Spread the batter over the top of the fruit. Bake on the middle shelf of the oven for 45 minutes, or until a skewer inserted into the centre of the cake comes out clean. Turn the pudding out on to a plate. Eat it while warm with whipped cream, fromage frais or vanilla ice cream.

- ★ 150g/5oz butter, softened, plus extra for greasing
- 125g/4oz golden caster sugar
- ★ 2 eggs
- 125g/4oz self-raising flour, sifted
- 60g/2oz soft brown sugar
- ★ 400g/13oz fresh fruit, such as pineapple, apricots, pears, weighed after peeling and cutting into chunks
- ★ a few cherries
- ★ whipped cream, fromage frais or vanilla ice cream, to serve

ginger fruit pudding

Serves 4

• Heat the oven to 180°C/350°F/gas 4. Lightly butter a 1.2 litre/2 pint capacity deep ovenproof dish.
• Sieve the flour, cinnamon, nutmeg, ginger, bicarbonate of soda and sugar into a bowl, tipping the bran left in the sieve into the mix. Mix in the egg.
• Melt the butter in a small saucepan and add the treacle to warm through. Add this to the flour-and-egg mixture, then pour in the milk. Using a balloon whisk, mix thoroughly so there are no lumps. Stir in the sultanas and preserved ginger.
• Pour the mixture into the prepared dish. Bake in the oven for 30–35 minutes. Do not overcook and don't worry if it subsides a bit in the middle; this gives a nice sticky centre to the pudding.
• Serve hot with chilled whipped cream. You can add some of the syrup from the preserved ginger to the whipped cream, if you wish.

★ 125g/4oz wholemeal self-raising flour
★ 2 tsp cinnamon
★ ½ tsp grated nutmeg
★ 1 tsp ground ginger
1 tsp bicarbonate of soda
125g/4oz soft dark brown sugar
★ 1 egg
★ 60g/2oz butter
90g/3oz black treacle
★ 300ml/½ pint milk
★ 60g/2oz sultanas
★ 4 pieces (more if you like) preserved ginger, chopped
★ whipped cream, to serve

blackberry & apple crumble

Serves 4

• Heat the oven to 180°C/350°F/gas 4. Butter a baking dish well.
• Peel, core and slice the apples, wash the blackberries and put both fruits in the baking dish. Add the sugar and sprinkle over the lemon juice.
• To make the topping, put the flour and brown sugar in a bowl and rub in the butter until the mixture resembles coarse breadcrumbs. Mix in the nuts. Sprinkle the topping over the fruit.
• Put the dish on a baking sheet and bake in the oven for 45 minutes–1 hour, or until the topping has crisped up a little.

★ 500g/1lb apples
★ 500g/1lb blackberries
1 tbsp soft brown sugar
★ 1 tsp lemon juice

For the topping:
★ 180g/6oz wholemeal flour
90g/3oz soft brown sugar
★ 90g/3oz butter, diced
★ 90g/3oz chopped mixed nuts

pancakes

Makes about 8

Pancakes are family fun in which everyone can join – and tossing pancakes is the kind of fun which men tend to take over, rather like barbecues, to make it a real family occasion. Quite small children can mix and make pancakes successfully, too – though perhaps without the tossing!

• Beat the eggs lightly and whisk in the flour, milk and sugar. Leave in the refrigerator for at least 30 minutes (or up to 24 hours, if necessary).

• When you're ready to make the pancakes, melt a little butter in a small omelette pan. When it is frothing, add about 4 tablespoons of the batter and cook for about 1 minute on each side – it is time to turn the pancake when little bubbles have appeared all over the surface. Keep the pancakes warm in the oven till everybody is ready – or serve them out as they're cooked. This should be a noisy, messy meal!

• Serve with a selection of accompaniments: lemon juice, sugar, apple purée, strawberries or raspberries stewed for just a couple of minutes to get their juices running, sugar-free fruit purée or ice cream.

★ **3 eggs**
★ **150g/5oz wholemeal flour**
★ **250ml/8fl oz milk**
1 tsp brown sugar
★ **butter, for cooking**

real rice pudding

Serves 4

This is a kids' treat for ever and totally unlike anything you can buy ready-made in cans or pots. A brilliant source of good calories and calcium, rice pudding can be served with any cooked fruit, apple purée or blackcurrant jelly.

• Heat the oven to 150°C/300°F/gas 2. Use a little of the butter to grease a shallow ovenproof dish.
• Put the rice, milk and sugar in the dish and stir well. Dot with tiny bits of the remaining butter and add freshly grated nutmeg.
• Transfer the dish to the oven. Bake for 15 minutes, then stir the pudding gently. Bake for another 15 minutes and stir again. Leave to cook for another 1½ hours, or until there is a crisp brown skin on top of the pudding.

★ 45g/1½oz butter
★ 3 tbsp pudding rice
★ 600ml/1 pint whole milk
2 tbsp soft brown sugar
★ pinch of nutmeg

stewed apple with mascarpone

Serves 4

This wonderful variation on traditional stewed apples has the added benefit of protein and calcium from mascarpone cheese. Depending on your children's taste you can add a sprig of mint, a few cloves, or both, while the apples are stewing.

• Put the water into a saucepan. Add the sugar and heat gently until the sugar has dissolved.
• Add the apple slices to the sugar mixture, cooking very gently. When the apples have cooked to a smooth purée, fold in the mascarpone.
• Put in individual dishes and chill in the refrigerator.

60ml/2fl oz water
30g/1oz caster sugar
★ 500g/1lb cooking apples, such as Bramleys, peeled, cored and sliced
★ 250g/8oz mascarpone cheese

prune purée

Serves 4

This simple dessert is super-rich in antioxidants and also has a little iron and lots of fibre.

• Put the prunes in a bowl, cover with boiling water and leave to soak overnight. Next day, remove the stones from the prunes and chop them coarsely.
• Put the remaining ingredients in a bowl and whisk until the mixture stiffens. Fold in the prunes and refrigerate for 2 hours. Serve with natural live yogurt containing zest from the second lemon, if liked, and a pinch of allspice.

★ 500g/1lb prunes
★ juice of 2 unwaxed lemons
★ zest of one of the lemons
45g/1½oz demerara sugar
★ 3 egg whites from guaranteed salmonella-free, free-range eggs (because the eggs are ucooked)
★ yogurt and allspice, to serve

delicious drinks

Children need to drink a lot. Fluids help avoid many nutritional deficiencies and common problems like constipation. Avoid high-sugar, high-caffeine soft drinks, and use a juicer or blender to make the great drinks here.

kiwi surprise

Serves 1–2

Illustrated top

This is an immunity-boosting glass of brain power which children love.
• Juice all the ingredients in a juicer.

★ **4 carrots**
★ **1 apple, quartered**
★ **1 kiwi fruit**

berry delight

Serves 1–2

Illustrated middle

Here is a drink that is high in energy, bursting with vitamin C and full of the most powerful immunity-boosting and cancer-protective plant chemicals.
• Put all the ingredients in a blender and process until smooth.

★ **150g/5oz natural live yogurt**
★ **300ml/1/2 pint milk (full-fat for the under 5s)**
★ **fresh or frozen berries – a mixture or all one variety, such as strawberries, blueberries, blackcurrants, raspberries**
a handful of ice cubes

coconut crush

Serves 2

Illustrated bottom

Older children will love the tropical smell and taste of this highly nutritious drink. It is especially good for girls because of its high calcium content and the phytoestrogens in the soya milk.
• Put all the ingredients in a blender and process until smooth.

★ **300ml/1/2 pint soya milk**
150ml/1/4 pint coconut milk
★ **150g/5oz frozen natural live yogurt**
1/2 tsp ground cinnamon
1/4 tsp ground cloves
a handful of ice cubes

pear power

Serves 1–2

Few people realize the nutritional value of a ripe pear. This drink provides a rich supply of natural sugars – just the thing for instant energy.
• Juice all the ingredients in a juicer.

★ 4 pears, quartered
★ 2 slices fresh pineapple
★ 2 apples, quartered
★ 12 grapes, black or white

tomatoes plus

Serves 1–2

This mind-and-body juice is super-rich in minerals to invigorate tired young muscles, and full of calming essential oils from the basil to revive the flagging mind and spirit.
• Juice the tomatoes, carrot, celery and basil in a juicer. Stir in the lemon juice, Worcestershire sauce and a twist of pepper.

★ 4 large ripe plum tomatoes
★ 1 carrot, roughly chopped
★ 1 stick celery
★ handful of basil leaves
★ juice of 1/2 lemon
dash of Worcestershire sauce
black pepper

nutty apple juice

Serves 1–2

This may sound like a kids' party treat, but it's also a real energy-boosting and nutritious smoothie. Instantly available calories from the fruit sugar in the apples, mixed with the slower release calories in bananas, make this suitable before sustained physical activity. Make sure you select one of the 'healthy' peanut butters, without added salt.
• Juice the apples in a juicer, add the bananas and peanut butter and blend together.

★ 6 apples, quartered
★ 2 bananas
★ 1 tbsp smooth peanut butter

jungle juice

Serves 1–2

Juice the mango and passionfruit in a juicer and blend with the yogurt and milk.

1 mango, peeled and stoned
2 passionfruit, flesh and seeds scooped from skins
★ 150g/5oz frozen live natural yogurt
★ 300ml/10fl oz whole milk

black stuff

Serves 1–2

Prunes are famed for their gentle laxative action, but because of their high potassium content they're good for maintaining normal blood pressure, too.
• Juice the apples and pears in a juicer. Purée the prunes in a blender, then add the juice, lecithin and molasses and whizz everything together.

★ 4 apples, quartered
★ 4 ripe pears, quartered
★ 6 prunes, soaked and stoned
2 tsp lecithin granules
2 tsp molasses

english lemonade

Serves 4–6

Make your own lemonade and avoid all the chemical additives, flavourings and colourings in the commercial squashes. The small amount of effort will be hugely repaid in taste and health benefits.
• Peel the lemons, leaving as much pith as possible on the fruit. Squeeze the juice from the peeled lemons into a large bowl and add the sugar.
• Put the peel and water into a saucepan, bring to the boil and simmer for 3 minutes. Strain the liquid into the juice, stirring until all the sugar has dissolved.
• Pour into a bottle with a tightly fitting cork or stopper and keep in the refrigerator. To drink the lemonade, dilute it to taste with ice-cold water.

> ★ 6 unwaxed lemons
> 500g/1lb granulated sugar
> 1.2 litres/2 pints water

sesame smoothie

Serves 1–2

This calcium- and energy-rich smoothie makes a great after-school reviver.
• Put the yogurt, tahini and ice cubes in a blender and process until smooth. Pour into glasses and sprinkle the sesame seeds on top.

> ★ 300g/10oz live natural yogurt
> ★ 1 tbsp tahini
> a handful of ice cubes
> ★ 1 tsp sesame seeds

tropical delight

Serves 1–2

Put the mango, pineapple, ginger and lime in a juicer and juice well together. Blend the juice with the yogurt and the ice cubes for a delicious fruit tea.

> 1 mango, peeled and stoned
> ★ 1 pineapple, top removed, cut into chunks
> ★ 2.5cm/1in piece fresh root ginger
> ★ 1 lime, peeled and sliced
> ★ 150g/5oz live natural yogurt
> a handful of ice cubes

b plus

Serves 1-2

This delicious drink is wonderfully high in B vitamins.
• Juice the tomatoes, celery and parsley in a juicer, then blend with the remaining ingredients.

> ★ 6 tomatoes, quartered
> ★ 2 sticks celery, chopped
> ★ handful of parsley, with stalks
> ★ 150g/5oz live natural yogurt
> ★ 125g/4oz cottage cheese
> 2 tsp brewer's yeast
> Worcestershire sauce, to taste

instant good food

You're home late and there isn't time to make the meal you planned. Or the children have just turned up with hungry friends in tow. Or the pizza place was full so you decided to have something at home instead. Or you all got home ravenous from a day's outing and your mind is a complete blank, even with a well-filled fridge, store cupboard and freezer.

Here are many suggestions for moments like this. They range from quick snacks to full-blown meals, with some ideas for quick healthy puddings, too. None of them is complicated: some don't even need a recipe. And some are from the Recipes section, with page references to get you to them quickly. Frozen herbs come into their own here: a teaspoon of chopped chives or parsley scooped out of a frozen potful can make a huge difference to the appeal of these quick meals. And if you also have frozen beans, petits pois, broccoli or spinach, you can turn a snack into a healthy meal.

Baked beans on toast with sliced tomatoes on top.

Oven-baked beans Heat the oven to moderately hot. Drain and thoroughly rinse a can of red kidney or cannellini beans. Heat a little oil in a saucepan, add the beans and toss. Turn the heat down very low, cover and gently heat the beans through for 5 minutes. Drizzle a little extra-virgin olive oil over thick slices of wholemeal bread or halved baps, spread a little mustard on them, put on a baking tray and top with the heated beans. Cover the beans with slices of tomato, top with grated cheddar cheese and put in the oven for 10 minutes, or until the cheese is melting and bubbly.

Beans 'n' onions Melt a good knob of butter in a pan, and gently fry a sliced onion in it until soft; add a dash of lemon juice. Add baked beans, toss, lower the heat, cover and let the beans heat through. Add black pepper and parsley, and serve on buttered wholemeal toast.

Canned tuna can be turned into at least half-a-dozen quick, easy meals.

Tuna and beans Flake canned tuna into rinsed and drained canned white beans (or borlotti or red kidney beans) and dress with plenty of olive oil, lemon juice and seasoning. Garnish with onion rings, tomato slices and parsley or chives.

Tuna and potato salad Boil and skin little new potatoes, put into a salad bowl with flaked tuna, sliced onion rings, and maybe a few black olives. Make a dressing with olive oil, lemon juice, black pepper, chopped garlic, mayonnaise and a touch of anchovy paste. Mix well and pour over the potatoes while still hot. Toss gently.

Tuna-eggs mayonnaise Hard-boil one egg per person. Arrange the shelled and halved eggs on a dish, mix a well-drained can of tuna with mayonnaise and cover the eggs with it. Serve with plenty of crusty bread.

Tuna and sweetcorn salad Put
some frozen sweetcorn in a pan with enough
water to cover, bring to the boil, simmer for
2–3 minutes, then drain. Add chunks of tomato,
beetroot, chopped spring onions, and some tuna.
Make a dressing with olive oil, lemon juice,
seasoning, a teaspoonful of mustard and a dollop
of mayonnaise. Pour over the salad and toss gently.

Wholemeal bread can be used in many
ways. Halve wholemeal baps, toast them, then
drizzle a little olive oil over the inner sides. Top
with slices of lightly seasoned beef tomato, then
slices of mozzarella, and a drizzle of pesto sauce.

Pizza-style bread Toast one side of
halved wholemeal baps, thick slices of wholemeal
bread, wholemeal pittas, or lengths of baguette.
Drizzle olive oil over the untoasted sides, top with
slices of tomato, season with dried oregano and a
little pepper. Grate cheddar cheese on top, and
put under a hot grill until the cheese bubbles.

Mushrooms on toast with
crumbly cheese uses mushrooms, any
hard cheese, and unsmoked bacon (see page 153).

Granny Smith's Welsh rarebit uses
Cheddar cheese, cream and apples (see page 155).

Bread and cheese bake Preheat
the oven to hot. For four people, butter four slices
of wholemeal bread and cut into squares. Finely
chop an onion. Grate a 180g/6oz piece of hard
cheese. Butter a pie dish, put a layer of bread
squares on the bottom, add half the onion, and
top with half the cheese. Repeat the bread, onion
and cheese layer. Then beat 4 eggs in 600ml/1 pint
milk, season and pour over. Bake in the oven for
about 30 minutes till golden brown on top.

Ploughman's lunch or supper
needs a decent cheese, and a few spring onions.
Serve the cheese with some interesting bread,
defrosted if frozen and warmed in the oven.

Coleslaw is quickly made. Shred a chunk
of white cabbage, a couple of carrots and a crisp
apple and dress with a good mayonnaise thinned
down slightly with a little olive oil and a touch of
lemon juice. Garnish with parsley or chives.

Chunks of mild cheese – Gouda,
Jarlsberg, Emmenthal or a mild Cheddar – served
with oatcakes, a glass of milk and an apple adds
up to a quick bedtime snack for small children.

Eggs are a good start for many a sustaining
snack. You can poach them, scramble them, make
them into an omelette, or just boil them and serve
with toast: 'a boiled egg and soldiers' is a favourite
nursery memory for countless grown-ups. Some
variations on the eggs theme:

Spanish omelette is an excellent quick
dish, needing only a salad to make it a satisfying
meal (see page 145 for recipe).

Eggs and spinach mornay Preheat
the oven to moderately hot. Hard-boil an egg per
person. Defrost a packet of spinach, stir in a knob
of butter and a good grinding of nutmeg, put it
into a baking dish, top with the hard-boiled eggs
sliced in two lengthways, cover with Sauce
Mornay (see below), top with grated cheese and
bake in the oven for 10–15 minute.

For Sauce Mornay for four, heat 300ml/½ pint
milk. In a nonstick pan melt 2 tablespoons butter
and add 2 tablespoons plain wholemeal flour
(or half white and half wholemeal), and stir until
the mixture is smooth. Add the milk, a little at a
time, stirring to keep the sauce smooth. Add
2 tablespoons grated hard cheese, a heaped
teaspoon French mustard, a little pepper and stir
again. Reduce the heat and cook for 5–10 minutes,
stirring from time to time.

Potato omelette is a simpler version of
the classic Spanish tortilla. Peel 2–3 potatoes,
grate, rinse and dry in a teatowel. Beat together
3 or 4 eggs, add a tablespoon of milk, the grated

potatoes, chopped parsley or chives and seasoning. Melt a little butter in a non-stick frying pan, add the mixture, lower the heat, cover and cook for 10 minutes. Flip the omelette over, cook for a little longer and serve with a salad or green vegetable.

Baked potatoes

If you have time in hand, bake one big potato for every two people, well pierced with a fork, in a very hot oven, for up to an hour: they are cooked when they give and feel slightly squashy. When done, halve them, scoop out most of the flesh into a basin, mash it with a little butter, milk, or cream cheese, and refill the potato skins. Make a hollow in the middle of each filling, break an egg into it, cover with grated cheese and return to the oven till the cheese is golden and bubbly and the egg has set.

Cooked rice

is a good stir-fry basic. Stir-fry sliced and diced vegetables, such as carrots, onions, leeks, cabbage, courgettes and tomatoes, in a wok. Add the cold cooked rice, a cupful of hot vegetable stock and simmer, covered, for 20 minutes.

Rice croquettes

also use cooked rice. Add grated cheese, chopped parsley and a beaten egg to the rice and form it into croquettes. Dust with seasoned flour and fry.

A sausage supper

Cook some peeled potatoes in boiling salted water. While they are cooking, grill the sausages. In a frying pan, heat some olive oil and fry a couple of onions cut into thick slices. When the potatoes and sausages are cooked, cut them both into chunks and put them in a serving bowl, with the drained fried onion. Add a little more oil to the pan in which the onions were fried, plus a teaspoon of mustard and a dash of vinegar, swirl around to mix and pour over the sausages and potatoes. Chopped celery would be a good crunchy addition.

Cottage cheese

makes a good base for a hot-day supper. Add to it chunks of cucumber, tomato and green pepper, onion rings and black olives. Dress with plenty of olive oil, lemon juice, fresh herbs and seasonings for a variation on Greek salad. If you have feta cheese you can make it authentic.

Pasta

, the original fast food, is ever-popular. Turn to pages 176–177 for some excellent sauces, including a quick tomato sauce, which can be made as you want them, or prepared in advance and kept in the refrigerator for several days.

Greek yogurt

is a great standby for quick and healthy puddings. Start with some creamy thick Greek yogurt and stir flaked almonds or chopped nuts into it with a drizzle of runny honey. Or stir in some puréed fruit, crushed strawberries and raspberries, or a spoonful of a no-sugar fruit spread. Or defrost a packet of frozen forest fruits, heat them through, adding slices of peach or nectarine or any other fresh fruit available, and serve with dollops of yogurt.

In summertime, cottage cheese makes a lovely pudding: serve it with fresh fruit, such as chunks of peach or nectarine, a few strawberries, or a handful of grapes, and a little orange juice and finely grated orange zest.

Pancakes

can be an uproarious family occasion as well as a memorable pudding: see page 190 for a good basic recipe and plenty of ideas for serving them.

And everyone loves baked apples. Core and slice them and lay in a thick layer on a buttered baking tray. Pour over the juice of a couple of lemons, a sprinkling of brown sugar and some chopped butter. Add a spoonful of apple juice, white wine or water and put in a very hot oven until the apple slices are soft and gilded. Serve with thick live yogurt or fresh cream.

special problems

Foods children eat contribute not only to the quality of their general health but also to their susceptibility to numerous food-related disorders. While the wrong foods can be a cause of eating disorders and other problems, switching to healthier foods can alleviate many of them.

food & disorders

Never before have the ingredients for a **healthy** and **delicious** diet been so **freely available** as they are to Western families today. Walk into any supermarket or food shop and you will see a cornucopia of **wonderful foods** from the world over. Despite this, diet-connected problems are increasing among children.

One of the reasons for this is that millions of children in the Western world live on poor and extremely limited diets featuring chiefly high-fat, high-sugar convenience foods that supply plenty of calories but disastrously few of the nutrients that growing children need. Deficiencies in the B vitamins, and in minerals such as zinc, magnesium and iron, can not only affect normal growth and development but also adversely affect the nervous system and crucial areas of brain function.

These deficiencies are increasingly common in today's children, with anaemia (caused by iron deficiency), scurvy (caused by a lack of vitamin C) and rickets (caused by a lack of vitamin D) all showing significant rises, especially among children living in inner cities.

children and food-related disorders

Parents today are encountering a whole new range of childhood food-related disorders for which there is no swift medical fix and, often, no real medical understanding either.

Allergic problems have become much more common, with the incidence of conditions such as asthma and eczema increasing inexorably. More and more children, boys as well as girls, are developing eating disorders such as anorexia. And attention deficit hyperactivity disorder (ADHD) affects all too many children in the West.

Many factors are known to contribute to the increase in these and other problems, stress and environmental pollution among them. But many careful studies suggest that what children eat, as well as what is missing from their diet, can be vital contributory causes.

the benefits of eating organic foods

A major problem is the numerous pesticides used in food production, traces of which turn up in many foods, with unknown consequences for children's health and development. Dr Vyvyan Howard, a leading foetal and infant toxicology expert at the University of Liverpool in the UK, is emphatic in his advice: 'One of the most positive things we can do is eat organic food. This considerably reduces the "body burden" of toxic chemicals in both parent and child.'

The right diet, rich in organic foods, certainly will not solve all these problems. But by feeding your children good, simple, healthy food from day one, and by teaching them the basic principles of good nutrition, you will certainly avoid the worst of them.

If, despite all your efforts, problems do arise, and a doctor is unable to help, consider seeking the advice of a trained, qualified and registered complementary therapist, such as a homeopath, naturopath or herbalist (see Resources, page 214).

allergies

An allergy is an inappropriate response from the body's immune system to a substance that is not normally harmful. The immune system is a complex mechanism which helps the body combat infections. It does this by identifying 'foreign bodies' and then mobilizing the white cells to destroy them.

Sometimes, the immune system mistakes an innocent substance for an invader. The white cells over-react, producing large quantities of the chemical histamine and the symptoms of asthma, hay fever, eczema and all the other allergic symptoms that plague so many people.

As our society has become more affluent, so the number of people suffering from allergies has risen. Our fresh air is polluted by traffic fumes; our homes are centrally heated, double glazed and carpeted, to the delight of the house-dust mite; our work places are often sealed boxes without a single opening window so they are too hot in the winter and air-conditioned in the summer.

identifying signs of allergic reaction

The other effect of affluence is the world-wide food production network which makes it possible for children to eat their favourite foods through the whole twelve months of the year, and in ever-increasing quantities. The more they eat the same foods, the more likely it is that allergies will develop. In fish-eating countries, fish allergies are more common; in countries where dairy products are a substantial part of the diet, allergy to these is more common.

The instant reactions which produce large quantities of histamine also produce instant symptoms. Blotchy skin, hives, swollen mouth and throat, streaming eyes, paroxysms of sneezing, are all immediately obvious. But it's also possible for food allergies to be delayed because killer T-cells, part of the body's immune-system defence mechanism, react to non-protein substances like nickel and other heavy metals, cosmetics, perfumes, and even food additives, delaying an allergic response by up to 48 hours. This makes the offenders difficult to identify. Common culprits are citrus fruits, garlic, mangoes, celery and even carrots. Chemicals added to food for colouring, flavouring or preserving can work in the same way.

Another example of non-acute food allergy is coeliac disease where sufferers are allergic to the gluten in wheat and other grains. Impaired nutrient absorption, weight loss and general malaise result.

allergy or intolerance?

There is a problem about deciding whether a child is suffering from food allergy (a reaction to allergens) or food intolerance (a condition for which allergic antibodies are not responsible). In the past decade there has been enormous media coverage of food allergies, and a mushrooming boom in dubious allergy clinics and allergy-testing methods. There is also a plethora of pseudo-scientific mumbo jumbo which has made huge numbers of people obsessed with what they eat, drink, breathe, wear and even where they live.

About half the world's population does not produce the enzyme needed to digest milk (see page 204), so milk intolerance is widespread, and common in children. Coffee, tea, cocoa, chocolate, cheese, beer, sausages, canned foods, red wine, wheat and tomatoes are all foods which the body may not tolerate.

Migraine, asthma, eczema, urticaria (hives), irritable bowel syndrome, colitis, Crohn's disease, hay fever and rheumatoid arthritis are just some of the illnesses which can involve food allergy or intolerance. They may all respond to the right dietary changes. Unfortunately, the only way to be certain that you are making appropriate dietary modifications to relieve the problem is to follow a lengthy and quite laborious exclusion diet.

It is essential, particularly when dealing with children, that any major change in eating habits is monitored by an expert nutritionist or doctor. It is not uncommon for allergy enthusiasts to recommend diets that are so restricted that their patients become severely malnourished, weak and very ill. If a child has a severe 'anaphylactic' allergy, which could be very serious, your physician will provide you with an emergency injection kit should the worst happen and the child unwittingly eats a peanut or a few sesame seeds, or gets stung by a bee or a wasp.

nutrition and allergies

While there has been little confirmatory scientific research, there is evidence that increasing consumption of some nutrients, either from foods or supplements, can lessen allergic reactions. B vitamins, particularly niacin and pantothenic acid, are thought to help with catarrh, nasal congestion and hay fever. Vitamin B_6 may reduce sensitivity to monosodium glutamate. Vitamin B_{12} is believed to reduce post-nasal drip and sensitivity to the sulphite preservatives. The essential fatty acids and omega-3 fatty acids in evening primrose oil and fish oils, together with magnesium have been shown to help reduce the allergic reaction in atopic (childhood) eczema.

foods that cause allergies

Several types of food are recognized as being common causes of allergic reactions among children. Some of these foods, such as berries, are seasonal and perhaps eaten less frequently; others are year-round basic superfoods.

If a child gets the occasional bout of something that looks like nettle rash for no obvious reason, or even red itchy patches that fade within a few hours, it is sensible to suspect a food allergy and to think back to what he has eaten in the past day. A common cause of such reactions among children, especially in the summer months, is berries, with strawberries near the top of the list.

Severe reactions are most likely from nuts, seeds, fish, shellfish and eggs. Less severe chronic symptoms are normally caused by milk and milk products, soya-based products, food additives (except for asthmatics who may react severely to some of these), and gluten-containing cereals, which include wheat, oats and barley. Other things that children may consume frequently when the summer comes, and which are common allergens, are cola drinks, pineapples, cherries and plums.

If your child is strongly allergic to any foods, you will soon know what they are, but slight reactions can sometimes go unrecognized.

References to the most common allergy-causing foods occur throughout this book. Here, their causes and symptoms are summarized.

Cow's milk and its dairy products head

the list of foods that may cause allergic reactions among children. The reaction is to a protein in the milk. Symptoms include diarrhoea, vomiting, colic in babies and abdominal pain in older children, eczema, and sinus and respiratory problems.

Babies and children allergic to cow's milk should be treated under the supervision of a doctor or nutritionist. Babies, if breast-feeding is not an option, may be given a hypoallergenic or soy-based formula milk. Older children may need to be fed a dairy-free diet.

Lactose intolerance is caused by a lack in the gut of a digestive enzyme, lactase, which normally digests lactose, the sugar in cow's milk. In Western countries, where most people retain lactase in the gut throughout life, lactose intolerance is usually caused by gastrointestinal bacteria or a virus damaging the gut and is a temporary problem.

Wheat is a fairly common cause of problems

in young children, probably because of the great amount of wheat-based foods eaten today. If your child has vague symptoms of digestive discomfort, lethargy, irregular bowel function and general malaise, for which no other specific cause can be found, it is worth trying a week or two without any wheat whatsover. Substitute rice cakes, rye crispbread, pumpernickel, products made with buckwheat, chickpea, rice or potato flour, or any other non-wheat product.

If there is a problem with gluten allergy, as in coeliac disease, all gluten-containing cereals, including wheat, oats, barley and rye, must be avoided. No babies should have gluten foods until six months old, or up to a year if there is a history of wheat or gluten intolerance in the family.

Nuts and seeds, particularly peanuts (or

groundnuts), but also walnuts, pecans and cashews, can cause rashes, asthma and eczema.

In severe cases – fortunately very rare – nuts can cause potentially fatal anaphylactic shock. If there is any history of food allergy in a child's family, nutritionists recommend that the child should not be given nuts in any form until he is at least five years old. If there is no history of allergy, children may be given an easily eaten form of peanuts, such as smooth peanut butter, from the time they are toddlers. Whole nuts should never be given to children under three years old because they could choke on them.

Eggs may cause rashes, swellings and stomach

upsets, asthma and childhood eczema (atopic eczema). Since the reaction is often to the egg white, rather than the whole egg, foods that should be avoided include desserts such as mousses and meringues, as well as cakes, mayonnaise and ice cream.

Fish, both fresh (such as cod and sole) and

smoked (kippers, smoked salmon, haddock and mackerel) can cause skin rashes, stomach upsets, nausea and migraine. Shellfish, both crustaceans and molluscs, can cause severe and prolonged stomach upsets as well as the migraine and nausea associated with fish.

dealing with allergy foods

The only treatment for food allergy in children is abstinence, and the way to find out what you should avoid giving your child is to follow an exclusion diet, such as the one set out on the opposite page.

This exclusion diet may look difficult, but it only needs to be followed rigorously for about two weeks, after which foods may be added back, provided you keep a record. You will soon be able to build a list of foods which your child can tolerate and eliminate the others.

Stick rigidly to the diet for a fortnight and keep a diary to pinpoint bad reactions. After two weeks things should improve. If they do not, food allergy or intolerance is probably not the problem and you should get further medical help.

exclusion diet for allergies

The diet is set out in two columns. In the 'not allowed' column are all those foods that a child should not eat in any form for the first two weeks of the diet. The list may seem rather long, but a glance at the 'allowed' column will show you such a good range of foods that, with a bit of careful planning, a child need never notice that he is being deprived of any favourite foods.

Foods for the first two weeks of the diet

Food	Not allowed	Allowed
Meat	Preserved or processed meats, bacon, sausages	All other meats
Fish	Smoked fish, shellfish	White fish
Vegetables	Potatoes, onions, sweetcorn, aubergine, chillies, sweet peppers, tomatoes	All other vegetables, salads, pulses, parsnip and swede
Fruit	Citrus fruit e.g. oranges, grapefruit	All other fruit, e.g. apples, bananas, pears
Cereals	Wheat, oats, barley, rye, corn	(Ground) rice, rice flakes and cakes, sago, rice cereals, tapioca, millet, buckwheat
Cooking oils	Corn oil, vegetable oil	Sunflower oil, soya oil, safflower oil, olive oil
Dairy products	Cow's milk, yogurt, butter, eggs, most margarines & cheese	Goat, sheep and soya milks and products made from them, dairy and trans-fat-free margarines
Beverages	Tea, coffee (beans, decaffeinated, instant), squashes, orange and grapefruit juices, alcohol, tap water	Herbal teas, fresh fruit juices, pure tomato juice (without additives), mineral and distilled water
Miscellaneous	Chocolate, yeast and yeast extracts, artificial preservatives, colourings and flavourings, monosodium glutamate, all artificial sweeteners	Carob, sea salt, herbs, spices and small amounts of sugar or honey

After two weeks re-introduce foods in this order: tap water, potatoes, cow's milk, yeast, tea, rye, butter, onions, eggs, porridge oats, coffee, chocolate, barley, citrus fruits, corn, cow's-milk cheese, white wine, shellfish, natural cow's-milk yogurt, vinegar, wheat and nuts.

Give only one new food every two days and, if there is a reaction, don't try it again for at least a month. Carry on with the list when any symptoms stop. Any diet which is very restricted puts children's health at risk and, although it is all right to experiment on your own for a few weeks, any long-term removal of major food groups should only be done under professional guidance, such as that of a doctor or nutritionist.

hyperactivity & ADHD

The symptoms of hyperactivity are all too familiar to many luckless parents and teachers. Hyperactive children are constantly overactive, have poor co-ordination, a short attention span and little concentration; they are emotionally unstable, prone to violent outbursts and find it hard to go to bed and often even harder to get to sleep.

In recent years there has been much controversy surrounding the question of hyperactive children, whose problem is called attention deficit hyperactivity disorder, or ADHD. This term does not apply to those who are simply naughty, badly behaved, or difficult. It applies to children who are impossibly disruptive, destructive to themselves and to property, and have learning difficulties.

For years these children were treated exclusively as behaviourally disturbed. Then, in the late 1960s, Dr Ben Feingold, an allergist working in America, stumbled across a possible chemical cause for hyperactivity while working on a project connected to flea-bite allergies in children. He devised a special diet which excluded a group of chemicals called salicylates, related to the aspirin family and similar to the substances produced by fleas. A number of children who were extremely allergic to flea bites were put on this diet and Feingold was astounded to discover that not only were the children reacting less severely to the flea bites, but their behaviour had improved as well.

He then began a major study on hyperactive children who had been institutionalized as they were beyond control. A considerable percentage of the children responded dramatically to the diet, their behaviour changing within days. When they were given a doughnut filled with artificially coloured and flavoured jam, their behaviour deteriorated within hours. Dr Feingold had established that many of the chemicals used as artificial food additives were salicylates, and he suggested that these very chemicals, together with natural salicylates occurring in some foods, were the root of the problem for some children.

chemical offenders

All children with ADHD may be sensitive to some of the chemicals used in processed foods. Among the worst offenders is the yellow colouring, tartrazine (E102), which is widely used in convenience foods, especially in many of the drinks, sweets and biscuits aimed directly at the children's market. Many children have been restored to reasonable behaviour and sleep by avoiding food additives – some of which can also be the trigger for asthmatic attacks, eczema, urticaria and other itches and irritations.

Phosphoric acid (E338-341), used in fizzy drinks to give them a fresh tingle in the mouth, may be a special problem. Phosphates turn up in other processed foods, including sausages and cooked or processed meats. Phosphoric acid was for a long time believed to be a harmless additive with no known adverse effects. But a German pharmacist, Hertha Hafer, has pointed out that phosphate use in foodstuffs has trebled since the 1960s, and she is firmly convinced that phosphates are a contributing cause to the rising epidemic of hyperactivity among children in many countries.

Hertha's own son Michael was hyperactive, and for a while both Hertha and her husband, and the boy's teachers were delighted with his obvious improvement on doses of Ritalin, the medication now given to millions of 'problem children' in the West (see page 210).

After learning of Feingold's work and putting it into practice, however, Hertha became particularly suspicious of the effects of phosphoric acid. In *The Hidden Drug*, published in France and Germany, she detailed cases where behavioural problems disappeared once phosphates were withdrawn from the diet. She also suggested a simple kitchen remedy for hyperactivity which she claimed is almost as effective as a tablet of Ritalin – a teaspoon of cider vinegar mixed into a glass of water.

Excess phosphates should be eliminated from children's diets for other reasons: they can, for instance, interfere with calcium uptake, leading to poor bone formation and osteoporosis in later life.

Nutritional deficiencies caused by poor diet may be at the root of many cases of hyperactivity. Too little zinc is one possible cause: in 1997 the British Hyperactive Children's Support Group tested 190 children with ADHD, and found that 183 were deficient in zinc. The Group has also researched essential fatty acid deficiency: they found that there was marked improvement in children given 2000–3000mg of evening primrose oil a day.

Other vital nutrients are the B-vitamin complex, found in meat and wholegrains; magnesium, found in bananas and dried fruits, cashews and peanuts; wholemeal flour, brown rice and green vegetables; and the healthy fats found in oily fish like sardines, mackerel, salmon and tuna.

the ADHD diet

For many hyperactive children, this diet is like turning a switch and going from darkness to light. Some children are just plain naughty and need discipline, and others have psychological problems, totally unrelated to food, that lead to their behavioural disorder. No matter what the cause, all children will benefit from the healthier eating patterns you can achieve with this diet.

It is not necessary to follow the plan under medical supervision, although it is easier if you have some help and guidance. You are not removing any entire food groups and you can continue to feed your child on a varied, well-balanced diet. The programme is suitable for children over the age of two years whom you suspect of having a behavioural problem and that it might be linked to food chemicals.

1. Keep a diet diary and write down everything your child eats. It is important to keep this diary going even after any improvements have occurred. Keep a column in the diary for general behaviour

and school progress. If the diet is working, but there is any sudden deterioration in behaviour, suspect that one or other of the baddies has crept in, either by accident or by cheating.

2. Any fruit or vegetable which is not on the prohibited list of Group 1 (see page 208) is allowed unless you suspect that it causes problems.

3. Be a label reader, rejecting anything that is not 100 per cent free of artificial additives. Permitted and not-permitted foods are in the Group 2 lists (see page 209).

4. All children enjoy the occasional sweet treat but you will have to make cakes, biscuits, pies, pastries, puddings and even simple sweets at home. Make your own ice cream, too, to avoid the additives in commercially manufactured ones.

5. The best way to ensure success is to get the whole family following the diet – would you like to watch while everyone else is eating goodies that you are not allowed? The restriction on fresh fruits and the two vegetables can be relaxed after

four to six weeks. Only give one new food in any 48-hour period so you can spot those that might still present a problem.

6. To succeed, the diet must be a 100 per cent effort. If an affected child has a mouthful of tartrazine on Sunday, and another on Wednesday, hyperactivity for a week could be the result.

7. Usually, a good response will be obvious within seven to 21 days. In some children behavioural improvements may be noticed within two or three days, in others it might take seven weeks. If your child is one of those sensitive to, or allergic to, these chemicals then you will see a benefit for all your efforts, so persevere.

8. Severely hyperactive children are frequently prescribed behaviour-modifying drugs, and you should never make changes without consulting the doctor who is overseeing your child.

group 1

The fruits and vegetables in this list contain natural salicylates, which have been found to be a cause of hyperactivity in children.

They must be omitted in any and all forms – fresh, frozen, canned, dried, as juice or as an ingredient of prepared foods.

Foods containing natural salicylates

Almonds
Apples
Apricots
Berries: blackberries, currants, gooseberries,
          raspberries, strawberries
Cherries
Cucumbers (pickles)
Grapes and raisins or any product made of
grapes (wine, wine vinegar, jellies, etc.)
Nectarines
Oranges
(grapefruit, lemon and lime are permitted)
Peaches
Plums and prunes
Tomatoes and all tomato products

After these foods have been left out of the diet for 4–6 weeks, try them again one at a time for 3 or 4 days. If there is no unfavourable reaction, another item can be added. This procedure is followed until all items in the group are tested and those to which there is no adverse reaction are restored to the diet.

group 2

All foods that contain artificial colours and artificial flavours are prohibited.

The list on the opposite page is a guide for shopping and food preparation. It does not list all foods that contain artificial colours and flavours because it would not be practical to do so. Do not use any foods that contain these substances.

The safest approach is to read food labels carefully and not to buy or use any that contain artificial colour and flavours. There is an increasing number of foods available that contain neither.

There are some permitted food items that must be prepared at home to avoid synthetics.

Note: it should be emphasized that this diet is not concerned with food preservatives except for Butylated Hydroxy Toluene (BHT). Occasionally, a child may show an adverse response to BHT.

Foods containing artificial colours and artificial flavours

Food	Not permitted	Permitted
Cereals	All cereals with artificial colours and flavours, all instant-breakfast preparations	Any cereal without artificial colours or flavours, dry or cooked
Bakery goods	All manufactured cakes, pastries, sweet rolls, doughnuts, etc., pie crusts, frozen baked goods, all commercial breads except egg bread and wholewheat bread, many packaged baking mixes	Any product without artificial colour or flavour, but most bakery items must be prepared at home 100 per cent wholewheat
Meats	Bologna, salami, frankfurters, sausages, meat loaf, ham, bacon, pork	All other meats
Poultry	All barbecued types, all turkeys, with prepared basting called 'self-basting', prepared stuffing	All poultry except stuffed
Fish	Frozen fish fillets that are dyed or flavoured; fish sticks that are dyed or flavoured	All fresh fish
Desserts	Manufactured ice creams, unless the label specifies no synthetic colouring or flavouring; the same applies to sherbet, ices, gelatins, junkets, puddings, and all powdered puddings; all dessert mixes; flavoured yogurt	Homemade ice cream without artificial colouring or flavouring; jellies, home-made from pure gelatins, with any permitted natural fruit or fruit juices; tapioca; home-made custards and puddings; plain yogurt – fresh fruits or juice may be added
Sweets	All manufactured types, hard or soft	Home-made sweets without almonds
Beverages	Cider, wine, beer, diet juices, soft drinks; all instant breakfast drinks; all quick-mix powdered drinks; tea, prepared chocolate milk, coffee	Grapefruit and pineapple juices, pear and guava nectars; home-made lemonade or limeade, made from fresh lemons or limes; milk
Miscellaneous	Any margarine containing artificial additives; coloured butter; mustard, cider vinegar, wine vinegar; all mint-flavoured items; soy sauce, if flavoured or coloured; commercial chocolate syrup; barbecue-flavoured potato chips; cloves; ketchup; chilli sauce Coloured cheeses	All cooking oils and fats; butter icing, not coloured or flavoured; mustard prepared at home from pure powder and distilled vinegar; honey; jams or jellies made from permitted fruits, not artificially coloured or flavoured; home-made mayonnaise; distilled white vinegar; home-made chocolate syrup All natural (white) cheeses
Sundry Items	All toothpastes and toothpowder; all mouthwashes, cough drops, throat lozenges; antacid tablets and perfumes	A salt-and-soda mixture can be used instead of toothpaste

diet changes or Ritalin?

Further evidence of the links between food additives and ADHD have became apparent through the work of the American criminologist Professor Steven Schoenthaler, at Cal-state University, Turlock, California. He conducted studies into the link between food additives and behaviour with juvenile delinquents who showed dramatic improvements in behaviour within weeks of being fed a monitored diet.

Schoenthaler subsequently carried out more studies, and concluded that a combination of improved diet and simple multivitamin-mineral supplements could change intelligence and behaviour in delinquent youngsters.

Penal institutions throughout the USA have followed his lead and replaced junk food full of additives with real food, high-fat and high-sugar items with healthier options, and introduced supplements. Even schools in the USA have followed suit, starting with the entire New York school system switching to healthier food and seeing an almost instant improvement in learning skills, behaviour and achievement.

The most disturbing feature of ADHD is the current vogue for the prescription of the drug Ritalin. This drug is believed to be taken by around a million children in the USA, including 12 per cent of boys in the 6–14 age group. In the United Kingdom, where nearly 70,000 children are believed to suffer from the most severe form of ADHD, Ritalin was recently approved by the National Institute for Clinical Excellence for use with children suffering from the most severe form of attention disorder.

The clinical advice is that Ritalin should only be used for children who fail to respond to psychotherapy, and the 'special precautions' say it must only be used under the supervision of a specialist in behaviour disorders. Many people, including concerned parents, suspect that it is routinely prescribed on the insistence of desperate parents, long before other treatments have been explored and without the specialist supervision considered so important.

Children are often on this drug for long periods, side effects are common, and withdrawal is often difficult. Ritalin is a 'controlled drug', classified with other highly addictive substances. Before you allow your child to take this drug for what may be a long time, it is surely worth a few weeks of your time and a bit of extra trouble to try the diet suggested here.

eating disorders

Researchers for the *British Medical Journal* recently found that as many as one in 100 young girls in the UK suffers from anorexia nervosa. The figures are rising among boys, too – one in 10 of the children being treated for anorexia at London's Great Ormond Street Hospital is now a boy.

Anorexia nervosa was once a disease of the late teens; therapists are now seeing victims as young as nine and ten. Similar figures are reported from other Western countries. The *BMJ* researchers also found that those who routinely skipped meals were 18 times more likely to develop anorexia, and even those who simply regularly cut down the amount they ate were five times more likely to develop it at some time.

It is essential to realize that parents themselves may be the chief negative influence on children's attitudes to food. If children see their parents constantly embarking on one diet after another, if they hear them counting calories and checking the fat content on every label, being obsessive about their own weight, or constantly worrying about the rest of the family's, they will receive a powerful message that thin is good and food is bad.

On the other hand, obese children are at considerable risk of becoming obese adults, which is not good for their health either. It is well recognized that some children have a greater tendency to put on weight than others. But the answer for such children can never be a slimming diet: it must always be a combination of healthy eating and exercise.

anorexia nervosa

Anorexia nervosa is a serious eating disorder that has grave long-term health consequences and is frequently a cause of death in young people. It is estimated that between 1 and 2 per cent of all schoolgirls suffer with this problem, which is almost exclusively confined to affluent Western society. Although the majority of sufferers are girls, up to 10 per cent are now young boys.

A major factor in the spread of anorexia nervosa is the influence of the media. Body images created by the advertising and fashion industries, and the multi-million dollar slimming industry pushing diet books, pills and potions are all putting pressure on young people to be thin.

Anorexia nervosa is a very complicated illness which inevitably involves social as well as psychological and biological factors, and there is some new evidence that there is a genetic factor as well. In principle, anorexics are turning their back on sexuality and adolescence, and in girls the cessation of periods frequently precedes the obvious and dramatic weight loss.

the signs of anorexia

Like alcoholics, anorexics become extremely clever at covering up their tracks. Be suspicious if your child starts wearing very baggy clothes, always has excuses not to sit down to family meals, or stops going out with friends to the burger bar or pizza parlour. Parents sometimes collude unwittingly by accepting a child's concern with food allergies, or a sudden switch to vegetarianism, veganism or some other extreme faddish diet, for moral or quasi-religious reasons.

More than half of anorexics become depressed and totally preoccupied with food and its calorie content and with their own body image. Anorexics seem to have fixed on a weight of 45kg/7 stone as their maximum supportable weight, and their lives revolve around staying below this.

Osteoporosis is a major hazard in anorexia. Many young anorexic girls in their late teens and early twenties have bones so thin and weak that they are at serious risk of spinal or hip fractures from the most minor injuries. The whole metabolic system shuts down in anorexics. The circulatory system suffers, fingers, toes and lips can be blue-tinged, and hair loss, bad skin and low blood pressure are all common symptoms.

Although they are obviously emaciated, sufferers become obsessed with the idea that they are fat. This often is the result of peer pressure, parents' over-concern with weight, and also a great fear of growing up. Difficult mother/daughter relationships are also common and there may well be a history of emotional trauma or disturbance before the onset of the illness. Divorce, and death of a parent or sibling, are also common triggers.

All forms of treatment are rejected by serious sufferers of anorexia and no amount of persuading will change their own perception of how they look.

treating anorexia nervosa

No parent should attempt to treat anorexia without medical help. The idea of easily getting seriously anorexic children or teenagers to follow a 'healthy diet' is ludicrous, just as pandering to the sufferer's eating obsessions is dangerous.

Many parents, especially those in the affluent, higher-income classes from which most cases of anorexia nervosa come, are so anxious about how they will look in the eyes of friends and colleagues if it becomes public knowledge that their child is anorexic, that they delay getting the right care.

Often, the only solution for doctors is to have the patient compulsorily admitted to a psychiatric unit, ideally one that specializes in treatment of the condition. As well as medical treatment to provide massive calorie input, psychotherapy that includes the whole family is essential once the patient's weight has increased to a non-critical level. Anorexics who have effective treatment have a great chance of survival – 20 years later 95 per cent will still be alive – but, left to their own devices and unhelped, 20 per cent of sufferers will probably have died.

bulimia nervosa

Bulimia nervosa involves alternate starving and bingeing. Sufferers can eat huge quantities of food in one sitting, then purge themselves with laxatives or make themselves vomit before returning to their starvation diet. Bulimics are not that easy to spot; they're usually older than anorexics, around the mid-20s being common. They are mostly independent, living away from home, and their normal 'diet' is just about socially acceptable. They are seldom emaciated; although sometimes very slim, they may also be overweight.

Bulimia is triggered by the same factors as anorexia: low self-esteem, pressure from ambitious parents, lack of parental affection and attention, and frequently an underlying thread of stress, anxiety and depression.

helping eating disorders through diet

A main route to helping children and young people with eating disorders is through diet. Anorexics must be encouraged to eat anything that contains calories and nutrients, especially high-zinc foods like shellfish, pumpkin seeds, liver, cheese, beef and sardines, as zinc stimulates appetite. All foods are acceptable for someone who is very underweight, but it is important to avoid bran and bran-based cereals as they interfere with zinc and iron absorption: anorexics are frequently obsessed with improving bowel function and may use bran as an alternative to laxatives.

The healthiest calories come from complex carbohydrates like wholemeal bread, oats, potatoes, pasta, rice and beans. But these are very bulky and there is a limit to how much can be eaten at one time. Do make sure that they contribute at least half the food intake.

Get extra calories from bananas, nuts – as long as they're unsalted or not covered in chocolate – and dried fruits. Raisins, sultanas, dates and dried apricots are excellent sources of energy, vitamins and minerals and also supply useful quantities of fibre. As snacks and nibbles throughout the day they supply a significant number of calories in comparatively small amounts of food. One of the best sources of healthy calories are seeds, and spreads made from seeds and nuts. Sunflower and sesame seeds are especially good and are rich in nutrients: tahini, a spread made from crushed sesame, and peanut butter provide a large number of calories and little bulk.

the value of frequent snacking

Try to encourage eating every two hours, starting at breakfast and finishing with a bedtime snack. Dips like guacamole, made from avocado and olive oil, or hummus, made with chickpeas and tahini, eaten with wholemeal pitta bread, make an excellent between-meals snack and, like all the best foods, provide a high proportion of nutrients along with their calories.

Finally, try this recipe. Make it up first thing in the morning, encourage your child to have a glass before breakfast, keep the rest in the refrigerator and make sure it's all gone by bedtime. Put 600ml/ 1 pint whole milk, one certified salmonella-free raw egg, one banana, 2 teaspoons each of molasses, honey, tahini, wheatgerm and brewer's yeast powder, and four dried apricots into a blender. Whisk all the ingredients together, pour into a jug and keep in the refrigerator. (The recipe could be made in a bowl or jug, using a hand blender.)

why zinc is important

Brains need zinc. Confusion, depression, including the 'baby blues', and even schizophrenia have been linked with low zinc levels. And since both appetite and taste depend on zinc, lack of this mineral can be one cause of anorexia nervosa. There have been well-documented cases of anorexics making spectacular recoveries when given extra zinc. High stress levels, growth and hormonal turmoil all make teenagers vulnerable to zinc deficiency, especially if they're dieting.

If your child is anorexic, it's well worth checking zinc levels, and there's a simple way to do it. Buy from a chemist a bottle of distilled or de-ionized water and a pack of zinc capsules containing 50mg elemental zinc. Open one up and stir the contents into 225ml/7½fl oz of the distilled water. To those well supplied with zinc, the water will have a strong metallic taste. If it tastes like water, they're dangerously low.

The supplemental dose is also 50mg of elemental zinc a day, taken with food or at least a fruit juice, until the sense of taste returns. Repeat the test dose to check. The dose can be increased up to three times a day, but no higher. It should be reduced as soon as possible.

If appetite does return, a good zinc-rich diet will be life-saving. Good sources of zinc include liver, red meat, turkey, crabmeat, sardines, eggs, kidney beans, chickpeas and wholegrain bread.

resources

British Homeopathic Association
15 Clerkenwell Close
London EC1R 0AA
tel: 020 7566 7800
web: www.trusthomeopathy.org
Contact this organization for a list of medically qualified homeopathic doctors.

British Society for Allergy and Environmental Medicine
PO Box 7,
Knighton LB7 1WT
tel: 0906 302 0010 (premier line)
Organization of practitioners who specialize in these problems. Send a SAE for general information, or telephone.

The Consumers' Association
PO Box 44,
Hertford X, SG14 1SH83.

The Food Commission
94 White Lion Street,
London N1 9PF
tel: 0207 837 2250
web: www.foodcomm.org.uk
A non-profit organization which campaigns for the right to safe, healthy food for everyone. Their excellent quarterly review, *The Food Magazine*, is packed with information the food industry would rather you didn't have.

Foresight: the Association for the Promotion of Pre-Conceptual Care
The Paddock,
Godalming,
Surrey GU7 1XD
A registered charity offering advice, information, lists of practitioners and a preconceptual health programme for couples planning a baby. Send an A5 SAE with a 33p stamp for information.

General Council and Register of Naturopaths
Goswell House, 2 Goswell Road,
Street,
Somerset BA16 0JG
tel: 01458 840072
Contact this organization to find a registered naturopathic practitioner.

Hyperactive Childrens' Support Group
71 Whyke Lane,
Chichester,
West Sussex PO19 2LD
tel: 01903 725182
web: www.hacsg.org.uk
Marvellous registered charity which has come to the rescue of thousands of desperate parents whose children suffer from ADHD or hyperactivity. Literature, advice, helpful information.

La Leche League (Great Britain)
BM3424,
London WC1N 3XX
tel: 020 7242 1278
For mothers experiencing problems with breast-feeding. Call them and they will put you in touch with a breast-feeding counsellor in your area.

National Association of Farmers' Markets
tel: 01225 787 914;
Wheatland Farmers' Markets Ltd
tel: 020 7704 9659
web: www.londonfarmersmarket.com
Farmers' markets are weekly markets where the farmers sell directly to the public. To find your nearest, contact the Association at the above telephone number; if you live in or near London, contact Wheatland Farmers' Markets.

National Childbirth Trust
tel: 08704 448707 (helpline)
The leading charity for help with every aspect of childbirth and parenting, including breast-feeding problems. Call helpline for information and advice.

National Institute of Medical Herbalists
56 Longbrook Street,
Exeter, EX4 6AH
tel: 01382 426022
To find a registered medical herbalist, telephone or send a SAE, stamped for up to 150g weight.

The Nutri Centre
7 Park Crescent,
London WIN 3HE
tel: 0207 436 5122.
web: www.nutricentre.com
Probably the largest suppliers in the UK of nutritional supplements and natural medicines of every kind. Their book shop (tel: 020 7323 2382) has a huge collection of books on every aspect of health, many imported from the USA.

Organics Direct
tel: 0207 729 2828
web: www.organicsdirect.co.uk
For a weekly or bi-weekly delivery of a box containing a selection of organic fruit and vegetables, get in touch with this very-good-value national scheme.

The Osteopathic Centre for Children
109 Harley Street,
London W!N 1DG
tel: 020 7486 6160
web: www.occ.com

Swaddles Green Farm
Hare Lane,
Buckland St Mary,
Chard,
Somerset TA20 3JR.
tel: 01460 234 387
web: www.swaddles.co.uk
An organic farm supplying a full range of organic produce, including readymade dishes, pâté, sausages, beef, lamb and pork, and the best turkeys you can buy. Deliveries by van over a wide range, including London.

The Vegetarian Society
Parkdale, Dunham Road,
Altrincham
Cheshire WA14 4QG
tel: 0161 925 2000
web: www.vegsoc.org
Teenage kids suddenly turned veggie? Call the Vegetarian Society for help, advice, information, lots of great recipe ideas, help with nutritional problems; or visit their well-organized website.

BABY FOODS
Organix, or Baby Organix
tel: 0800 393 511
web: http://www.babyorganix.co.uk
One of the original organic baby foods producers, with 42 different foods. Registered with the Soil Association. Their products are available from supermarkets, most health food stores, Boots, Mothercare, or from Lobster (www.lobster.co.uk).

Babynat
Hundred per cent organic baby food, produced in France. Gluten-free and guaranteed GMO-free; no sugar, preservatives. Milk formula, biscuits, cereals are stocked in some supermarkets. Also available in the UK via Organico (contact tel. no. 020 8340 0401 or website www.organico.co.uk to find out your nearest stockist).

HIPP
tel: 0800 195 0906 for a leaflet; 0845 050 1352 for help and information.
Complete range of organic foods for all stages. Available in supermarkets and health food stores.

Holle
tel: 01386 792 622 (for mail order)
Cereal products, which are 99 per cent organic and biodynamic (Demeter certified), include millet, semolina and oat flakes, and contain no sugar or additives. Available in some health food shops.

books to read

The Allergy Bible
Linda Gamlin, consultant Prof. Jonathan Brostoff
QUADRILLE 2001
Up-to-the-minute compendium of practical
information and advice about allergy problems,
and how to cope, together with a full Resources
section with useful names and addresses.

E for Additives
Maurice Hanssen
THORSONS PUBLISHING, Wellingborough 1986
Lists and names all the E numbers permitted
in manufactured foods.

The Food Our Children Eat
Joanna Blythman
FOURTH ESTATE, London 1999

Food Your Miracle Medicine
Jean Carper
SIMON & SCHUSTER 1993

Natural Treatment for ADD and Hyperactivity
Skye Weintraub
WOODLAND PUBLISHING INC, USA 1997.
Written by a naturopath, this book looks at
all the complex possible causes of ADHD and
hyperactivity, including nutritional deficiencies,
hypoglycemia and allergies, and suggests
natural treatments.

*Nutritional Medicine: a Comprehensive Guide
to Nutrition in Medicine*
Dr Stephen Davies and Dr Alan Stewart
PAN BOOKS 1987
Includes useful sections on individual nutrients,
their function, food sources of them and
deficiency symptoms.

Organic Baby and Toddler Cookbook
Lizzie Vann
DORLING KINDERSLEY, London 2000

Planning for a Healthy Baby
Belinda Barnes and Suzanne Gail Bradley
FORESIGHT (see page 214 for address)

Poisoned Harvest
Christopher Robbins
GOLLANCZ, London 1991

Superfast Foods
Michael van Straten and Barbara Griggs
DORLING KINDERSLEY, London 1994

Superfoods
Michael van Straten and Barbara Griggs
DORLING KINDERSLEY, London 1990

Super Organic Foods
Michael van Straten
MITCHELL BEAZLEY, London 1999.

What Are you Eating?
Isabel Skypala
MICHAEL O'MARA BOOKS LTD, London 1998

Books listed here may be available from the
Nutri Centre Bookshop, London
(tel: 020 7323 2382).

index

acknowledgments & credits

The authors would like to thank Corinne Roberts for her enthusiasm and encouragement; Janice Anderson for her patient and indefatigable editing; art editor Glenda Fisher, who transformed the book into a work of art; and Fiona Lindsay of Limelight Management, our delightful, efficient literary agent.

They would also like to thank Victoria Heath for recipes tested at her child-friendly Cookery School; Mia Perren for original recipes and for recipe-testing; Aldo Zilli for Cream of Smoked Haddock & Potato Soup from *Zilli Fish* (Metro Publishing); Emily Sharman, pupil of a Cookie Crumbles' cookery class for Chicken Salad with Honey & Chilli; and Lizzie Vann of Organix for Banana Porridge. Broccoli with Spinach © Madhur Jaffrey, 1998, is reproduced by permission of the author, c/o Rogers Coleridge & White, Ltd, 20 Powis Mews, London W11 1JN.

Dorling Kindersley would like to thank Toni Kay for design and Helen Blanchard for design assistance; Caroline Barty for food styling for photography; Claire Cross for editorial assistance; Jane Knott for proof-reading; and Sue Bosanko for the index.

Many thanks to the models

Catherine Chambers, Eleanor Chambers, Laura Chambers, Adam Jogee, Kamilah Jogee, Alexander Kay, Charlotte Kay, Richard Kay and Eloise Newton.

Picture credits

Gettyone Stone Christopher Bissell jacket front br; David Oliver 4tl, 79b.
Rex Interstock Ltd 75br; Organic Picture Library 23br.
Telegraph Colour Library Ed Horn 26–27, 28–29, 30–31; Masterfile 34–35, 36–37, 38–39, 40–41.